ENDORSEMENTS

"For almost a decade Pastor Carter passionately led worship for our local congregation and our Kingdom Agenda Pastors and Leaders Conference. His fiery pursuit of the presence of God and for spiritually authentic worship has touched many hearts throughout the years. He has demonstrated a strong desire to mentor and disciple the leaders under his care. As a spiritual son, his love for me, my late wife, Lois, and my family has been greatly appreciated.

"I have witnessed his tenacity to rebound, recover, and reclaim his rightful position as a kingdom man for his marriage, family, and ministry.

"*Letters to Leaders* is a compelling and powerful devotional tool from A to Z, for leaders to muse and meditate daily on biblical truth regarding roles, responsibilities, and relationships required to thrive in their calling. I highly recommend this resource for every worship leader and church leader seeking to ignite their heart ablaze to worship God in spirit and in truth, in song and in service."

—DR. TONY EVANS, SENIOR PASTOR, OAK CLIFF BIBLE
FELLOWSHIP; PRESIDENT, THE URBAN ALTERNATIVE

"*Letters to Leaders* is the most profound book I have ever read on worship. It's transformational. Nothing will better prepare you for entrance into the presence of God. It's practical, which we all desperately need, instructive, encouraging, at times corrective, and most of all, anointed.

"I love the layout. So creative and inviting. Pastors need to read it as well, to help them in selecting their leadership. I would suggest you purchase it yesterday and dispense it to everyone on the worship leadership team. Better yet, have them buy their own so they will value its contents and act on its suggestions. I can't imagine any worship team being the same after reading this book."

—LARRY TITUS, FOUNDER AND PRESIDENT EMERITUS,
KINGDOM GLOBAL MINISTRIES, DALLAS, TEXAS

"I have had the honor and privilege of knowing, loving, respecting, and admiring Rodney in so many capacities. I've encountered the teenager, singer, songwriter, worshipper, worship leader, writer, minister, man, husband, father, and so much more over the last thirty years and counting! I've seen him live these letters each and every day, and I am ecstatic that he is investing his life and lessons learned in others through this work.

"Rodney has always had a gift for masterfully organizing information. He could've called it the ABCs of worship leading. In *Letters to Leaders,* he wraps this gift in a lovely package from A to Z. The format with the devotional letter, scripture, and word study somehow is filled with spiritual and practical nutrition in small consumable bites. It's simple enough for our teenage son to pore through and initiate forethought on servant leadership, humility, integrity, art, and heart. Conversely, it's deep enough to coach a worship leader or any leader through navigating the sometimes treacherous waters that flow through ministry.

"He's throwing a lifeline in seas where he almost drowned. I'm so glad he held on, grabbed hold of the lifeline he was thrown, and now is a lighthouse for worship leaders making sense of themselves and their assignment. As an English graduate, the language delights me. As an educator, the message instructs me. As a worshipper and musician, the themes inspire me. As a proud wife, the entire work revives me. I hope, pray, and believe it will have a similar effect on all who consume it."

—ANGELA M. CARTER, EDUCATOR, EC–4 GENERALIST AND MUSIC
K–12; SINGER, SONGWRITER, MUSICIAN, WORSHIP LEADER

"What a tool! What a resource. What a gift. These pages highlight relatable, practical reminders of things we often overlook as ministry leaders and worship leaders—truths that are sometimes placed on the back burner as we give ourselves to the work of the ministry. In *Letters to Leaders,* I am greatly encouraged, knowing that I'm not ever alone on this beautiful journey of highs, lows, and everything in between. All throughout, my brother, whom I admire, respect, and love, cheers me, and countless others on, as we live, worship, and lead."

—AYIESHA WOODS-HILLERY, GRAMMY AND DOVE AWARD-
NOMINATED SINGER, SONGWRITER, MUSICIAN, WORSHIP LEADER

"I've known and respected Pastor Carter and his work as a worship leader for over fifteen years. There are lots of books on worship and a plethora of books on leadership. However, this is one of the most encouraging and straightforward books for worship leaders I've ever read. It's a very heartfelt inspirational treasure chest of tools for worship leaders—packed with biblical truths, practical applications, and personal testimonies that can help shape the spiritual journey of any worship leader.

"It has been one of my greatest joys to walk with Rodney in ministry over the years. To witness him embrace the redeeming love of God on his life has been nothing short of amazing. As a worship leader, I trust him to teach and lead worship with our congregation monthly. I have repeatedly experienced God's Spirit through him and Angela's worship ministry because the Carters always take everything back to scripture.

"*Letters to Leaders* is a must-read for anyone who longs to be a more dynamic worship leader. I highly recommend this book. When the Holy Spirit fills a leader, and the passion and love for God's people fills their heart, they then can become God's instrument of His divine providence. This is why every worship leader needs this devotional. It will challenge them to have a much greater passion as a worship leader!"

—DR. CHARLES M. WOLFORD II, SENIOR PASTOR, CROSSPOINT BIBLE FELLOWSHIP; CEO, UNION GOSPEL MISSION OF TARRANT COUNTY

"As a hospital chaplain and former worship leader, I find that *Letters to Leaders* would enhance the ministry of any church leader. Pastor Carter and his wife's passion for helping somebody as they pass this way is demonstrated in these letters.

"I would encourage you to read the devotionals and enter the presence of the Lord. Sit back, put on your seat belt, and prepare to laugh, cry a little, and experience the travails of life through the rearview mirror of a couple who pushed, prayed, and persevered."

—RONALD BULLOCK, CEO, FRESH PERSPECTIVES MEDIATION AND RECONCILIATION

"*Letters to Leaders* is authored by my dear friend Rodney Carter. I have a deep love and appreciation for him and his amazingly gifted wife, Angela. It is with great enthusiasm and a profound sense of honor that I write this endorsement for a book that is not just a mere compilation of words but a treasure trove of wisdom and spiritual enlightenment.

"At its core, this book is a confluence of biblical wisdom, practical advice, and deeply personal reflections. Each page is imbued with the rich practical experiences of the author, making it a unique blend of scholarly insight and spiritual maturity. The author, through his authentic voice, shares insights from the triumphs and challenges he has faced on his professional and spiritual journey.

"One of the most striking aspects of this book is its applicability beyond the sphere of worship leadership. While it is undoubtedly an invaluable resource for worship leaders, its principles and insights are equally relevant to all spiritual leaders seeking to deepen their relationship with God. *Letters to Leaders* encourages leaders to reflect, engage, and grow in their faith, fostering a deeper understanding of their spiritual journey and greater effectiveness in their practical ministry.

"Rodney's ability to weave together scriptural references with real-life applications is a testament to his love for the scripture and experience in ministry. Each letter serves as a standalone piece of wisdom while also contributing to the larger narrative of building a strong, faith-led leadership style. This devotional is not just a guide; it is a companion for those who are navigating the often complex path of spiritual leadership. I wholeheartedly endorse *Letters to Leaders*. It is a must-read for anyone who aspires to lead with grace, wisdom, and a heart attuned to God's calling."

—DR. LARRY A. MERCER, PRESIDENT AND FOUNDER, THERAPON
LEADERSHIP SERVICES; EXECUTIVE ADMINISTRATOR OF
CHRISTIAN EDUCATION, OAK CLIFF BIBLE FELLOWSHIP

"Failure teaches what success cannot, which is what makes this book valuable. The most remarkable individuals are those who have endured suffering, faced failure, experienced grief, encountered adversity, and not only survived but also emerged transformed by their experiences. What makes *Letters to Leaders* meaningful is the fact that Pastor Rodney doesn't come from the perspective of how he got it right, but rather comes from the perspective of love, humility, and brokenness."

—RICK REYNOLDS, PRESIDENT AND FOUNDER, AFFAIR RECOVERY

"It is quite easy to merely complain about the problems that we see—within our families, on our jobs, at our churches, throughout the world—and even easier to do nothing about them. My brother and my friend Rodney L. Carter, by way of the Holy Spirit Himself, bucks against this trend in brilliant fashion by offering *Letters to Leaders* to his generation and prayerfully many to follow. Rodney recognized a void in the resources available to help worship leaders navigate the everyday ebbs and flows of ministry and decided to boldly pursue filling that void with this work.

"Rodney is the only person throughout my forty-five years of life who has ever volunteered to personally invest in my spiritual maturity as a man, a husband, and a worship leader. The Lord used him well over a decade ago to change the trajectory of my life as he shared many of the principles now presented in this book. I'm so excited that the same truths will now be able to have the same impact on the rest of the world. You will be encouraged and challenged as you hear from his heart in each letter."

—MICHAEL T. THOMAS, SINGER, SONGWRITER, WORSHIP LEADER

"I have known Rodney for five years. I had the pleasure of serving with him during one of the toughest seasons to be in church leadership. We served together during the 2020 pandemic. He was a phenomenal mentor that demonstrated pastoral care, biblical counsel, 'family first ministry,' and genuine transparency. I've experienced some of the pages of this book in real life.

"Rodney's mentorship and heart for ministry are unique and anointed. The passion and biblical teaching that come from him are inspiring and ignite a fire in anyone who has a yearning to grow spiritually, express their creativity, and go deeper in their worship. These letters from A to Z are essential for every worship leader and music minister.

"I can't wait to walk through this devotional with my church worship team and purchase copies to give this book to all my friends who also lead worship. *Letters to Leaders* is what I would call 'mandatory orientation and spiritual development' for all worship leaders."

—JOANIE DAWSON, MBA, SINGER, SONGWRITER, WORSHIP LEADER

"Authentic, spiritual, enlightening, energetic, and practical. This is one book to keep accessible! It will be a staple in your library and great to repeatedly go back to for inspiration and focus. Rodney has provided a practical, powerful pathway forward for any worship leader who understands their assignment as 'witnesses' unto Christ and His kingdom. *Letters to Leaders* is more than a devotional. It's a tool to sharpen your walk with Christ so you can more effectively lead people into His presence. I highly recommend it!"

—TRINA TITUS LOZANO, PRESIDENT, THE HOME EXPERIENCE; AUTHOR, PASTORAL COUNSELOR

"Pastor Rodney Carter is a great person, friend, brother, godfather of my youngest child, and indeed a man of God. I am so proud of him for using his life experiences as imprints of spiritual life tools for this world.

"*Letters to Leaders* is an innovative, practical guideline for anyone wanting to grow and develop into the best version of themselves. This out-of-the-box devotional tool from A to Z can be used for teaching, training, and daily life ingredients—to enhance a person's mental, emotional, physical, and spiritual development—and is appropriate for all ages. If I were to describe this devotional tool in three phrases, they would be words of knowledge, nuggets of wisdom, and life-changing."

—DR. MOSES CHISM JR., LPC-S, MASTER LIFE COACH; CEO AND CLINICAL DIRECTOR, INNOVATIVE-CENTERED COUNSELING

LETTERS TO LEADERS: WORSHIP EDITION

(WHAT I WISH I HAD KNOWN)

RODNEY L. CARTER

WESTBOW
PRESS®
A DIVISION OF THOMAS NELSON
& ZONDERVAN

WestBow Press books may be ordered through booksellers or by contacting:

WestBow Press
A Division of Thomas Nelson & Zondervan
1663 Liberty Drive
Bloomington, IN 47403
www.westbowpress.com
844-714-3454

Scripture quotations are taken from the New King James Version.
Copyright © 1982 by Thomas Nelson, Inc. Used by permission. All rights reserved.

ISBN: 979-8-3850-2644-9 (sc)
ISBN: 979-8-3850-2645-6 (e)

Library of Congress Control Number: 2024910949

Print information available on the last page.

WestBow Press rev. date: 08/09/2024

To my only son, our little leader, Josiah.

You are our epistle written in our hearts, known and read by all men; clearly you are an epistle of Christ, ministered by us, written not with ink but by the Spirit of the living God, not on tablets of stone but on tablets of flesh, that is, of the heart.

(2 Corinthians 3:2–3 NKJV)

CONTENTS

Spiritual Checkup: INSPIRE

Spiritual Checkup: INSPIRE

Spiritual Checkup: INSPIRE

Spiritual Checkup: INSPIRE

WEEKLY SCHEDULE

Week	Letter 1	Letter 2	Week	Letter 1	Letter 2
W1	Apprenticeship	Appreciation	W2	Anointing	Atmosphere
W3	A cappella	Ad-lib	W4	Authenticity	Brokenness
W5	Boundaries	Burn Out	W6	Boldness	Blended
W7	Being	Creativity	W8	Clapping	Congregation
W9	Commitment	Courage	W10	Care	Connect
W11	Compliment	Calling	W12	Counseling	Discipleship 1
W13	Discipleship 2	Discipleship 3	W14	Discipleship 4	Devotion
W15	Disciplines	Delegation	W16	Deliverance	Dancing
W17	Distraction	Discord	W18	Elitism	Example
W19	Enjoyment	Emotionalism	W20	Filled	Fight
W21	Faith	Fear	W22	Feelings	Friends
W23	Forgiveness	Grace	W24	Glory	Growth
W25	Gospel	Gifts	W26	Guard	Goodness
W27	Honor	Health	W28	Hymns	Investment
W29	Inspiration	Illiteracy	W30	Intimacy	Identity
W31	Integrity	Jesus	W32	Kingdom	Kindness
W33	Love	Levites	W34	Leadership	Mentorship
W35	Music	Meditation	W36	Marriage	Mind
W37	Necessary	Organism	W38	Organization	Order
W39	Preparation	Prayer	W40	Psalms	Proverbs
W41	Politics	Quiet	W42	Releaser	Roles
W43	Recovery	Servants	W44	STEAM 1	STEAM 2
W45	Sex	Safety	W46	Songwriting	Scripture
W47	Success	Theology	W48	Tabernacle	Transition
W49	Understanding	Unity	W50	Vision	World Changer
W51	Χριστός	Yielding	W52	Your Letter	Zenith

LETTER GUIDE

Keyword defined

Singing through Colossians

Scripture

Personal Letter

Hebrew or Greek

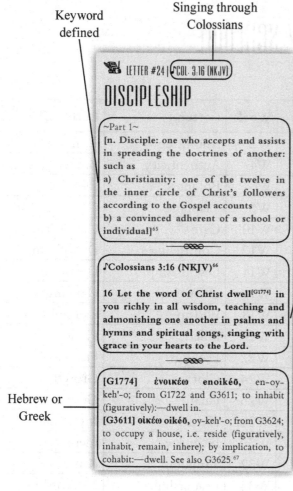

LETTER #24 | ♪COL. 3:16 (NKJV)

DISCIPLESHIP

~Part 1~

[n. Disciple: one who accepts and assists in spreading the doctrines of another: such as
a) Christianity: one of the twelve in the inner circle of Christ's followers according to the Gospel accounts
b) a convinced adherent of a school or individual][65]

♪Colossians 3:16 (NKJV)[66]

16 Let the word of Christ dwell[G1774] in you richly in all wisdom, teaching and admonishing one another in psalms and hymns and spiritual songs, singing with grace in your hearts to the Lord.

[G1774] ἐνοικέω enoikéō, en-oy-keh'-o; from G1722 and G3611; to inhabit (figuratively):—dwell in.
[G3611] οἰκέω oikéō, oy-keh'-o; from G3624; to occupy a house, i.e. reside (figuratively, inhabit, remain, inhere); by implication, to cohabit:—dwell. See also G3625.[67]

Dear Worship Leader,

Discipleship in Christ is about dwelling and abiding in Christ (John 15). I first learned this through ♪Colossians 3:16, which has become my life verse. God uses it to train me, and I, others. It's "Discipleship through Music." When my tank is low, it fuels, energizes, enriches, and enlightens me. It's a wellspring that I've been drinking from and dwelling with for years now.

Colossians is a love letter from Paul to the church of Colosse. He alarms them because the city, previously known for its wealth, is under the threat of an enemy seeking to steal their spiritual riches, or their dwelling, in Christ. The enemy wants to confuse (2:4), cheat (2:8, 18), and condemn them (2:16).

So as any protective father would, Paul responds with a command for his children: You're under attack! Everyone, lock up your spiritual riches and hide them in your hearts! Or in the NKJV, "Let the word of Christ **dwell** in you richly in all wisdom ..." That is, *receive the Word indwelt, in abundance, and in all wisdom.* Let it be housed or tabernacled in you. Let it reside and remain there. Let it occupy and fill the house. Let it have

your keys, inform your decisions, and make you rich. You need great intake, excess, and access. Let it go viral in you! Eat, drink, and digest it. Become indoctrinated, intoxicated, impregnated, implanted, infused, imprinted, and invested.

Paul then surrounds the imperative [G1774] ἐνοικέω enoikéō, dwell, with three other participles: teaching, admonishing, and singing. By interweaving and interlocking them, he says the following: whenever you're singing kingdom truth (psalms, hymns, and spiritual songs), you're actually teaching and admonishing one another, thereby, helping each other with "dwelling," which is key to

References and notes

[1] Merriam-Webster dictionary | www.merriam-webster.com | www.learnersdictionary.com
[2] Matt. 28:16–20 | Rom. 8:11; 2 Cor. 6:16; 2 Tim. 1:5, 14 | Rom. 7:17–18, 20; 8:9, 11; 1 Cor. 3:16; 7:12–13; 1 Tim. 6:16
[3] *Strong's Exhaustive Concordance of the Bible* | Blue Letter Bible | www.blueletterbible.org

discipling. So through music, you can help disciple the nations and prevail against the enemy!

Love, grace, and peace …

♪Colossians 3:16,

Rodney

Take a moment to meditate, muse, and memorize God's word. What is the Holy Spirit saying to you right now?

_____
_____
_____
_____
_____
_____
_____
_____
_____
_____
_____
_____
_____
_____
_____

Personal
Reflection

BIBLE ABBREVIATIONS

Book Name	Abbreviation	Book Name	Abbreviation	Book Name	Abbreviation
Genesis	Gen.	Isaiah	Isa.	Romans	Rom.
Exodus	Exod.	Jeremiah	Jer.	1 Corinthians	1 Cor.
Leviticus	Lev.	Lamentations	Lam.	2 Corinthians	2 Cor.
Numbers	Num.	Ezekiel	Ezek.	Galatians	Gal.
Deuteronomy	Deut.	Daniel	Dan.	Ephesians	Eph.
Joshua	Josh.	Hosea	Hosea	Philippians	Phil.
Judges	Judg.	Joel	Joel	♪Colossians	♪Col.
Ruth	Ruth	Amos	Amos	1 Thessalonians	1 Thess.
1 Samuel	1 Sam.	Obadiah	Obad.	2 Thessalonians	2 Thess.
2 Samuel	2 Sam.	Jonah	Jon.	1 Timothy	1 Tim.
1 Kings	1 Kings	Micah	Mic.	2 Timothy	2 Tim.
2 Kings	2 Kings	Nahum	Nah.	Titus	Titus
1 Chronicles	1 Chron.	Habakkuk	Hab.	Philemon	Philem.
2 Chronicles	2 Chron.	Zephaniah	Zeph.	Hebrews	Heb.
Ezra	Ezra	Haggai	Hag.	James	James
Nehemiah	Neh.	Zechariah	Zech.	1 Peter	1 Pet.
Esther	Esther	Malachi	Mal.	2 Peter	2 Pet.
Job	Job	Matthew	Matt.	1 John	1 John
Psalms	Ps.	Mark	Mark	2 John	2 John
Proverbs	Prov.	Luke	Luke	3 John	3 John
Ecclesiastes	Eccles.	John	John	Jude	Jude
Song of Solomon	Song of Sol.	Acts	Acts	Revelation	Rev.

★♪– In this work, a musical note (♪) is placed before Colossians scriptures and references in an effort to encourage spiritual growth through singing, musing, and meditating on God's word. (See Colossians 3:16 and The Colossians Project: https://soundcloud.com/col316/sets/colossians-project-writings.)

ACKNOWLEDGMENTS

First and foremost, if it had not been for the Lord on my side, where would I be? All my life, You have been faithful! I am forever indebted to You for Your unconditional love, grace, and mercy. You are my strength, song, and salvation. I often feel like one of the ten lepers cleansed, that when he saw he was healed returned to Jesus with a loud voice glorifying God and fell down on his face at His feet, giving Him thanks. That is my story. I am forever changed. I owe You this praise!

To Angela, my precious wife of more than twenty-five years of marriage, and over thirty years of friendship, my beloved and friend. You are the wife of my youth, my good thing, my fruitful vine, the apple of my eye. You are proof that fine wine gets better with time. From the University of Iowa until now, I am intoxicated with your love. You are my dream come true. The sunshine of my life. My angel. Your worth is far above rubies. My heart safely trusts in you. Because of you, I am known in the gates and seated among the elders. Without your grace, double determination, and sacrifice, there would be no letters. Thanks for investing your time, talent, and treasure into my vision.

To Josiah Benjamin—whom Jehovah (Yahweh) heals, son of my right hand—our miracle from God. It's the honor of a lifetime watching you grow. As Josiah in scripture was eight years old when he became king, early on we saw your God-given natural ability to lead. As I wrote each letter, I thought of you. I prayed long and hard about what I wanted to say to you—and all the other young Josiahs in this world. If this work blesses no one else but you, my labor was not in vain! You are my letter, my legacy, and my treasure. You are my heart wrapped up in a thirteen-year-old body. Thanks for coming to check on me from time to time while writing this book. All of this is for you.

To the best mom (Angel), dad (Daddio), and twin brothers (the Dudes) I could ever have. Each of you inspires me to live, laugh, and love. To the greatest grandma ever, now the matriarch of our family, thank you for naming me and setting the bar high with class, grace, and style. To my late grandparents, I miss you all every day. Thanks for passing on such a rich heritage. To my mother-in-love and the most amazing in-laws, you have given me the gift of a lifetime. I will spend the rest of my life unwrapping her, loving her, and honoring you. To the rest of my family and friends, those alive as well as those now with the Lord, I hope I make you proud.

To all the pastors, first ladies, and elders who have entrusted me to lead God's people in worship, thank you for the enormous opportunity and responsibility! I'm blessed beyond measure. I can say I've never served a pastoral family that I didn't truly love. Thanks for investing and believing in me and for taking me under your wings. In spite of my flaws, you've given me a place at the table. I don't take that for granted.

To Dr. Tony Evans, Dr. Larry Mercer and my OCBF Accountability Team (the A Team), thank you for strategically, tenderly, and graciously carrying me back to Jesus. You embodied Mark 2:4 for me. You are my forever community.

To the believers at Antioch, ACOG, Victory Temple, Shekinah Glory/New City, OCBF, Covenant, Gateway, Abundant Life, NLF, OCC, Crosspoint, and Wheeler Ave, we love you all dearly.

To Rick Reynolds and Affair Recovery, I can't believe we get to work together full time. When we finally met you in person, God expanded our family. Thanks for warmly receiving us and for teaching and modeling that we learn from failure what we could never learn from success.

To Criswell College, the University of Iowa, Marie Sklodowska Curie Metro High School of Performing Arts, Walt Whitman and the Soul Children of Chicago, along with every teacher, preacher, leader, pastor, and musician I studied, I am your letter.

To all my spiritual family and friends who have encouraged me down through the years and labored to make this vision a reality—whether contracted or volunteer—you share in my reward for every heart and life touched by this work. I love you dearly.

Finally, to you the reader, thank you for your support. I commend you for investing in yourself and the lives you will in turn sow into. That is how the kingdom of God expands. While much effort has been made to present you a book free from flaw and error, only God is perfect. I pray you will receive the λόγος word of Christ with all readiness of mind, and like the Bereans in Acts 17:11, you will search the scriptures daily. May you forever be changed by the rich truth of this living, powerful, infinite, infallible, inerrant word of God!

*Photo by Donald Fuller, courtesy of The Urban Alternative.

Special thanks to our spiritual parents,
Larry and Devi Titus and Drs. Tony and Lois Evans.

For though you might have ten thousand instructors in Christ, yet you do not have many fathers; for in Christ Jesus I have begotten you through the gospel.
(1 Corinthians 4:15 NKJV)

In loving memory of Devi Titus and Dr. Lois Evans.

INTRODUCTION

In your hands is the culmination of over thirty years of lessons learned while serving in worship leadership ministry. Although it has been a blessed journey, none of it has been easy. Twenty-five of those years were served at three churches. I was minister of music for ten years at Shekinah Glory in Cedar Rapids, Iowa. Afterward, I joined Oak Cliff Bible Fellowship (OCBF) in Dallas, Texas, for ten years, where I was hired full time as associate pastor of worship. And for five years I led at New Life Fellowship in Arlington, Texas, as pastor of worship and arts. The remaining five years were mostly spent in transition either helping out other churches for shorter periods of time or taking twelve to eighteen months for recovery and sabbatical.

Ministry is not for the faint of heart. Prior to my need for an emergency sabbatical at OCBF in 2014, I had experienced major burnout. The Energizer Bunny in me got tired, weary, discouraged, disheartened, and overwhelmed. I was drowning and didn't know it. I was still leading and singing but pretending normal and mechanically going through the motions. My battery died. My ship had sunk. My vehicle was on the side of the road. But no one really knew it. Suffering burnout in silence or oblivion is such a dangerous place to be because our defenses are low and we are most vulnerable to poor choices and decisions. And I made a number of them. Eventually, I had to be sidelined and benched due to moral failure and personal breakdown. I needed a 911 rescue.

That's where I could have used a resource like this. I needed someone with 911 experience who could counsel, encourage, and correct me. If that's where you are, please allow these letters to be a starting point for you to do something different. Cry out for help! We all need help. We all need change. For me, the answer was Christ through community and counseling. I call them "the 3 Cs." Even today, after ten years of sobriety and freedom, they are just as important now as they were back then.

Here's the truth: we all need Christ, we all need a community, and we all need some level of counseling. I know that's a hard sell for some, but I'm convinced of it. I'm a huge advocate for crisis prevention. Let's not wait until we have a heart attack to get serious about our health. If we make the necessary changes now, in advance, we might be able to prevent it from ever happening.

After a year and a half of intense self-work—with the blessing of my wife and my Accountability Team—Dr. Tony Evans, senior pastor of OCBF, restored me and recommissioned me back into ministry. There wasn't a dry eye in the place. God showed up! In that little Green Room, my family experienced the ministry of reconciliation. After which, we were ready for our new life at New Life Fellowship! There we birthed The Colossians Project, where we wrote and recorded (in our little home studio) seventy-eight scripture songs to cover all ninety-five verses in Colossians—for meditation, memorization, manifestation, and ministry.

And now we offer *Letters to Leaders: Worship Edition (What I Wish I Had Known)*. From A to Z, one hundred heartfelt letters covering today's critical topics. In a year, that allows for two fillings per week—since most of us expend massive fuel and energy at midweek rehearsals and weekend services. We've even added four "Life Application Letters" at the very end, to take you through all fifty-two weeks of the year. Nevertheless, please pace yourself as needed. If it takes you more than one year to complete this devotional, please give yourself the gift of grace. Create your own schedule. This is a marathon, not a sprint. Grab a few others to join you in the race. Take your self-care seriously. You never know what crisis you are preventing or preparing for! And lastly, enjoy the journey.

Let the word of Christ dwell in you richly in all wisdom, teaching and admonishing one another in psalms and hymns and spiritual songs, singing with grace in your hearts to the Lord.

(♪Colossians 3:16 NKJV)

PART 1
LETTERS A TO G

LETTER #1

APPRENTICESHIP

[n. Apprenticeship: a position as an apprentice: an arrangement in which someone learns an art, trade, or job under another][1]

Matthew 28:18–20 (NKJV)[2]

18 And Jesus came and spoke to them, saying, "All authority has been given to Me in heaven and on earth.
19 "Go therefore and make disciples[G3100] of all the nations, baptizing them in the name of the Father and of the Son and of the Holy Spirit,
20 "teaching them to observe all things that I have commanded you; and lo, I am with you always, even to the end of the age." Amen.

[G3100] μαθητεύω mathēteúō, math-ayt-yoo'-o; from G3101; intransitively, to become a pupil; transitively, to disciple, i.e. enrol as scholar:—be disciple, instruct, teach.[3]

Dear Worship Leader,

To the next generation, I say, "You will replace me. This position. This platform. This place of influence. You will hold this microphone. You will stand in these shoes. You will wear this uniform. You will carry this cross. I hope that's not a surprise to either of us. It's the circle of life. As my voice fades, your voice will increase. As my hair grays, your hair grows. The camera shot is about to change, from me to you."

Let's prepare now. Ask me anything. Ask me everything. While I can still hear you and answer. I want you to learn from my triumphs and my trials. The good, the bad, and the ugly. A few years ago, my grandfather, age seventy-eight, passed from this life to glory. But in my mind, I can still hear his voice today. The wisdom. The advice. The stories. Some funny, some not so funny. I would listen for hours, so intensely, almost trying to memorize them verbatim. Many of them he would tell me over and over again. I could almost finish his sentences. But I dared not give him the impression that I had already heard this or that

I didn't want to hear it again. "Please, Granddaddy, tell me again. And again." I tear up now, knowing that I will not audibly hear his voice on this side of heaven anymore. I will, however, feast off the precious memories. I'm so glad we had that time together.

I am now in my late forties, with over thirty years of worship leading experience. I long to share the lessons I've learned with those behind me. It's therapeutic for me. It's my history, but it's your future. I hope my Fs become your As. And that my As become your A+s. Each generation has a calling to get wiser, stronger, and better than the one preceding it.

---

[1] Merriam-Webster dictionary | www.merriam-webster.com | www.learnersdictionary.com
[2] 2 Pet. 1:12–15; Acts 1:8; Eccles. 12; 2 Tim. 2:1–2; Phil. 2:19–24; 1 Cor. 11:1; Acts 9:36–42; 2 Cor. 3:2–3; John 14:12; Luke 9:23; Deut. 31:1–8; Num. 27:12–23; 1 Sam. 22:2; 2 Sam. 23:8–39; 1 Chron. 11:10–47; 2 Kings 2:9–14; Ruth 1
[3] *Strong's Exhaustive Concordance of the Bible* | Blue Letter Bible | www.blueletterbible.org

Each round, higher and higher. Let's maximize the moments we have now. Because sooner than later, tomorrow cometh.

Love, grace, and peace …

♪Colossians 3:16,

Rodney

Take a moment to meditate, muse, and memorize God's word. What is the Holy Spirit saying to you right now?

_____

_____

_____

_____

_____

_____

_____

_____

_____

_____

_____

_____

_____

_____

_____

 LETTER #2

APPRECIATION

[n. Appreciation: a feeling or expression of admiration, approval, or gratitude][4]

⁂

1 Thessalonians 1:2–3 (NKJV)[5]

**2 We give thanks[G2168] to God always for you all, making mention of you in our prayers,
3 remembering without ceasing your work of faith, labor of love, and patience of hope in our Lord Jesus Christ in the sight of our God and Father,**

⁂

[G2168] εὐχαριστέω eucharistéō, yoo-khar-is-teh'-o; from G2170; to be grateful, i.e. (actively) to express gratitude (towards); specially, to say grace at a meal:—(give) thank(-ful, -s).[6]

Dear Worship Leader,

One of the greatest characteristics of being an effective leader is the ability to say two words: *thank you.* Not out of duty, obligation, or manipulation but sincerely, from the heart. As an overflow of what you truly think and feel on the inside. People know when they're really appreciated. Similar to a bouquet of flowers or roses, they can smell it. They can feel it. They see it in your eyes. They can hear it in your voice.

Over the years, I've worked to make this a practice. Having an attitude of gratitude. During rehearsal. Before service. During service. After service. Before and after meetings. Publicly and privately. Rehearse this. Get really good at it—creative even. *The Five Love Languages,* by Gary Chapman, is a great resource for ideas. Jesus, our example, was full of grace and truth. Both are extremely important.

During my earlier years in ministry, I have to admit this was not a priority. Receiving their compliance was most important back then. But after many hard lessons, I've learned, like the apostle Paul, to give thanks. It is truly more blessed to give.

Give thanks to God for their presence. For their work. For their sacrifice. For them following our leadership amid our own personal weaknesses and flaws. Without someone following us, we have no one to lead. No matter how magnificent the leader, none of us can harmonize all by ourselves. We need others. We need teams. We need groups. We need congregants. We need partnerships. We need relationships. We need family. We need friendships. That's why Jesus called the disciples, because they were needed in the kingdom. Gratitude doesn't deny errors or mistakes; it simply says that people are loved and valued in spite of them.

Love, grace, and peace …

♪Colossians 3:16,

---

4 Merriam-Webster dictionary | www.merriam-webster.com | www.learnersdictionary.com
5 1 Thess. 2:13; Acts 20 | Rom. 1:8; 1 Cor. 1:4; Eph. 1:16; Phil. 1:3; ♪Col. 1:3; 2 Thess. 1:3; 2:13; 2 Tim. 1:3; Philem. 1:4
6 *Strong's Exhaustive Concordance of the Bible* | Blue Letter Bible | www.blueletterbible.org

Rodney

Take a moment to meditate, muse, and memorize God's word. What is the Holy Spirit saying to you right now?

_____

_____

_____

_____

_____

_____

_____

_____

_____

_____

_____

_____

_____

_____

_____

_____

LETTER #3

ANOINTING

[v. Anoint: 1) to smear or rub with oil or an oily substance
2a) to apply oil to as part of a religious ceremony
2b) to choose by or as if by divine election][7]

1 John 2:20–21, 26–27 (NKJV)[8]

**20 But you have an anointing[G5545] from the Holy One, and you know all things.
21 I have not written to you because you do not know the truth, but because you know it, and that no lie is of the truth.**

**26 These things I have written to you concerning those who try to deceive you.
27 But the anointing[G5545] which you have received from Him abides in you, and you do not need that anyone teach you; but as the same anointing[G5545] teaches you concerning all things, and is true, and is not a lie, and just as it has taught you, you will abide in Him.**

[G5545] χρῖσμα chrîsma, khris'-mah; from G5548; an unguent or smearing, i.e. (figuratively) the special endowment ("chrism") of the Holy Spirit:—anointing, unction.
[G5548] χρίω chríō, khree'-o; probably akin to G5530 through the idea of contact; to smear or rub with oil, i.e. (by implication) to consecrate to an office or religious service:—anoint.[9]

Dear Worship Leader,

There is no substitute for God's anointing. His oil is like no other. In the heat of the battle, you can count on it. It's on us. It's in us. It connects us with God Himself. It's spiritual. It's supernatural. It's mysterious. It's remarkable. But one thing it is not—it is not superstitious. It is sure, tried, and true.

Because the spiritual realm is mainly unseen and intangible, it has been marketed as the spooky realm. But don't believe this nonsense. Yes, humanly speaking, there is mystery behind it, but don't be fooled. God has clearly spoken on it. The Holy Spirit is a person. And not just a person but the Person of God. And not just God somewhere far out in space. He is God abiding in us. And us in Him. He is God, teaching us. Filling us. Empowering us. Calling us. Sending us. Directing us. Guiding us. Protecting us. Like David sings in Psalm 23:5, He anoints our heads with oil and our cups runneth over.

We need the oil. It's heaven's seal of approval. A holy unction. A divine impartation. The fingerprint of God. Like sheep need the shepherd's oil for protection and healing. Like vehicles need fresh oil to keep the engine running well. Like the ten virgins in Matthew 25 needed oil to keep their lamps trimmed and burning. Like the oil the prophet Samuel poured on David in 1 Samuel 16, anointing him as the next king of Israel. We need it. The type of oil that whenever David played the harp before King Saul the evil spirit departed!

Never let this become a fad, take this for granted, or underestimate the Spirit's power. We are a people oiled for war. For battle against the evil one and all his lies. It's our superpower

---

[7] Merriam-Webster dictionary | www.merriam-webster.com | www.learnersdictionary.com
[8] Luke 4:18–19; 7:38, 46; Acts 4:27; 10:38; 2 Cor. 1:21; Heb. 1:9; Matt. 6:17; Mark 6:12–13; 16:1; John 11:2; 12:3
[9] *Strong's Exhaustive Concordance of the Bible* | Blue Letter Bible | www.blueletterbible.org

and secret weapon. In a spiritual war that we've already won—through Jesus the Christ, the Anointed One!

Love, grace, and peace …

♪Colossians 3:16,

Rodney

Take a moment to meditate, muse, and memorize God's word. What is the Holy Spirit saying to you right now?

_____

_____

_____

_____

_____

_____

_____

_____

_____

_____

_____

_____

LETTER #4

ATMOSPHERE

[n. Atmosphere: a surrounding influence or environment][10]

Luke 7:37–38 (NKJV)[11]

37 And behold, a woman in the city who was a sinner, when she knew that Jesus sat at the table in the Pharisee's house, brought an alabaster flask of fragrant oil,[G3464]

38 and stood at His feet behind Him weeping; and she began to wash His feet with her tears, and wiped them with the hair of her head; and she kissed His feet and anointed them with the fragrant oil. [G3464]

[G3464] μύρον mýron, moo'-ron; probably of foreign origin (compare H4753, G4666); "myrrh", i.e. (by implication) perfumed oil:—ointment.[12]

Dear Worship Leader,

When we're leading worship, we're setting a table. A table for His presence. For us to dine with the King. To worship at His feet. Wash them with our tears. Wipe them with our hair. Kiss and anoint them with fragrant oil. Perfumed oil. Expensive oil. Oil that changes the atmosphere.

Worship like this is intimate. It's costly. It's uncomfortable to our flesh but life to our spirits. It bids that we come out from cultural norms. Where others around us may whisper that we've gone too far. That we're making too big of a deal. They want us to keep worship perfectly wrapped in a nice, neat, little box. And to a certain degree, I can appreciate that. I do believe in order, in boundaries, in not drawing a lot of attention to myself—not making a big scene. Personally, I'm more of an introvert. So I certainly understand that type of quietness. And in most cases, privately, I prefer it.

But there comes a time when we must break the box. The box of position, personality, and personal preference. God's been far too good for that. Here's the principle: To whom little is forgiven, the same loves little, but for those of us who realize we've been forgiven for much, we can't help but love Him much. Worship Him much. Praise Him much. Sing to Him much. Yes, and even dance before Him much. Like David, in 2 Samuel 6:14, we're dancing before the Lord, with all our might. He gave His all for me. I owe Him this praise!

To all the naysayers, don't push us on this. Because we feel like David did when he told his wife, Michal, "I'm not dancing for you! I'm dancing before the One who chose me! The One who appointed me! The One who called me! The One who anointed me! And when I think of His goodness, and all He's done for me, I will be even more undignified than this!"

Love, grace, and peace …

---

[10] Merriam-Webster dictionary | www.merriam-webster.com | www.learnersdictionary.com

[11] Luke 7:36–50 (47); Matt. 26:6–13; Mark 14:3–9; John 12:1–8 | 2 Sam. 6:1–23 (22); 1 Chron. 15 | 1 Kings 12:28–30

[12] *Strong's Exhaustive Concordance of the Bible* | Blue Letter Bible | www.blueletterbible.org

♪Colossians 3:16,

Rodney

Take a moment to meditate, muse, and memorize God's word. What is the Holy Spirit saying to you right now?

_____

_____

_____

_____

_____

_____

_____

_____

_____

_____

_____

_____

_____

_____

_____

_____

LETTER #5

A CAPPELLA

[a. A cappella: without instrumental accompaniment][13]

Acts 16:25–26 (NKJV)

25 But at midnight Paul and Silas were praying and singing hymns to God, and the prisoners were listening[G1874] to them. 26 Suddenly there was a great earthquake, so that the foundations of the prison were shaken; and immediately all the doors were opened and everyone's chains were loosed.

[G1874] ἐπακροάομαι epakroáomai, ep-ak-ro-ah'-om-ahee; from G1909 and the base of G202; to listen (intently) to:—hear.[14]

Dear Worship Leader,

One of the sweetest moments we can lead God's people into is a cappella singing. As much as I love and appreciate what instruments add to the worship experience, I have to admit sometimes they can get in the way. And depending on the sound system and the volume of the musicians, there are times that the voices simply can't be heard. It's not that God can't hear us; we can't hear ourselves. One of the richest parts of the worship experience is us hearing the collective sound of our voices praying and singing to God.

In congregational worship, we're not the audience; God is. And as great as the worship leader or praise team may be, they can't sing for us. Whether we're flat, sharp, out of tune, or off beat, our song is to God. And He loves our singing.

Lord, help us to never lose this truth: that we're leading Your people to sing to You. They're not gathered to watch us. To be entertained by us. To be mesmerized by our talent and skill. If Sunday worship becomes *Showtime at the Apollo,* then let's not call it congregational worship. Let's call it a show. An event. A performance. And if so, we're not paying tithes; we're buying tickets. And if that's the case, count me out!

I want God's people to experience what Paul and Silas did in prison. At midnight, at the darkest hour of the day, without any instrumental accompaniment, the prisoners intently listened to them praying and singing to God. Without distraction or fanfare. Scripture doesn't tell us what song, what key, or at what tempo they were singing. But they could hear each other, and most importantly, God heard them.

I hope and pray that no matter how creative our services become, we always treasure and make time for the simple things: God and His people, enjoying one another.

Love, grace, and peace …

♪Colossians 3:16,

---

[13] Merriam-Webster dictionary | www.merriam-webster.com | www.learnersdictionary.com
[14] *Strong's Exhaustive Concordance of the Bible* | Blue Letter Bible | www.blueletterbible.org

Rodney

Take a moment to meditate, muse, and memorize God's word. What is the Holy Spirit saying to you right now?

_____

_____

_____

_____

_____

_____

_____

_____

_____

_____

_____

_____

_____

_____

_____

_____

LETTER #6

AD-LIB

[v. Ad-lib: to deliver spontaneously; to improvise, especially lines or a speech][15]

Exodus 15:20–21 (NKJV)

20 Then Miriam the prophetess, the sister of Aaron, took the timbrel in her hand; and all the women went out after her with timbrels and with dances.
21 And Miriam answered[H6030] them:

"Sing to the LORD,
For He has triumphed gloriously!
The horse and its rider
He has thrown into the sea!"

[H6030] עָנָה 'ânâh, aw-naw'; a primitive root; properly, to eye or (generally) to heed, i.e. pay attention; by implication, to respond; by extension to begin to speak; specifically to sing, shout, testify, announce:—give account, afflict (by mistake for 6031), (cause to, give) answer, bring low (by mistake for 6031), cry, hear, Leannoth, lift up, say, × scholar, (give a) shout, sing (together by course), speak, testify, utter, (bear) witness. See also H1042, H1043.[16]

Dear Worship Leader,

When it comes to leading worship, I don't call singers BGVs, or background vocalists. I believe everyone on the platform is in the foreground leading worship. Yes, everyone. Obviously, there is typically someone assigned to be the worship leader, but even so, they are not the center of attention; they are simply directing traffic. Thus, the worship leader is not the only one leading the congregation. Everyone on the platform is being watched and observed by someone somewhere in the congregation.

That is why I personally love ad-libs sprinkled throughout the worship set. I know this makes some leaders nervous, but if led appropriately, orderly, and at the appointed time, it can be so effective. Yes, it requires instruction, training, patience, management, monitoring, and special skill, but it's worth it.

For me, praying and singing go hand in hand. And just as I wouldn't have a problem with multiple people praying aloud at a given time, the same is true for singing. I don't have to control every miniscule detail of the service. Sometimes I want the Upper Room experience like on the Day of Pentecost in Acts 2. While there was unity, there was also personal expression and freedom. They were all filled and all speaking as the Spirit gave utterance, in multiple languages!

Here we have organized chaos. Some even mocked that they must be drunk. As with Miriam and all the women in Exodus 15:20–21, they didn't preplan, pre-orchestrate, prepackage, or prerehearse this moment. It spontaneously sounded like a rushing mighty wind hit the house—like someone instantly in labor—and suddenly the Holy Ghost had taken over! He's driving the service, baptizing the people, and birthing the church! He's completely in charge and at total liberty.

Love, grace, and peace …

---

[15] Merriam-Webster dictionary | www.merriam-webster.com | www.learnersdictionary.com
[16] *Strong's Exhaustive Concordance of the Bible* | Blue Letter Bible | www.blueletterbible.org

♪Colossians 3:16,

Rodney

Take a moment to meditate, muse, and memorize God's word. What is the Holy Spirit saying to you right now?

_____

_____

_____

_____

_____

_____

_____

_____

_____

_____

_____

_____

_____

_____

_____

 LETTER #7

AUTHENTICITY

[a. Authentic: 1) not false or imitation: real, actual
2) true to one's own personality, spirit, or character][17]

John 4:23–24 (NKJV)[18]

23 "But the hour is coming, and now is, when the true[G228] worshipers will worship the Father in spirit and truth; for the Father is seeking such to worship Him.
24 "God is Spirit, and those who worship Him must worship in spirit and truth."

[G228] ἀληθινός alēthinós, al-ay-thee-nos'; from G227; truthful:—true.
[G227] ἀληθής alēthés, al-ay-thace'; from G1 (as a negative particle) and G2990; true (as not concealing):—true, truly, truth.
[G2990] λανθάνω lanthánō, lan-than'-o; a prolonged form of a primary verb, which is used only as an alternate in certain tenses; to lie hid (literally or figuratively); often used adverbially, unwittingly:—be hid, be ignorant of, unawares.[19]

Dear Worship Leader,

I wish all our churches were a safe place for us to take off our masks, remove our capes, and step outside the Batmobile. But I know worship is that place for me. There I can fully and authentically be myself. I'm free to be me.

Good, bad, or ugly—I don't have to pretend normal. I don't have to hide my thoughts and feelings. I can permanently take off the fig leaves. Like a lost child, I can run to the Father with outstretched arms—ready for Him to pick me up. Regardless of what has happened or how many times, I know that I am unconditionally loved, accepted, significant, and secure in Christ. Through the finished work of the cross.

There I am safe. Like the prodigal son, the Father embraces me. With abandonment issues, abuse, addiction, trauma, sickness, wounds, bruises, offenses, sin, shame, and all. Fill in the blank. He loves me. He heals me. He washes me. He hears me. He sees me. He knows me. He shapes me. He corrects me. He disciplines me. He counsels me. He sings to me. He revives me. He restores me. He rejuvenates me. And so on.

That's why worship happens in the spirit realm. It's the deepest part of man. Plus God is Spirit. So it connects the deepest part of me with the highest Power and Person there is: God Himself. In Spirit and truth—His way, His terms.

It's also why worship is so intensely personal, even in public. Because before Him, we are naked and uncovered. Yet it's where He covers us. In His presence is fullness of joy, and at His right Hand are pleasures forevermore (Psalm 16:11).

---

[17] Merriam-Webster dictionary | www.merriam-webster.com | www.learnersdictionary.com
[18] John 4:7–30; 8:1–12; 19:30; Ps. 16:11; Gen. 2:25; 3:7–10, 21; Luke 15:17–24; ♪Col. 1:20; 2:14; Heb. 4:16; 10:19–25
[19] *Strong's Exhaustive Concordance of the Bible* | Blue Letter Bible | www.blueletterbible.org

In worship He trains me to be authentic, naked, and not ashamed—with God, self, and others. It starts right there.

Love, grace, and peace …

♪Colossians 3:16,

Rodney

Take a moment to meditate, muse, and memorize God's word. What is the Holy Spirit saying to you right now?

_____

_____

_____

_____

_____

_____

_____

_____

_____

_____

_____

_____

_____

_____

_____

LETTER #8

BROKENNESS

[a. Broken: 1a) made weak or infirm
1b) subdued completely
1c) bankrupt
1d) reduced in rank][20]

Psalm 34:17–18 (NKJV)[21]

**17 The righteous cry out, and the LORD hears,
And delivers them out of all their troubles.
18 The LORD is near to those who have a broken**[H7665] **heart,
And saves such as have a contrite spirit.**

[H7665] שָׁבַר **shâbar,** shaw-bar'; a primitive root; to burst (literally or figuratively):—break (down, off, in pieces, up), broken (-hearted), bring to the birth, crush, destroy, hurt, quench, × quite, tear, view (by mistake for H7663).[22]

Dear Worship Leader,

Sometimes life hurts. Most of us don't have to live long before it breaks us; even Jesus experienced it (Hebrews 4:15; Isaiah 53). And there are many ways to be broken.

Broken people. This is a true depiction of us, our audience, congregation, praise team, choir, musicians, technical support, etc. As we're planning our grandiose celebratory song list, remember them. Remember that. That doesn't always mean we change our setlists, but have they been considered at all in the planning? Are we open to change?

If the Lord is near to them, why are we so far? It's hard to admit this, but from my experience, many of our churches and church leaders don't know how to handle the brokenhearted. The service wasn't planned with them in mind. There's no room for them to grieve, fall apart, cry, or heal. We've given them no place in the worship service, meeting, or rehearsal to emote. Instead, we force feed them religious legalistic food. Commanding them to "get over it" because "the joy of the Lord" is their strength. Inadvertently creating a climate where it's never OK to not be OK.

Lord, please forgive me for the times I didn't even stop to ask for prayer requests. Or the times I slightly shamed the person for not clapping, dancing, lifting their hands, or standing up for praise and worship. What if, for some reason, they really couldn't do it? How lonely of a place?

As worship leaders, we're leading a hospital of broken and sick people. Some in the valley, some in a storm, some in ICU, and some are clueless. Believers and unbelievers alike. As a body, may we always remember them. Pray for them. Reach out to them. Love them so that they never suffer alone.

Love, grace, and peace …

---

20 Merriam-Webster dictionary | www.merriam-webster.com | www.learnersdictionary.com
21 Isa. 61:1; Luke 4:18; 5:29–32; Ps. 51:8, 17; 1 Cor. 12:20–26; Matt. 9:12–13, 35–38; 25:35–36; James 1:27; 5:13–18
22 *Strong's Exhaustive Concordance of the Bible* | Blue Letter Bible | www.blueletterbible.org

♪Colossians 3:16,

Rodney

Take a moment to meditate, muse, and memorize God's word. What is the Holy Spirit saying to you right now?

_____

_____

_____

_____

_____

_____

_____

_____

_____

_____

_____

_____

_____

_____

_____

LETTER #9

BOUNDARIES

[n. Boundary: something that indicates or fixes a limit or extent][23]

1 Timothy 3:1–5 (NKJV)[24]

1 This is a faithful saying: If a man desires the position of a bishop, he desires a good work.

2 A bishop then must be blameless, the husband of one wife, temperate, sober-minded, of good behavior, hospitable, able to teach;

3 not given to wine, not violent, not greedy for money, but gentle, not quarrelsome, not covetous;

4 one who rules[G4291] his own house well, having his children in submission with all reverence

5 (for if a man does not know how to rule[G4291] his own house, how will he take care of the church of God?);

[G4291] προΐστημι proḯstēmi, pro-is'-tay-mee; from G4253 and G2476; to stand before, i.e. (in rank) to preside, or (by implication) to practise:—maintain, be over, rule.[25]

Dear Worship Leader,

I'm not married to the church. I'm the husband of one wife; her name is Angela. I have one son; his name is Josiah. Outside Christ, they are my number one priority. No matter how great of a worship leader or pastor I am, if I'm failing at home, I'm failing everywhere else. That was a hard lesson to learn.

As much as I feel the tug and pull of trying to do a lot simultaneously, there's really only one way to win: family first. All else is secondary. I cannot win the church and world at the expense of losing my family. To the church and world I am easily replaced, but to Angela and Josiah, I am not. What I do at home privately is the foundation for everything else I do publicly. I would rather have the applause of these two than the ovation of two thousand. This requires hard choices to be made each day. The people-pleaser in me has to die daily. The Superman complex of wanting to be everyone's hero has to be slaughtered on the altar. Lord, make me a hero at home first. At the end of the day, that's what matters most.

Please hear me. For years, my home suffered while I sought to make the house of God soar. For this, I had to repent. It is truly "Backward, Christian Soldiers." Practically, that means learning to say no to others so that I can say yes to home. I hope it never comes to this, but if I have to fight the church for my family, call me Sugar Ray Leonard. I'm here for it!

My family needs a day off each week. We require a family vacation away every year. It's important that we eat at the table together regularly. Family prayer and devotion are essential. Recreational exercise is vital. It's necessary that we all help with family chores. My wife and son need things only a husband and father can provide. Now I draw a line in the sand so that when all is said and done, they win first.

---

[23] Merriam-Webster dictionary | www.merriam-webster.com | www.learnersdictionary.com

[24] Titus 1:5–9; 2:1–8; Ps. 127–128; Deut. 6:4–9; 1 Tim. 5:8; 6:6; ♪Col. 3:18–21; Eph. 5:22–6:4; 1 Pet. 3:1–7; 1 Cor. 7

[25] *Strong's Exhaustive Concordance of the Bible* | Blue Letter Bible | www.blueletterbible.org

Love, grace, and peace …

♪Colossians 3:16,

Rodney

Take a moment to meditate, muse, and memorize God's word. What is the Holy Spirit saying to you right now?

_____

_____

_____

_____

_____

_____

_____

_____

_____

_____

_____

_____

_____

_____

LETTER #10

BURN OUT

[v. Burn out: to cause to fail, wear out, or become exhausted, especially from overwork or overuse][26]

Genesis 2:1–3 (NKJV)

1 Thus the heavens and the earth, and all the host of them, were finished.
2 And on the seventh day God ended His work which He had done, and He rested[H7673] on the seventh day from all His work which He had done.
3 Then God blessed the seventh day and sanctified it, because in it He rested[H7673] from all His work which God had created and made.

[H7673] שָׁבַת **shâbath,** shaw-bath'; a primitive root; to repose, i.e. desist from exertion; used in many implied relations (causative, figurative or specific):—(cause to, let, make to) cease, celebrate, cause (make) to fail, keep (sabbath), suffer to be lacking, leave, put away (down), (make to) rest, rid, still, take away.[27]

Dear Worship Leader,

Many of us laughed at the viral video of the six-year-old boy that was supposed to give a speech at church one day but instead chose to say these words: "I'm tired of this church." As he handed the microphone back and protested to his seat, the church audibly gasped. And the rest of the world fell out laughing because we can relate.

We all need a break. We are not robots and machines. And even if we were, we would still need to be shut off and rebooted sometimes. God is all wise. As our Creator, on the seventh day, He modeled for us what to do at the end of our workday or week: Rest. Relax. Reboot. Rejuvenate. Refresh.

Without it, burnout is inevitable and everything suffers. Strength decreases. Vulnerabilities increase. Awareness is lowered. Decisions turn irrational. Passion dissipates. Values weaken. We become Grouchy Smurf—cranky, moody, and easily irritated. Why? Because we have aborted God's original plan and the way He preprogrammed us.

Like Chick-fil-A (which closes on Sundays) has proven as the number one fast-food restaurant of our time: God's plan is best. It's better to trust God with six days than to have seven without Him. It's kingdom arithmetic. Even working God's program, it's unwise to skip breaks. You'll pay for it later. I'm a witness!

We are not more than human. Superman, Batman, and Wonder Woman were all fictitious characters. We as human beings need sleep. We need rest. We need Sabbaths. So take the day off. Use all of your paid vacation time. Unplug. Go for a hike or a swim. Do something fun. Write in yourself on your own calendar. And just as you wouldn't cancel someone else in need, don't cancel yourself. You're the one in need this time!

Love, grace, and peace …

---

26 Merriam-Webster dictionary | www.merriam-webster.com | www.learnersdictionary.com
27 *Strong's Exhaustive Concordance of the Bible* | Blue Letter Bible | www.blueletterbible.org

♪Colossians 3:16,

Rodney

Take a moment to meditate, muse, and memorize God's word. What is the Holy Spirit saying to you right now?

_____

_____

_____

_____

_____

_____

_____

_____

_____

_____

_____

_____

_____

_____

_____

SPIRITUAL CHECKUP: INSPIRE

Review the last ten letters and record any key highlights. Has the Holy Spirit revealed any …

Instruction?

_____

_____

_____

_____

Needs?

_____

_____

_____

_____

Scripture?

_____

_____

_____

_____

Principles?

_____

_____

_____

_____

Interests?

_____

_____

_____

_____

Reproof?

_____

_____

_____

_____

Encouragement?

_____

_____

_____

_____

LETTER #11

BOLDNESS

[a. Bold: 1a) fearless before danger 1b) showing or requiring a fearless daring spirit][28]

Acts 4:13, 29, 31 (NKJV)[29]

13 Now when they saw the boldness[G3954] of Peter and John, and perceived that they were uneducated and untrained men, they marveled. And they realized that they had been with Jesus.

29 "Now, Lord, look on their threats, and grant to Your servants that with all boldness[G3954] they may speak Your word,

31 And when they had prayed, the place where they were assembled together was shaken; and they were all filled with the Holy Spirit, and they spoke the word of God with boldness.[G3954]

[G3954] παῤῥησία parrhēsía, par-rhay-see'-ah; from G3956 and a derivative of G4483; all out-spokenness, i.e. frankness, bluntness, publicity; by implication, assurance:—bold (X -ly, -ness, -ness of speech), confidence, × freely, × openly, × plainly(-ness).[30]

Dear Worship Leader,

Leadership requires bold moves to be made. Personally, I tend to be more of a timid person. That is, until I'm filled with the Spirit (4:8, 31). When He takes over, all bets are off. Like Peter and John in Acts 4, there's no room for the spirit of fear. Too much is at stake! We can't allow passivity to lose the service, the team, or the congregation. We are at war and in high battle. Direction always needs to be loving and respectful but also clear, concise, and without compromise.

At warship (war + worship), I've noticed that I become a different person. I'm not worried about hurting feelings or stepping on toes. Hopefully, at this point they know my heart. If not, we can discuss it later. But right now, I'm leading an army. And now is no time for coddling and pampering. Someone's life is on the line! Luke 4:18–19 (NKJV) says it best

The Spirit of the LORD is upon Me,
Because He has anointed Me
To preach the gospel to the <u>poor</u>;
He has sent Me to heal the <u>brokenhearted</u>,
To proclaim liberty to the <u>captives</u>
And recovery of sight to the <u>blind</u>,
To set at liberty those who are <u>oppressed</u>;
To proclaim the acceptable year of the LORD.

As soldiers, let nothing and no one get us off course. We have a job to do, a mission to accomplish, and a work to finish. We need laser focus. And we will not be distracted, hijacked, or hindered. This is a matter of life or death. Heaven or hell. Now or never. And with the Holy Spirit in charge, we choose life, healing, liberty, sight, and deliverance. In the bold name of Jesus, by His blood and His authority!

---

[28] Merriam-Webster dictionary | www.merriam-webster.com | www.learnersdictionary.com

[29] Acts 4:1–31; 5:17–42; 6:8–7:60; 9:27–29; 13:46–52; 14:3; 17:1–9; 18:26; 19:8; 20:24; Isa. 61:1; Eph. 4:15; 5:18–21; 6:19–20; ♪Col. 4:6; 2 Tim. 1:7; 2:3–4; 1 Cor. 14:8; Prov. 28:1; 29:25; Exod. 3:1–4:17; Heb. 11:1–40 (6); 13:5–6; Dan. 3; 6

[30] *Strong's Exhaustive Concordance of the Bible* | Blue Letter Bible | www.blueletterbible.org

Love, grace, and peace …

♪Colossians 3:16,

Rodney

Take a moment to meditate, muse, and memorize God's word. What is the Holy Spirit saying to you right now?

_____

_____

_____

_____

_____

_____

_____

_____

_____

_____

_____

_____

_____

_____

_____

LETTER #12

BLENDED

[v. Blend: 1) mix, especially: to combine or associate so that the separate constituents or the line of demarcation cannot be distinguished
2) to prepare by thoroughly intermingling different varieties or grades][31]

♪Colossians 3:16 (NKJV)[32]

16 Let the word of Christ dwell in you richly in all wisdom, teaching and admonishing one another in psalms and hymns and spiritual songs, singing[G103] with grace in your hearts to the Lord.

[G103] ᾄδω áidō, ad'-o; a primary verb; to sing:—sing.[33]

Dear Worship Leader,

As it relates to worship music, I like to offer blended styles—something that resonates with everyone. Yes, this requires that I continue to expand my repertoire, but that's perfectly fine. The goal is to have everyone singing God's truth. Regardless of age, race, or culture—traditional or contemporary—we all need to eat. And I like to musically offer the medley of a well-balanced, colorfully plated, spiritually nutritious meal. Psalms, hymns, and spiritual songs.

While leading, I have been known to prayerfully burst into a well-known chorus or hymn totally unplanned. Now this is risky and has to be done carefully because it has the potential to crash and burn. In fact, sometimes I will do it a cappella or even accompany myself on the keyboard, in order to transition in and out smoothly. But for me, strategically making a sharp right turn is worth the risk, if it deepens our worship, heightens our expression, and unifies the room.

It really grieves me to see people just watching us sing during praise and worship. I immediately go into problem-solving mode. We're here to worship, not to observe a performance or concert. And worship is participatory, generational, and global. It's also instructional and therapeutic. We all need it. Let's offer to God all that we are in response to all that He is.

All of creation belongs to Him! So don't deify or demonize anything musical. ♪Colossians 1:16 teaches that *all things* were created by Him, through Him, and for Him. Romans 11:36 (NKJV; emphasis mine) says, "For of Him and through Him and to Him are *all things,* to whom be glory forever. Amen." So as the body of Christ, for the glory of God, let's broaden our musical scope to reach all people, types, and nations. And let's creatively sing the word of Christ, in all styles, rhythms, and languages.

Love, grace, and peace …

♪Colossians 3:16,

---

[31] Merriam-Webster dictionary | www.merriam-webster.com | www.learnersdictionary.com
[32] Eph. 5:19; 2 Chron. 5:11–14; Matt. 26:30; Mark 14:26; Acts 16:25; Rom. 14:11; Phil. 2:9–11; Rev. 5:8–10; 7:9–17
[33] *Strong's Exhaustive Concordance of the Bible* | Blue Letter Bible | www.blueletterbible.org

Rodney

Take a moment to meditate, muse, and memorize God's word. What is the Holy Spirit saying to you right now?

_____

_____

_____

_____

_____

_____

_____

_____

_____

_____

_____

_____

_____

_____

_____

LETTER #13

BEING

[v. Be: 1a) to equal in meaning: have the same connotation as: symbolize
1b) to have identity with: to constitute the same idea or object as
1c) to constitute the same class as
1d) to have a specified qualification or characterization
1e) to belong to the class of][34]

Matthew 5:13–14 (NKJV)

13 "You are[G2075] the salt of the earth; but if the salt loses its flavor, how shall it be seasoned? It is then good for nothing but to be thrown out and trampled underfoot by men.
14 "You are[G2075] the light of the world. A city that is set on a hill cannot be hidden.

♪Colossians 2:10 (NKJV)

10 and you are[G2075] complete in Him, who is the head of all principality and power.

[G2075] ἐστέ esté, es-teh'; second person plural present indicative of G1510; ye are:—be, have been, belong.[35]

Dear Worship Leader,

We are human beings, not human doings. There is peace in knowing who you are. Identity is a life-changing concept to grasp; it encompasses everything. It's where we find value. Say these words: I am a spirit. I have a soul. I live in a body.

Here's one of life's greatest questions: who are you? For me, the answer is not Rodney. That's my name. It can be changed. It's also not worship leader. That's what I do. What about when I'm not working? I love saying that I'm Angela's husband or Josiah's father. But those are still roles. Who was I before I knew them? Answering that I'm Black or African American doesn't work because that's my color or ethnicity. Yes, I'm an American, but that's not my identity either. That's where I live. And thank God the answer is not in my weight, height, talent, possessions, notoriety, family, friends, or social media status.

Here's the true answer. As a believer in Christ, He gave me a whole new identity. I am now a child of God. A spiritual son. A Christian. A Saint. And because of the finished work of the cross, that will *never* change! Based on Ephesians 1, we are

Chosen in Christ (vv. 4–6)—chosen, holy, blameless, adopted, accepted
Heirs in Christ (vv. 11–12)—inheritance, predestined, purpose, praise
Redeemed in Christ (vv. 7–10)—redemption, forgiveness, riches, grace
Identified in Christ (vv. 13–14)—sealed with the Holy Spirit of promise
Spiritually blessed in Christ (v. 3)—every spiritual blessing in heaven
Trusted in Christ (vv. 1–2)—saints, faithful, grace, peace, Father, Lord

Now that we're in Christ, our identity informs our behavior, not the reverse. We're all He says we are. We're salt. We're light. We're complete. We don't work to become this; we're already

---

[34] Merriam-Webster dictionary | www.merriam-webster.com | www.learnersdictionary.com
[35] *Strong's Exhaustive Concordance of the Bible* | Blue Letter Bible | www.blueletterbible.org

this. Eternally secure. Christ finished the job on our behalf. At the moment of our salvation, we received it all simply—by *grace alone* through *faith alone* in *Christ alone!*

Love, grace, and peace …

♪Colossians 3:16,

Rodney

Take a moment to meditate, muse, and memorize God's word. What is the Holy Spirit saying to you right now?

_____

_____

_____

_____

_____

_____

_____

_____

_____

_____

_____

_____

_____

 LETTER #14

CREATIVITY

[n. Creativity: 1) the ability to create 2) the quality of being creative][36]

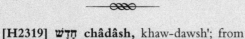

Psalm 40:1-3 (NKJV)[37]

To the Chief Musician. A Psalm of David.
1 I waited patiently for the LORD;
And He inclined to me,
And heard my cry.
2 He also brought me up out of a horrible pit,
Out of the miry clay,
And set my feet upon a rock,
And established my steps.
3 He has put a new[H2319] song in my mouth—
Praise to our God;
Many will see it and fear,
And will trust in the LORD.

[H2319] חָדָשׁ **châdâsh,** khaw-dawsh'; from H2318; new:—fresh, new thing.
[H2318] חָדַשׁ **châdash,** khaw-dash'; a primitive root; to be new; causatively, to rebuild:—renew, repair.[38]

Dear Worship Leader,

We serve a creative God. The very first thing we see Him doing in Genesis 1:1 is creating the heavens and the earth. And we are made in His image (Genesis 1:27). How exciting!

I wholeheartedly believe that one of the ways we lead God's people is by writing or singing a new song. One that fits that house, that moment, and that congregation. In scripture, five times God tells us to sing to Him a new song (Psalm 33:3; 96:1; 98:1; 149:1; Isaiah 42:10). In 1 Kings 4:32 we learn that Solomon wrote 1,005 new songs! The entire book of Psalms is a collection of songs to be sung, not simply read. This is no small thing, but it is a massive miss for many.

I appreciate the many talented and well-known songwriters of our day, past and present. But they are not the only ones gifted to write new songs. So are you! Yes, you. Look closely at your hands. Do you see your fingerprints? None of us has the same fingerprint. Your arch, loop, and whorl are uniquely yours. That's how gifted you are. Have you considered using your creativity to glorify God in a way that is unique to your story, your praise, and your testimony? Crafted with your fingerprint. Your handprint. Your voiceprint. Your *songprint.*

On occasion, just because I love my wife, I enjoy presenting her a Hallmark greeting card to express how much she means to me. But that's a card Hallmark wrote. You should see her face when I present her with something I wrote. With my mark on it. From my *heartprint.* It's the same with God. Singing songs to Him that others have written is great. But on occasion, just because you love Him, sing to Him a new song that you write—from your own heart and pen. Heaven will touch earth in a way that's special between you and Him.

---

[36] Merriam-Webster dictionary | www.merriam-webster.com | www.learnersdictionary.com
[37] Exod. 15:1–21; Deut. 31:19–32:47; Judg. 5; 1 Sam. 2:1–10; 2 Sam. 1:17–27; Luke 1:46–55; Rev. 5:9–10; 14:3; 15:3–4
[38] *Strong's Exhaustive Concordance of the Bible* | Blue Letter Bible | www.blueletterbible.org

Love, grace, and peace …

♪Colossians 3:16,

Rodney

Take a moment to meditate, muse, and memorize God's word. What is the Holy Spirit saying to you right now?

_____

_____

_____

_____

_____

_____

_____

_____

_____

_____

_____

_____

_____

_____

LETTER #15

CLAPPING

[v. Clap: 1) to strike (two things, such as two flat, hard surfaces) together so as to produce a sharp percussive noise
2) to strike (the hands) together repeatedly usually in applause
3) to strike with the flat of the hand in a friendly way][39]

Psalm 47:1–2 (NKJV)[40]

To the Chief Musician. A Psalm of the sons of Korah.
1 Oh, clap[H8628] your hands, all you peoples!
Shout to God with the voice of triumph!
2 For the LORD Most High is awesome;
He is a great King over all the earth.

[H8628] תָּקַע tâqaʻ, taw-kah'; a primitive root; to clatter, i.e. slap (the hands together), clang (an instrument); by analogy, to drive (a nail or tent-pin, a dart, etc.); by implication, to become bondsman by handclasping):—blow (a trumpet), cast, clap, fasten, pitch (tent), smite, sound, strike, × suretiship, thrust.[41]

Dear Worship Leader,

Whenever I see a psalm written by the sons of Korah, such as in Psalm 47, I pause in amazement. Their father, Korah, died as a rebel leader against Moses and Aaron. In public display, the earth opened its mouth and swallowed him and his companions alive. Numbers 26:11 (NKJV) says, "Nevertheless, the children of Korah did not die." So the sons of Korah are walking miracles of the mercy and grace of God. Their dad led a rebellion against God, but here they are—marvelously leading worship, praise, and celebration for God!

And oh, what a celebration it is when God's people come together and make a big deal about the Lord! Clapping their hands, singing praises, and shouting with joyful voices of victory. Why all the noise? Because the Lord Most High is awesome! He is God and a great King over all the earth!

It's culturally acceptable to go wild at sport events or at concerts headlining the hottest artist or band of the day. When teams win championships, you can hardly hear the announcer because the crowd is thunderous with claps and cheers echoing throughout the stadium. All this fanfare for celebrities who do not know our names. Yet we've made them stars, kings, queens, and idols.

How much more does the one who rescued us deserve? The one who has given us the victory! The one who gives us brand-new mercies every day. The one who supplies oxygen for us to take the next breath. He not only knows our names but also has the very hairs on our heads all numbered, according to Matthew 10:30. Let's clap, sing, and shout to His name! To our Champion—the King eternal, immortal, invisible, who alone is wise—be honor and glory forever and ever! Amen (1 Timothy 1:17).

---

39 Merriam-Webster dictionary | www.merriam-webster.com | www.learnersdictionary.com
40 Num. 16:1–50; 26:9–11; 1 Tim. 1:17; Lam. 3:22–23; Ps. 103; 118; 136; 150:1–6 | Ps. 42; 44–49; 84–85; 87–88
41 *Strong's Exhaustive Concordance of the Bible* | Blue Letter Bible | www.blueletterbible.org

Love, grace, and peace …

♪Colossians 3:16,

Rodney

Take a moment to meditate, muse, and memorize God's word. What is the Holy Spirit saying to you right now?

_____

_____

_____

_____

_____

_____

_____

_____

_____

_____

_____

_____

_____

LETTER #16

CONGREGATION

[n. Congregation: 1a) an assembly of persons: gathering
1b) a religious community such as: an organized body of believers in a particular locality][42]

Numbers 14:6–9 (NKJV)[43]

6 But Joshua the son of Nun and Caleb the son of Jephunneh, who were among those who had spied out the land, tore their clothes;
7 and they spoke to all the congregation[H5712] of the children of Israel, saying: "The land we passed through to spy out is an exceedingly good land.
8 "If the LORD delights in us, then He will bring us into this land and give it to us, 'a land which flows with milk and honey.'
9 "Only do not rebel against the LORD, nor fear the people of the land, for they are our bread; their protection has departed from them, and the LORD is with us. Do not fear them."

[H5712] עֵדָה 'êdâh, ay-daw'; feminine of H5707 in the original sense of fixture; a stated assemblage (specifically, a concourse, or generally, a family or crowd):—assembly, company, congregation, multitude, people, swarm. Compare H5713.[44]

Dear Worship Leader,

What message are you carrying to the congregation? Out of the twelve spies sent into the Promised Land, only two proved to be good worship leaders: Joshua and Caleb. The other ten spies were bad worship leaders because they brought back a bad report. It's as simple as that.

Most of us would not consider the twelve spies worship leaders because they weren't singing, but they absolutely were. Their attitudes and actions were singing loud and clear. Ten were singing fear, and two were singing faith. In unison, the congregation harmonized with the ten and aborted God's plan. That's bad worship leading, with or without music.

It's tempting to simply look at the lyrics of the songs we're singing and assume that's our message, but that might not be altogether true. Our attire is sending a message. Our spirits are sending a message. What we say during or in between songs is sending a message. How we honor or dishonor our leaders is a message. How we treat others is a message. How we respond to distraction or technical difficulty is a message. How prepared we are for spiritual warfare is a message. How we handle God's word is a message. How we worship on and off the platform is a message. How we handle criticism or failure is a message. We're sending lots of messages.

But here is the ultimate question: are we pointing people toward God or away from Him? Fear is away from Him. Idolatry is away from Him. People-pleasing is away from Him. The love of money is away from Him. Pride, lust, and division are away from Him. Emotionalism, traditionalism, legalism, materialism, racism, elitism, and perfectionism are all pointing people

---

[42] Merriam-Webster dictionary | www.merriam-webster.com | www.learnersdictionary.com
[43] Num. 13:1–33; 14:1–45; Deut. 1:19–33; Heb. 3:16–19; 4:1–16; 10:22–23, 38; 11:1–40; 12:2; Ps. 100:1–5 (3); 23:1–6
[44] *Strong's Exhaustive Concordance of the Bible* | Blue Letter Bible | www.blueletterbible.org

away from God. He wants us all running toward Him in faith. We are His people and the sheep of His pasture.

Love, grace, and peace …

♪Colossians 3:16,

Rodney

Take a moment to meditate, muse, and memorize God's word. What is the Holy Spirit saying to you right now?

_____

_____

_____

_____

_____

_____

_____

_____

_____

_____

_____

_____

LETTER #17

COMMITMENT

[n. Commitment: 1a) an agreement or pledge to do something in the future 1b) something pledged 1c) the state or an instance of being obligated or emotionally impelled][45]

―――∞∞∞―――

Luke 14:27–30 (NKJV)[46]

27 "And whoever does not bear his cross and come after Me cannot be My disciple.
28 "For which of you, intending to build a tower, does not sit down first and count the cost, whether he has enough to finish[G535] it—
29 "lest, after he has laid the foundation, and is not able to finish,[G1615] all who see it begin to mock him,
30 "saying, 'This man began to build and was not able to finish.'[G1615]

―――∞∞∞―――

[G535] ἀπαρτισμός apartismós, ap-ar-tis-mos'; from a derivative of G534; completion:—finishing.
[G1615] ἐκτελέω ekteléō, ek-tel-eh'-o; from G1537 and G5055; to complete fully:—finish.[47]

Dear Worship Leader,

I hope others can count on us to keep our word, follow through with our commitments, and finish what we started. Some days ago, I was offered an opportunity to lead worship for a sizable church. As honored as I was to be invited, I graciously declined because I had already committed to lead for another church, which happens to be considerably smaller. I do not regret that decision because I made a commitment and I want my name and word to matter (Proverbs 22:1).

God's word matters, so why shouldn't mine? As His disciple, I am a reflection of Him. In His kingdom, we are not ruled by fame, fortune, or riches. We're not accepting ministry assignments from whoever is the highest bidder as if we're climbing some corporate ladder of success. We're called to be good financial stewards, but we're also foot-washing servants. We've been enlisted as soldiers to serve wherever our King, the Commander in Chief, assigns us. And to stay there until He says the work is finished—no AWOL over here!

Sometimes He sends us into some difficult places. Some tough terrains. Some wilderness experiences. But if ministry were easy, everyone would do it. It's not for the faint of heart. We have to have spines of steel. Matthew 10:16 says for us to be wise as serpents and harmless as doves because He's sending us out as sheep in the midst of wolves. Matthew 10:22 alerts us that we'll be hated for His name's sake, but those who endure to the end will be saved. He's got us!

As our Leader, He's not asking us to do anything that He didn't first model (John 13:14). There was nothing easy about Jesus's assignment. As the old hymn taught, must Jesus bear the cross alone and all the world go free? No, there's a cross for everyone, and there's a cross for me.

―――――――

45 Merriam-Webster dictionary | www.merriam-webster.com | www.learnersdictionary.com
46 Luke 14:15–33; 22:24–30; 1 Pet. 5:1–4; 1 Cor. 4:1–2; 2 Tim. 2:1–4; Matt. 10:16–26; 20:20–28; Heb. 12:2; Prov. 25:19
47 *Strong's Exhaustive Concordance of the Bible* | Blue Letter Bible | www.blueletterbible.org

Love, grace, and peace …

♪Colossians 3:16,

Rodney

Take a moment to meditate, muse, and memorize God's word. What is the Holy Spirit saying to you right now?

_____

_____

_____

_____

_____

_____

_____

_____

_____

_____

_____

_____

_____

_____

LETTER #18

COURAGE

[n. Courage: mental or moral strength to venture, persevere, and withstand danger, fear, or difficulty][48]

Joshua 1:6–7, 9, 18 (NKJV)

6 "Be strong and of good courage,[H553] for to this people you shall divide as an inheritance the land which I swore to their fathers to give them.
7 "Only be strong and very courageous,[H553] that you may observe to do according to all the law which Moses My servant commanded you; do not turn from it to the right hand or to the left, that you may prosper wherever you go.

---

9 "Have I not commanded you? Be strong and of good courage;[H553] do not be afraid, nor be dismayed, for the LORD your God is with you wherever you go."

---

18 "Whoever rebels against your command and does not heed your words, in all that you command him, shall be put to death. Only be strong and of good courage."[H553]

[H553] אָמֵץ 'âmats, aw-mats'; a primitive root; to be alert, physically (on foot) or mentally (in courage):—confirm, be courageous (of good courage, stedfastly minded, strong, stronger), establish, fortify, harden, increase, prevail, strengthen (self), make strong (obstinate, speed).[49]

Dear Worship Leader,

We all need courage to move forward and persevere in life. Have you ever been stuck or stranded in a car that wouldn't start or go any further? I have. Maybe you ran out of gas or needed someone to come and give you a jump. In essence, you needed the power and fuel of courage or encouragement.

In Joshua 1, after the death of Moses, four times in one chapter, God commands Joshua to be *strong* and of *good courage*. As the next leader of the children of Israel, God knew he would need it. The Hebrew word for "strong" here, [H2388] חָזַק châzaq, khaw-zak', has also been translated "courage" several times in the KJV. Combined with "good courage," [H553] אָמֵץ 'âmats, aw-mats' in Joshua 1, it could now mean double the courage! It's as if God was saying Joshua would need four double doses of courage! Spiritual "liquid" courage, if you will. That's a lot of power and fuel!

In the New Testament, Timothy seemed to have a problem with timidity. In 1 Timothy 5:23, Paul told him to drink a little wine for his stomach's sake and for his frequent infirmities. In Ephesians 5:18, Paul told the church of Ephesus not to be drunk with wine, in which is dissipation, but be filled with Spirit—like we see in Acts 2:1–4—on the Day of Pentecost!

That's what we need for spiritual mobility today: a continual drinking or filling of the Holy Spirit! According to Ephesians 5:19–21, then we'll be speaking in the Spirit, singing in the Spirit, giving thanks in the Spirit, and submitting in the Spirit.

---

48 Merriam-Webster dictionary | www.merriam-webster.com | www.learnersdictionary.com
49 *Strong's Exhaustive Concordance of the Bible* | Blue Letter Bible | www.blueletterbible.org

In Joshua 1:8, we see the answer is in Joshua's mouth. God told him not to let the Word depart from his mouth but to meditate in it day and night. Drinking and digesting the Word leads to us doing the Word. Doing the Word leads to our ways being prosperous, which ends in good success. A drink, anyone?

Love, grace, and peace ...

♪Colossians 3:16,

Rodney

Take a moment to meditate, muse, and memorize God's word. What is the Holy Spirit saying to you right now?

_____

_____

_____

_____

_____

_____

_____

_____

_____

_____

LETTER #19

CARE

[n. Care: 1a) painstaking or watchful attention
1b) maintenance
2) charge, supervision, especially: responsibility for or attention to health, well-being, and safety][50]

1 Peter 5:2–4 (NKJV)[51]

2 Shepherd[G4165] the flock of God which is among you, serving as overseers, not by compulsion but willingly, not for dishonest gain but eagerly;
3 nor as being lords over those entrusted to you, but being examples to the flock;
4 and when the Chief Shepherd appears, you will receive the crown of glory that does not fade away.

[G4165] ποιμαίνω poimaínō, poy-mah'-ee-no; from G4166; to tend as a shepherd of (figuratively, superviser):—feed (cattle), rule.
[G4166] ποιμήν poimēn, poy-mane'; of uncertain affinity; a shepherd (literally or figuratively):—shepherd, pastor.[52]

Dear Worship Leader,

I love this saying: before people care how much you know, they want to know how much you care. I have found this to be true. We are not only called to care for the program of the church, but first and foremost, our call is to care for the people of the church. Christ died for people (John 3:16; Mark 10:45).

It's in our titles. We are not called worship leaders because we are leading an event or project but because we are leading people. While that does not give us license to be sloppy in our skillfulness as musicians, it does highlight the need to have a heart for the people—and their need for leadership. David shepherded the people according to the integrity of his heart and guided them by the skillfulness of his hands, Psalm 78:72. Integrity—>Heart. Skillfulness—>Hands.

We are undershepherds. God is the Chief Shepherd. As He cares for us, we care for the people. He's our example; we are theirs. Of all the responsibilities required to care for sheep, know that their number one need is for a shepherd that loves them. If the shepherd loves them, all of the needed care will follow.

That's why I don't currently own a dog. I grew up cleaning their poop as a responsibility of living in my parents' house, but I never learned to love them, which is relationship. I don't have fond memories of petting our dogs or playing with them. All I remember is poop. But I've noticed that poop doesn't really bother owners that love their dog. They feed them out of love. They clean them out of love. They walk them out of love. And yes, they handle their poop out of love.

God says, "I need shepherds that love My people. More than a title, role, or paycheck. Along with that comes poop. But as I clean up your poop out of love, I want you to do the same."

---

[50] Merriam-Webster dictionary | www.merriam-webster.com | www.learnersdictionary.com
[51] Ps. 23; Jer. 23; Ezek. 34; Matt. 9:35–38; 23; Luke 20:45–47; ♪Col. 1:7–8; 4:7–15; Eph. 6:21–22; 1 Thess. 2:8; 2 Cor. 11
[52] *Strong's Exhaustive Concordance of the Bible* | Blue Letter Bible | www.blueletterbible.org

40

Love, grace, and peace …

♪Colossians 3:16,

Rodney

Take a moment to meditate, muse, and memorize God's word. What is the Holy Spirit saying to you right now?

_____

_____

_____

_____

_____

_____

_____

_____

_____

_____

_____

_____

_____

_____

_____

LETTER #20

CONNECT

[v. Connect: 1) to become joined 2) to have or establish a rapport 3) to establish a communications connection][53]

Ephesians 4:16 (NKJV)[54]

16 from whom the whole body, joined[G4883] **and knit together**[G4822] **by what every joint supplies, according to the effective working by which every part does its share, causes growth of the body for the edifying of itself in love.**

[G4883] συναρμολογέω synarmologéō, soon-ar-mol-og-eh'-o; from G4862 and a derivative of a compound of G719 and G3004 (in its original sense of laying); to render close-jointed together, i.e. organize compactly:—be fitly framed (joined) together.
[G4822] συμβιβάζω symbibázō, soom-bib-ad'-zo; from G4862 and βιβάζω bibázō (to force; causative (by reduplication) of the base of G939); to drive together, i.e. unite (in association or affection), (mentally) to infer, show, teach:—compact, assuredly gather, intrust, knit together, prove.[55]

Dear Worship Leader,

Part of winning is establishing and maintaining true life-giving connection, care, and community within our teams, which is vital to growth and effectiveness. One of my favorite games to play is Connect 4. I always enjoy trying to beat my opponent in making the winning connection.

Here is what I call "Connect 4 for Every Leader!" Practically, this could help you plan meetings and rehearsals.

Connect 1: The Administrative Connection: The Order of Christ

- Relate administratively by regularly communicating pertinent information in a professional, clear, timely, orderly, and effective manner. We share facts/data: who, what, where, when, and how.

Connect 2: The Brotherly/Sisterly Connection: The Family of Christ

- Relate personally and graciously as the members of the family of God and of the body of Christ. We share what's going on relationally. Family fun. Family discussion. Family bonding. Fellowship. Friendship.

Connect 3: The Comfort/Care Connection: The Heart of Christ

- Relate compassionately and empathetically in times of personal need and crisis. We share by praying, celebrating life, crying, giving, grieving, visiting, loving, and supporting one another.

---

[53] Merriam-Webster dictionary | www.merriam-webster.com | www.learnersdictionary.com
[54] Eph. 1:3–14; 2; 3:12; 4:11–24 (16); 5:1–2; Rom. 12:3–21; 1 Cor. 12; ♪Col. 2:2, 19; Heb. 10:24; Acts 2:40–47; 6:1–7
[55] *Strong's Exhaustive Concordance of the Bible* | Blue Letter Bible | www.blueletterbible.org

Connect 4: The Discipleship Connection: The Word of Christ

- Relate spiritually, personally, and practically through the word of God and prayer. We share life on life. Spiritual formation. Who God is. Who we are in Christ. What He's saying to us. Our responses, walk, and testimony. Q&A.

I regularly use this as a tool to set agendas and create checkpoints for me and my leaders. I've learned that failure in any one of these connections can lead to division, disarray, dissolution, distraction, and dissension. We are one body. Every member is important. No part can survive on its own.

Love, grace, and peace …

♪Colossians 3:16,

Rodney

Take a moment to meditate, muse, and memorize God's word. What is the Holy Spirit saying to you right now?

_____

_____

_____

_____

_____

_____

_____

_____

_____

_____

SPIRITUAL CHECKUP: INSPIRE

Review the last ten letters and record any key highlights. Has the Holy Spirit revealed any …

Instruction?

_____

_____

_____

_____

Needs?

_____

_____

_____

_____

Scripture?

_____

_____

_____

_____

Principles?

_____

_____

_____

_____

Interests?

_____

_____

_____

_____

Reproof?

_____

_____

_____

_____

Encouragement?

_____

_____

_____

_____

LETTER #21

COMPLIMENT

[n. Compliment: 1a) an expression of esteem, respect, affection, or admiration, especially: an admiring remark
1b) formal and respectful recognition: honor][56]

Proverbs 27:2 (NKJV)[57]

2 Let another man praise[H1984] you, and not your own mouth;
A stranger, and not your own lips.

[H1984] הָלַל **hâlal,** haw-lal'; a primitive root; to be clear (orig. of sound, but usually of color); to shine; hence, to make a show, to boast; and thus to be (clamorously) foolish; to rave; causatively, to celebrate; also to stultify:—(make) boast (self), celebrate, commend, (deal, make), fool(-ish, -ly), glory, give (light), be (make, feign self) mad (against), give in marriage, (sing, be worthy of) praise, rage, renowned, shine.[58]

Dear Worship Leader,

How do you handle compliments? For many of us, it just seems awkward. Sometimes it's how the compliment is given. Or maybe it's who the compliment is coming from that makes it weird. It could also be bad timing. "Never" might feel better!

I used to wonder what a good way to handle it is. Clap? Take a bow? Gesture for more? Or like we see at the award ceremonies, start down a long list of acknowledgments and credits? Should we even allow others to praise us since we're not God and aren't supposed to be people-pleasers? Should we care what they think?

The response that really makes me laugh out loud (LOL) is when the intended recipient aggressively shakes their head no while repeatedly pointing upward, demanding that the compliment or encouragement should only be to God. As if to say, "Don't thank or idolize me. Worship God."

Well, the best advice I've ever heard regarding this topic comes from Larry Titus. He says, "Receive it, and give glory to God." Wow. This blesses me and has changed my perspective.

First of all, receive it because it comes across as rude not to do so. This person is offering you a gift. Death and life are in the power of the tongue. And scripture tells us to exhort and edify one another daily, because we need it! We all need encouragement, edification, and healthy praise. The giver is probably not being insincere or idolizing you; they just want to thank you. You've blessed them and they want you to know it. Next time, maybe try replying, "Thank you. Praise God."

Finally, give glory to God because that's where it needs to land. Matthew 5:16 (NKJV) says, "Let your light so shine before men, that they may see your good works and glorify your Father in heaven." Let praise flow through you—to God!

56 Merriam-Webster dictionary | www.merriam-webster.com | www.learnersdictionary.com
57 Phil. 4:15–20; Heb. 10:25; Prov. 18:21; Eph. 4:29, 32; Acts 4:36; Philem. 1:7; 1 Thess. 2:1–12 (3–6); 2 Cor. 7:6, 13–16
58 *Strong's Exhaustive Concordance of the Bible* | Blue Letter Bible | www.blueletterbible.org

Love, grace, and peace …

♪Colossians 3:16,

Rodney

Take a moment to meditate, muse, and memorize God's word. What is the Holy Spirit saying to you right now?

_____

_____

_____

_____

_____

_____

_____

_____

_____

_____

_____

_____

_____

_____

LETTER #22

CALLING

[n. Calling: 1) a strong inner impulse toward a particular course of action especially when accompanied by conviction of divine influence
2) the vocation or profession in which one customarily engages][59]

Acts 13:36 (NKJV)[60]

36 "For David, after he had served[G5256] his own generation by the will of God, fell asleep, was buried with his fathers, and saw corruption;

[G5256] ὑπηρετέω hupēretĕō, hoop-ay-ret-eh'-o; from G5257; to be a subordinate, i.e. (by implication) subserve:—minister (unto), serve.
[G5257] ὑπηρέτης hupēretēs, hoop-ay-ret'-ace; from G5259 and a derivative of ἐρέσσω ĕrĕssō (to row); an under-oarsman, i.e. (generally) subordinate (assistant, sexton, constable):—minister, officer, servant.[61]

Dear Worship Leader,

Have you ever felt like you were called to do something bigger than yourself? And that whatever it is, you can't die until you've finished it? Something on the inside won't let you put it to rest. It's your life calling, passion, purpose, and service—part of your reason for being here on planet Earth.

When God calls you to a work, you're never the same. It changes you. Even if it doesn't make sense to you or others, it compels you. Even if you don't have all the details worked out, it constrains you. Even without all the resources, it's calling your name. You were made for this. This is your moment. All of life has been preparing you for now.

Somehow, like Noah, God gives you grace to see beyond the natural, into the supernatural. You're building an ark, and it has never rained before. When was the last time you read Hebrews 11, "The Hall of Faith"? These heroes and heroines of the faith were not flawless, but they were faithful. Hebrews 11:38 (NKJV) says "of whom this world was not worthy."

From birth until now, God has been orchestrating the symphony of your life. Jeremiah 1:5 teaches that before He formed you, He knew you. Before you came out of the womb, He sanctified and ordained you. Ephesians 2:10 says that you are His workmanship created in Christ Jesus for good works, which God prepared beforehand that you should walk in them. Romans 8:29–30 proclaims that who God foreknew, He also predestined; who He predestined, He also called; who He called, He also justified; and who He justified, He also glorified. From start to finish, God is ordering your steps.

No matter how big or small the work, your generation is counting on you. Serve until the Master calls you home.

---

[59] Merriam-Webster dictionary | www.merriam-webster.com | www.learnersdictionary.com
[60] Gen. 6–9; 2 Cor. 5:7; Rom. 8:28; Ps. 37:23; 1 Tim. 1:12–17; 2 Tim. 1:8–12; 1 Pet. 2:9; Eph. 1:11; Phil. 2:13; 1 Sam. 22
[61] *Strong's Exhaustive Concordance of the Bible* | Blue Letter Bible | www.blueletterbible.org

Love, grace, and peace …

♪Colossians 3:16,

Rodney

Take a moment to meditate, muse, and memorize God's word. What is the Holy Spirit saying to you right now?

_____

_____

_____

_____

_____

_____

_____

_____

_____

_____

_____

_____

_____

_____

_____

LETTER #23

COUNSELING

[n. Counseling: professional guidance of the individual by utilizing psychological methods especially in collecting case history data, using various techniques of the personal interview, and testing interests and aptitudes][62]

———⚬⚬⚬———

Proverbs 11:14; 15:22; 24:6 (NKJV)[63]

———⚬⚬⚬———

14 Where there is no counsel, the people fall; But in the multitude of counselors[H3289] **there is safety.**

———⚬⚬⚬———

22 Without counsel, plans go awry, But in the multitude of counselors[H3289] **they are established.**

———⚬⚬⚬———

6 For by wise counsel you will wage your own war, And in a multitude of counselors[H3289] **there is safety.**

———⚬⚬⚬———

[H3289] יָעַץ yâ'ats, yaw-ats'; a primitive root; to advise; reflexively, to deliberate or resolve:— advertise, take advise, advise (well), consult, (give, take) counsel(-lor), determine, devise, guide, purpose.[64]

Dear Worship Leader,

Prior to my life falling apart in 2014, and twenty-two years of ministry, I hadn't considered my own need for professional Christian counseling. After my fall, I'm thoroughly convinced that I wouldn't have survived without it! God used therapy and an emergency sabbatical to help restore and recommission me back into service. Unfortunately, many don't make it back.

If I were to do it all again, I would have started out with professional help, support, and tools. Preventive care. Crisis prevention. But here's the problem: denial. I, along with many other leaders, tend to reside in the land of denial where we think we're OK, but internally something is catastrophically wrong—and without correction and alignment, disaster awaits. This leads us to what I call the ABCs of Recovery.

- **Abuse.** We all experience some level of abuse or trauma. If nothing else, we're in a fallen world, with a real enemy (the world, the flesh, and the devil) seeking to steal, kill, and destroy us—along with everyone else connected to us.
- **Brokenness.** As a result of abuse or trauma, we all experience some level of brokenness. You can't take a hammer and repeatedly beat against a piece of wood and claim that the piece of wood remains unaffected.

- **Coping.** Because of brokenness, we all experience some level of coping. Positive or negative, healthy or unhealthy, godly or ungodly—over time, we all develop habits, skills, and techniques attempting to deal with the pain.
- **Deliverance and discipleship.** Consequently, we all need deliverance and discipleship from poor patterns, behaviors, and coping—to help us learn to replace

[62] Merriam-Webster dictionary | www.merriam-webster.com | www.learnersdictionary.com
[63] Ps. 1; 37:37; 1 Cor. 10:12; John 10:10; Rom. 7:14–25; Exod. 1:8–14; 2:24; Acts 7:34; Eph. 2:1–10; 4:1, 17; 5:2, 8, 15
[64] *Strong's Exhaustive Concordance of the Bible* | Blue Letter Bible | www.blueletterbible.org

50

them with what's rich, good, and beneficial. We all need *Christ* through *community* and *counseling.* Isaiah 9:6 says that His name is Counselor!

The earlier, the better. Why wait until we crash and burn before learning to fly correctly—with proper boundaries, resources, tools, and safety protocol in place? This is where counseling can help us. Get help now. Later might be too late.

Love, grace, and peace …

♪Colossians 3:16,

Rodney

Take a moment to meditate, muse, and memorize God's word. What is the Holy Spirit saying to you right now?

_____

_____

_____

_____

_____

_____

_____

_____

_____

_____

_____

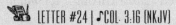 LETTER #24 | ♪COL. 3:16 (NKJV)

DISCIPLESHIP

~Part 1~

[n. Disciple: one who accepts and assists in spreading the doctrines of another: such as
a) Christianity: one of the twelve in the inner circle of Christ's followers according to the Gospel accounts
b) a convinced adherent of a school or individual][65]

♪Colossians 3:16 (NKJV)[66]

16 Let the word of Christ dwell[G1774] in you richly in all wisdom, teaching and admonishing one another in psalms and hymns and spiritual songs, singing with grace in your hearts to the Lord.

[G1774] ἐνοικέω enoikéō, en-oy-keh'-o; from G1722 and G3611; to inhabit (figuratively):— dwell in.
[G3611] οἰκέω oikéō, oy-keh'-o; from G3624; to occupy a house, i.e. reside (figuratively, inhabit, remain, inhere); by implication, to cohabit:—dwell. See also G3625.[67]

Dear Worship Leader,

Discipleship in Christ is about dwelling and abiding in Christ (John 15). I first learned this through ♪Colossians 3:16, which has become my life verse. God uses it to train me, and I, others. It's "Discipleship through Music." When my tank is low, it fuels, energizes, enriches, and enlightens me. It's a wellspring that I've been drinking from and dwelling with for years now.

Colossians is a love letter from Paul to the church of Colosse. He alarms them because the city, previously known for its wealth, is under the threat of an enemy seeking to steal their spiritual riches, or their dwelling, in Christ. The enemy wants to confuse (2:4), cheat (2:8, 18), and condemn them (2:16).

So as any protective father would, Paul responds with a command for his children: You're under attack! Everyone, lock up your spiritual riches and hide them in your hearts! Or in the NKJV, "Let the word of Christ **dwell** in you richly in all wisdom …" That is, *receive the Word indwelt, in abundance, and in all wisdom.* Let it be housed or tabernacled in you. Let it reside and remain there. Let it occupy and fill the house. Let it have your keys, inform your decisions, and make you rich. You need great intake, excess, and access. Let it go viral in you! Eat, drink, and digest it. Become indoctrinated, intoxicated, impregnated, implanted, infused, imprinted, and invested.

Paul then surrounds the imperative [G1774] ἐνοικέω enoikéō, dwell, with three other participles: teaching, admonishing, and singing. By interweaving and interlocking them, he says the following: whenever you're singing kingdom truth (psalms, hymns, and spiritual songs), you're actually teaching and admonishing one another, thereby, helping each other

---

[65] Merriam-Webster dictionary | www.merriam-webster.com | www.learnersdictionary.com
[66] Matt. 28:16–20 | Rom. 8:11; 2 Cor. 6:16; 2 Tim. 1:5, 14 | Rom. 7:17–18, 20; 8:9, 11; 1 Cor. 3:16; 7:12–13; 1 Tim. 6:16
[67] *Strong's Exhaustive Concordance of the Bible* | Blue Letter Bible | www.blueletterbible.org

with "dwelling," which is key to discipling. So through music, you can help disciple the nations and prevail against the enemy!

Love, grace, and peace …

♪Colossians 3:16,

Rodney

Take a moment to meditate, muse, and memorize God's word. What is the Holy Spirit saying to you right now?

_____

_____

_____

_____

_____

_____

_____

_____

_____

_____

_____

_____

_____

_____

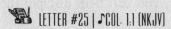 LETTER #25 | ♪COL. 1:1 (NKJV)

DISCIPLESHIP

~Part 2~

[n. Disciple: one who accepts and assists in spreading the doctrines of another: such as
a) Christianity: one of the twelve in the inner circle of Christ's followers according to the Gospel accounts
b) a convinced adherent of a school or individual][68]

♪Colossians 3:16 (NKJV)[69]

16 Let the word of Christ dwell in you richly in all wisdom, teaching[G1321] and admonishing[G3560] one another in psalms and hymns and spiritual songs, singing[G103] with grace in your hearts to the Lord.

[G1321] διδάσκω didáskō, did-as'-ko; a prolonged (causative) form of a primary verb δάω dáō (to learn); to teach (in the same broad application):—teach.

[G3560] νουθετέω noutheteō, noo-thet-eh'-o; from the same as G3559; to put in mind, i.e. (by implication) to caution or reprove gently:—admonish, warn.

[G103] ᾄδω áidō, ad'-o; a primary verb; to sing:—sing.[70]

Dear Worship Leader,

As a child, I always wanted to become a teacher when I grew up but had no idea that God would use music to do it. As worship leaders, according to ♪Colossians 3:16, we serve as teachers and admonishers (or advisors) in the body of Christ.

For their safety, not only does Paul command the Colossian church to receive the Word indwelt, in abundance, and in all wisdom—as a help to that, but he also wants them *to reflect the Word through service, song, and singing.* He knows that music serves as a pipeline and messenger to the mind/heart.

God designed us in such a way that we all live in a gated community. The brain (which is a gateway to the mind/heart) is surrounded by four types of gates: ear gate, eye gate, nose gate, and mouth gate. These gates are meant to protect us from unwanted guests who could negatively impact or infect our most prized possessions: the way we think and feel.

That's why singing is key. It opens our gates and carries its message right into the control center of our minds/hearts. So Paul urges the Colossians, along with us, to sing the Word because the message matters, music is powerful, and we are all musical. God preprogrammed us to remember and respond to music. The world knows this, which is why they use it to serve the fallen worship leader and god of this world. As a result, his poor message has musically gone viral, while the King of king's rich message and playlist has yet to do so.

Paul knows the enemy's chances to steal our riches are greatly diminished by biblical singing, teaching, and admonishing. The Word will go viral, we'll be watching out for each other

---

[68] Merriam-Webster dictionary | www.merriam-webster.com | www.learnersdictionary.com
[69] Prov. 4:20–27; Phil. 4:6–7; Heb. 10:16; 2 Cor. 4:3–4; Rom. 12:2; Eph. 5:15–21; 1 John 2:16; Ps. 19:7–14; 119:97, 103
[70] *Strong's Exhaustive Concordance of the Bible* | Blue Letter Bible | www.blueletterbible.org

(as teachers and advisors do), and as sheep, we'll have peace and safety in a strengthened community.

Love, grace, and peace …

♪Colossians 3:16,

Rodney

Take a moment to meditate, muse, and memorize God's word. What is the Holy Spirit saying to you right now?

_____

_____

_____

_____

_____

_____

_____

_____

_____

_____

_____

_____

_____

 LETTER #26 | ♪COL. 1.2 (NKJV)

DISCIPLESHIP

~Part 3~

[n. Disciple: one who accepts and assists in spreading the doctrines of another: such as

a) Christianity: one of the twelve in the inner circle of Christ's followers according to the Gospel accounts

b) a convinced adherent of a school or individual][71]

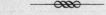

♪Colossians 3:16 (NKJV)[72]

16 Let the word of Christ dwell in you richly in all wisdom, teaching and admonishing one another in psalms and hymns and spiritual songs,[G5603] singing with grace in your hearts to the Lord.

[G5603] ῷδή ōidḗ, o-day'; from G103; a chant or "ode" (the general term for any words sung; while G5215 denotes especially a religious metrical composition, and G5568 still more specially, a Hebrew cantillation):—song.[73]

Dear Worship Leader,

The potential we have as a community is staggering. Through our service as biblical teachers and advisors to one another, we can have such great impact. Plus we have a great message! There is no song more potent and timeless than one drawn from the eternal wellspring of life, the Word of God Himself (John 1:1–5, 14). And that combined with singing really makes for great music—music that divinely touches hearts/minds.

When God's people sing, we are unstoppable. Singing unifies us, unleashes God's power, upsets the devil, and unlocks the soul. Singing is messaging. It's universal and therapeutic. When we sing, we invest in one another. Have you ever had an earworm? It's a song or melody that keeps repeating in your mind. Well, someone planted that seed to go through your gates, to your control center, and play on loop. That's how powerfully dangerous music is, which is why Paul wants us to be intentional, strategic, and deliberate about our singing.

Music helps us to muse or meditate on the word of God. It also helps us with memorization. If you think back, that's how we learned our ABCs. Songs are creatively crafted to refrain and repeat over and over again, ingraining the message of the song deeper and deeper within our souls. In fact, great songs are written with a hook, something that will reel in its listeners. It's musical bait in the hands of skillful fishermen.

The goal is clear. Paul wants kingdom singing, teaching, and warning to lead to kingdom behavior for greater kingdom impact on behalf of the King of kings! I call this God's divine M4 weaponry: meditation, memorization, manifestation, and ministry. We want to manifest fruit in our lives that will minister to others globally, generationally, and eternally.

---

[71] Merriam-Webster dictionary | www.merriam-webster.com | www.learnersdictionary.com
[72] Exod. 32:18; 1 Sam. 18:6; 2 Sam. 19:35; 1 Chron. 13:8; 2 Chron. 23:18; 30:21; 35:25; Neh. 12:27; Ps. 100:2; 126:2; Song of Sol. 2:12; Isa. 14:7; 16:10; 35; 44:23; 48:20; 49:13; 51:11; 54:1; 55:12; Zeph. 3:17; Acts 16:25; Eph. 5:17–21
[73] *Strong's Exhaustive Concordance of the Bible* | Blue Letter Bible | www.blueletterbible.org

Love, grace, and peace …

♪Colossians 3:16,

Rodney

Take a moment to meditate, muse, and memorize God's word. What is the Holy Spirit saying to you right now?

_____

_____

_____

_____

_____

_____

_____

_____

_____

_____

_____

_____

_____

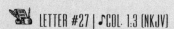 LETTER #27 | ♪COL. 1:3 (NKJV)

DISCIPLESHIP

~Part 4~

[n. Disciple: one who accepts and assists in spreading the doctrines of another: such as
a) Christianity: one of the twelve in the inner circle of Christ's followers according to the Gospel accounts
b) a convinced adherent of a school or individual][74]

♪Colossians 3:16 (NKJV)[75]

16 Let the word of Christ dwell in you richly in all wisdom, teaching and admonishing one another in psalms and hymns and spiritual songs, singing with grace in your hearts to the Lord.[G2962]

[G2962] κύριος kýrios, koo'-ree-os; from κῦρος kŷros (supremacy); supreme in authority, i.e. (as noun) controller; by implication, Master (as a respectful title):—God, Lord, master, Sir.[76]

Dear Worship Leader,

Ultimately, our singing is to the Lord. There is an inward receiving, an outward reflecting, and an upward rejoicing. No matter what others think or feel about our singing, our song is to the Lord. He loves to hear the voices of His children singing to Him! Psalm 100:2 (NKJV) says, "Come before His presence with singing." Verse 4 adds, "Enter into His gates with thanksgiving, And into His courts with praise. Be thankful to Him, and bless His name." Notice the divine entry code He offers us: singing, thanksgiving, blessing, and praise.

The King of kings doesn't want leftover worship that's crusty, last minute, and thrown together. He deserves our best sacrifices. That which is first, fresh, and fiery. In ♪Colossians 3:16, Paul says to *rejoice in the Word with perspective, passion, and purpose*. Singing with grace, that's perspective. Singing with grace in our hearts, that's passion. Singing with grace in our hearts to the Lord, that's purpose. That's worship filled with great gratitude, depth, and inspiration.

Each dimension—receiving, reflecting, and rejoicing (the inward, outward, and upward)—is critical for an enriching 3D experience. Let's personalize ♪Colossians 3:16 in reverse.

With grace in our hearts to the Lord, we're singing psalms and hymns and spiritual songs, teaching and admonishing one another, so that the word of Christ will dwell in us richly in all wisdom.

What a revelatory discipleship message to the Colossians and to Christians all around the globe. It's a call to awareness, action, and accountability. For imprinting hearts and minds with kingdom truth. In Deuteronomy 31, right before Moses's death, of all the things to do, God had Moses write and teach a song to the children of Israel. This was his final investment into their lives: a song. What a legacy and example for us all!

[74] Merriam-Webster dictionary | www.merriam-webster.com | www.learnersdictionary.com
[75] Mal. 1:6–8; 2 Sam. 24:24; Deut. 31:19–32:47; 1 Pet. 5:10; 2 Pet. 3:18; 1 Cor. 15:10; 2 Cor. 8:9; 9:8; 12:9; ♪Col. 1:28
[76] *Strong's Exhaustive Concordance of the Bible* | Blue Letter Bible | www.blueletterbible.org

Love, grace, and peace …

♪Colossians 3:16,

Rodney

Take a moment to meditate, muse, and memorize God's word. What is the Holy Spirit saying to you right now?

_____

_____

_____

_____

_____

_____

_____

_____

_____

_____

_____

_____

_____

_____

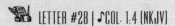 LETTER #28 | ♪COL. 1:4 (NKJV)

DEVOTION

[n. Devotion: 1a) religious fervor: piety 1b) an act of prayer or private worship—usually used in plural // morning devotions 1c) a religious exercise or practice other than the regular corporate worship of a congregation][77]

Luke 9:23 (NKJV)[78]

23 Then He said to them all, "If anyone desires to come after Me, let him deny himself, and take up his cross daily, and follow[G190] Me.

Matthew 4:18–20 (NKJV)

18 And Jesus, walking by the Sea of Galilee, saw two brothers, Simon called Peter, and Andrew his brother, casting a net into the sea; for they were fishermen. 19 Then He said to them, "Follow Me, and I will make you fishers of men." 20 They immediately left their nets and followed[G190] Him.

[G190] ἀκολουθέω akolouthéō, ak-ol-oo-theh'-o; from G1 (as a particle of union) and κέλευθος kéleuthos (a road); properly, to be in the same way with, i.e. to accompany (specially, as a disciple):—follow, reach.[79]

Dear Worship Leader,

I've wrestled a lot with guilt and shame when it comes to doing "devotions." When I think of all the morning devotions I've missed, I can feel like a failure. Because of past abuse, the question "How was your devotion this morning?" can trigger me and seem more like an interrogation than an inquiry!

I do believe in spending time with Jesus daily. But my mind had to shift from a religious checklist to a loving relationship of following and walking with Jesus each day, full of grace and truth. When people ask me how my wife and son are doing, I'm never ashamed to answer because I instantly see the faces of two dear people that I love from the bottom of my heart.

Some people throw away the term *religion* because of the legalistic connotations attached to it, but I don't. For me, religious duty, or exercise, is an outflow of relationship. James 1:27 (NKJV) teaches us about true religion. It says, "Pure and undefiled religion before God and the Father is this: to visit orphans and widows in their trouble, and to keep oneself unspotted from the world." I love that! More than its usage of the word *religion,* I see relationships with God the Father, orphans, widows, and myself. It's pure, undefiled worship!

It helps me to replace the word *religion* with the word *time.* Time spent with the people I love is always an outflow of our relationship. I'm not spending time with them to get or earn a relationship; we already have one. However, if I were to never spend time with Angela and Josiah, our relationships would drastically suffer. They would rightfully feel abandoned. And

---

77 Merriam-Webster dictionary | www.merriam-webster.com | www.learnersdictionary.com

78 Matt. 4:19; 8:22; 9:9; 10:38; 14:23; 16:24; 19:21; Mark 1:17, 35; 2:14; 6:46; 8:34; 10:21; Luke 5:27; 6:12; 9:23, 59; 11:1; 18:22; John 1:43; 10:27; 12:26; 13:36; 17:1–26; 21:19, 22; Ps. 1; Acts 4:13; Gen. 5:21–24 (24); 6:9; Ps. 103:7–14

79 *Strong's Exhaustive Concordance of the Bible* | Blue Letter Bible | www.blueletterbible.org

it would be hard to argue that I'm devoted to them without prioritizing quality time with them. Both relationship and time are essential, but a loving relationship is where it all begins.

Love, grace, and peace …

♪Colossians 3:16,

Rodney

Take a moment to meditate, muse, and memorize God's word. What is the Holy Spirit saying to you right now?

_____

_____

_____

_____

_____

_____

_____

_____

_____

_____

_____

_____

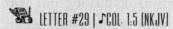 LETTER #29 | ♪COL. 1:5 (NKJV)

DISCIPLINES

[v. Discipline: 1) to train or develop by instruction and exercise especially in self-control
2a) to bring (a group) under control
2b) to impose order upon][80]

Hebrews 12:11 (NKJV)

11 Now no chastening seems to be joyful for the present, but painful; nevertheless, afterward it yields the peaceable fruit of righteousness to those who have been trained[G1128] by it.

1 Timothy 4:7–8 (NKJV)

7 But reject profane and old wives' fables, and exercise[G1128] yourself toward godliness.
8 For bodily exercise[G1129] profits a little, but godliness is profitable for all things, having promise of the life that now is and of that which is to come.

[G1129] γυμνασία **gymnasía,** goom-nas-ee'-ah; from G1128; training, i.e. (figuratively) asceticism:—exercise.
[G1128] γυμνάζω **gymnázō,** goom-nad'-zo; from G1131; to practise naked (in the games), i.e. train (figuratively):—exercise.
[G1131] γυμνός **gymnós,** goom-nos'; of uncertain affinity; nude (absolute or relative, literal or figurative):—naked.[81]

Dear Worship Leader,

Spending alone time with Jesus is one of the most intimate and rewarding experiences you can have. It's a heavenly, divine relationship. While there can be structure, it's not always required. The marital relationship ruled by a daily planner is less of a honeymoon and more of a nightmare. Scheduling has its place, but no one wants to be in bed with a clock or stopwatch.

Intimate time with Jesus will look and feel different from season to season and person to person. Obviously, there will be similarities, but we're not in love with a ritual or a template. We're in love with a Person.

Through the years, I've truly been blessed by reading daily devotional books. But quite honestly, if that's the extent of our intimacy with Jesus, I wonder just how limited of an experience we're really having. Just as there are many ways to exercise, there are many ways to spend time with Jesus.

We have spiritual disciplines, such as Bible reading, studying, memorization, meditation, worship, prayer, fasting, confession, consecration, self-examination, silence and solitude, journaling, rest, serving, stewardship, fellowship, evangelism, discipleship, and so on. These are foundational to our faith walk, but please don't stop there.

You can also go fishing with Jesus. Personally, I like to go walking with Him early in the morning, near sunrise. My absolute favorite is for us to go swimming together. In the pool, as lifelong best friends, we talk about everything—past, present, and future. We laugh, cry, and sing. He corrects me, coaches me, and trains me. I pray, meditate, and worship. It's my workout. It's my altar. It's my sanctuary. And nothing is off-limits. In His presence, I am naked and not ashamed.

---

[80] Merriam-Webster dictionary | www.merriam-webster.com | www.learnersdictionary.com
[81] *Strong's Exhaustive Concordance of the Bible* | Blue Letter Bible | www.blueletterbible.org

Love, grace, and peace …

♪Colossians 3:16,

Rodney

Take a moment to meditate, muse, and memorize God's word. What is the Holy Spirit saying to you right now?

_____

_____

_____

_____

_____

_____

_____

_____

_____

_____

_____

_____

_____

_____

LETTER #30 | ♪COL. 1:6 (NKJV)

DELEGATION

[v. Delegate: 1) to entrust to another // delegate authority
2) to appoint as one's representative][82]

Exodus 18:21 (NKJV)[83]

21 "Moreover you shall select from all the people able men, such as fear God, men of truth, hating covetousness; and place[H7760] **such over them to be rulers of thousands, rulers of hundreds, rulers of fifties, and rulers of tens.**

[H7760] שׂוּם **sûwm,** soom; or שׂים **sîym;** a primitive root; to put (used in a great variety of applications, literal, figurative, inferentially, and elliptically):—× any wise, appoint, bring, call (a name), care, cast in, change, charge, commit, consider, convey, determine, disguise, dispose, do, get, give, heap up, hold, impute, lay (down, up), leave, look, make (out), mark, name, × on, ordain, order, paint, place, preserve, purpose, put (on), regard, rehearse, reward, (cause to) set (on, up), shew, stedfastly, take, × tell, tread down, (over-)turn, × wholly, work.[84]

Dear Worship Leader,

Trust is a big deal for leaders. I've seen newer leaders rejoice over a promotion, assuming they had been entrusted to bring about great change, only to find out that they had all the responsibilities but little to none of the authority. Responsibility without the rights and privileges of authority and empowerment leads to frustration, fury, and failure.

I've also seen younger leaders who had been empowered to make the touchdown actually fumble the ball and fail. Their lack of training, discipline, dedication, resources, and skill left them shattered, disillusioned, and unable to score.

Whether frustrated or fumbling, I've been both. And in both scenarios, the senior leader ends up like Moses in Exodus 18: burdened down, worn out, and alone. Great leaders need groomed leaders for the work, or the entire team suffers.

Is this a leadership issue or a followership issue? It could be both. To make delegation work, it takes established leaders who are willing to select, invest, train, and entrust—and it takes trustworthy followers with proven ability to be faithful and teachable. Second Timothy 2:2 implores us to commit, or deposit, to faithful men who will be able to teach others also.

Every servant leader needs to be a grace-recipient and a grace-dispenser. We have to know when to catch the ball, when to pass the ball, and when to take the shot. No more ball-hogging celebrities or ball-dodging cowards in the kingdom. We need team players. The Acts 2 church was sharing, caring, and empowering. They appointed deacons in Acts 6. They passed the ball. As a result, the team multiplied and grew. Eventually, if we keep losing, the owner Himself will appoint new coaches and draft new winning teams.

Mistakes will be fixed.

[82] Merriam-Webster dictionary | www.merriam-webster.com | www.learnersdictionary.com
[83] Exod. 18; Acts 2:40–47; 6:1–7; Num. 11:10–30; 14:26–38; Judg. 7:2–3 | Luke 6:12–16; Matt. 10:1–4; Mark 3:13–19
[84] *Strong's Exhaustive Concordance of the Bible* | Blue Letter Bible | www.blueletterbible.org

Love, grace, and peace …

♪Colossians 3:16,

Rodney

Take a moment to meditate, muse, and memorize God's word. What is the Holy Spirit saying to you right now?

_____

_____

_____

_____

_____

_____

_____

_____

_____

_____

_____

_____

_____

SPIRITUAL CHECKUP: INSPIRE

Review the last ten letters and record any key highlights. Has the Holy Spirit revealed any …

Instruction?

_____

_____

_____

_____

Needs?

_____

_____

_____

_____

Scripture?

_____

_____

_____

_____

Principles?

_____

_____

_____

_____

Interests?

_____

_____

_____

_____

Reproof?

_____

_____

_____

_____

Encouragement?

_____

_____

_____

_____

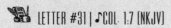 LETTER #31 | ♪COL. 1:7 (NKJV)

DELIVERANCE

[v. Deliver: 1) to set free
2a) to take and hand over to or leave for another
2b) hand over, surrender][85]

2 Corinthians 1:8–10 (NKJV)[86]

8 For we do not want you to be ignorant, brethren, of our trouble which came to us in Asia: that we were burdened beyond measure, above strength, so that we despaired even of life.
9 Yes, we had the sentence of death in ourselves, that we should not trust in ourselves but in God who raises the dead, 10 who delivered[G4506] us from so great a death, and does deliver[G4506] us; in whom we trust that He will still deliver[G4506] us,

[G4506] ῥύομαι rhýomai, rhoo'-om-ahee; middle voice of an obsolete verb, akin to G4482 (through the idea of a current; compare G4511); to rush or draw (for oneself), i.e. rescue:—deliver(-er).[87]

Dear Worship Leader,

God is truly our Deliverer! He loves us so much that He offers us deliverance in three tenses and phases: deliverance past, deliverance present, and deliverance future. We see this represented in 2 Corinthians 1:10. As believers, by grace, we were saved the moment we placed faith alone, in Christ alone, for the forgiveness of sins. But in many ways, He is presently and actively delivering us in our everyday lives.

I can't count all the times God has delivered me. From strongholds and addictions. From fear, guilt, and shame. From sickness and disease. From dangers seen and unseen. From unhealthy thoughts, decisions, and actions. From others who sought to do me harm. Even from my own self, when I considered giving up on life altogether. I am a living testimony that there is nothing too hard for God!

Many times in leading worship, we emphasize what God has delivered us from, but most importantly, let's remember what God has delivered us to: Himself. In Exodus, several times God tells Pharaoh, "Let My people go, that they may serve Me." He saves, sanctifies, and delivers us to Himself. That's what's at stake. He calls us to a person, to a relationship, to our Lord and Savior Jesus Christ—to love, serve, and worship our Father, our Shepherd, the Great I Am.

In my own recovery and as a certified sexual recovery pastoral counselor, I've learned that *the antidote to addiction is not sobriety but intimacy.* We're created for healthy, intimate relationships. There's no greater commandment in all of scripture than these: love God and love your neighbor as yourself. That's true deliverance, identity, and intimacy. His kingdom come. His will be done on earth, as it is in heaven.

Love, grace, and peace …

---

85 Merriam-Webster dictionary | www.merriam-webster.com | www.learnersdictionary.com
86 Rom. 10:9–10; Eph. 2:8–9; John 3:16; ♪Col. 1:13–14, 19–23; Jer. 32:17, 27; Matt. 19:26; Luke 1:37; Heb. 6:18; Rom. 8:35–39; Ps. 18; 23; 34:19; 91; Exo. 4:23; 7:16; 8:1, 20; 9:1, 13; 10:3; 2 Cor. 11:22–33; Matt. 6:9–13; 22:34–40
87 *Strong's Exhaustive Concordance of the Bible* | Blue Letter Bible | www.blueletterbible.org

♪Colossians 3:16,

Rodney

Take a moment to meditate, muse, and memorize God's word. What is the Holy Spirit saying to you right now?

_____

_____

_____

_____

_____

_____

_____

_____

_____

_____

_____

_____

_____

_____

_____

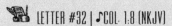

DANCING

[v. Dance: 1) to move one's body rhythmically usually to music: to engage in or perform a dance
2) to move or seem to move up and down or about in a quick or lively manner][88]

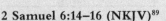

2 Samuel 6:14–16 (NKJV)[89]

14 Then David danced[H3769] before the LORD with all his might; and David was wearing a linen ephod.
15 So David and all the house of Israel brought up the ark of the LORD with shouting and with the sound of the trumpet.
16 Now as the ark of the LORD came into the City of David, Michal, Saul's daughter, looked through a window and saw King David leaping and whirling[H3769] before the LORD; and she despised him in her heart.

[H3769] כָּרַר **kârar,** kaw-rar'; a primitive root; to dance (i.e. whirl):—dance(-ing).[90]

Dear Worship Leader,

Have you ever danced before the Lord with all your might? Sometimes my wife and I will catch each other at home spontaneously singing, praising, worshipping, and dancing before the Lord, "as if no one is watching." It's beautiful.

David is bringing the ark of the Lord, which represents the very presence of God, into the city of David. And in His presence David is leaping, whirling, and dancing. There are times your heart is so full you have to dance. When you think of how far the Lord has brought you and know where your life could have ended up if it had not been for the Lord who was on your side, you have to dance. You forget about whoever is watching and their opinion. You're expressing a deep love and passion for the one who rescued you, who delivers you time after time; you have to dance. He's your first love. The apple of your eye. The rose of Sharon. The lily of the valleys. You have to dance. He deserves your praise. You were created to praise Him. If you didn't, you'd lose your mind. The rocks would cry out in your place. You have to dance!

Not only is David dancing before the Lord, but he's also dancing with all his might. The Lord gave His all for you. Isaiah 53:5 (KJV) says, "But he was wounded for our transgressions, he was bruised for our iniquities: the chastisement of our peace was upon him, and with his stripes we are healed." He died so you could live. He became poor so you could be rich. He's your source, your strength, your life, your all in all. You can't afford to give Him half-hearted worship or mediocre praise. Our great God deserves great praise. Nothing but the best for your Savior, your Lord, and your King. He's your world. You whirl because He turned your world around. He turned your weeping into joy and turned your mourning into dancing!

Love, grace, and peace …

♪Colossians 3:16,

---

[88] Merriam-Webster dictionary | www.merriam-webster.com | www.learnersdictionary.com
[89] 1 Chron. 15; Ps. 16:11; 18; 30:11; 124; 149:3; 150:4; Eccles. 3:4; 1 Sam. 13:14; Rev. 2:4; Prov. 2:12, 16; 7:2; Song of Sol. 2:1; Luke 19:40; Rom. 7:24; 12:1; 2 Cor. 1:10; 8:9; Jer. 31:13; ♪Col. 1:13; 2 Tim. 3:11; 4:17–18; 2 Pet. 2:9; Gal. 1:4
[90] *Strong's Exhaustive Concordance of the Bible* | Blue Letter Bible | www.blueletterbible.org

Rodney

Take a moment to meditate, muse, and memorize God's word. What is the Holy Spirit saying to you right now?

 LETTER #33 | ♪COL. 1:9 (NKJV)

DISTRACTION

[v. Distract: 1a) to draw or direct (something, such as someone's attention) to a different object or in different directions at the same time
1b) to turn aside: divert
2) to stir up or confuse with conflicting emotions or motives][91]

Revelation 2:4–5 (NKJV)[92]

4 "Nevertheless I have this against you, that you have left your first love.
5 "Remember therefore from where you have fallen;[G1601] repent and do the first works, or else I will come to you quickly and remove your lampstand from its place—unless you repent.

[G1601] ἐκπίπτω ekpíptō, ek-pip'-to; from G1537 and G4098; to drop away; specially, be driven out of one's course; figuratively, to lose, become inefficient:—be cast, fail, fall (away, off), take none effect.[93]

Dear Worship Leader,

Leading a worship service is similar to performing a wedding ceremony. The goal is to let nothing distract us from the bride and groom uniting in holy matrimony. So it is with a church service. Our eyes are on Jesus. He is the Groom, and the church is His bride (Song of Solomon).

When the bride enters the sanctuary, we long to see her and the groom connect. We want their eyes laser focused and interlocked, as if no one else is in the room. Let the groom be overwhelmed and enamored by her beauty. Let the bride's eyes gleam from his adoration and praise. Let there be love songs. Let there be passion, affection, and tears. Let there be an atmosphere conducive for covenant. All of the rehearsing and planning prior to this moment is for this moment.

As worship leaders, it is with this intensity and intentionality that we lead. We're not stopping the wedding ceremony or the worship service for technical difficulties. Worship anyway! If something goes haywire musically, or if the air conditioner goes out, we're not canceling service. We'll make the necessary adjustments and continue singing. While elements as these were meant to be a help for why we came, we won't allow any of them to hinder us or hold us hostage from our purpose, our mission, and our calling.

We're not here to worship the service, the creativity, the music, the band, the light show, the worship leader, the sermon, or the pastor. We came to see Jesus (John 12:21). As long as they're assisting us to that end, praise God. But if any of it becomes the center of attention instead of the arrow it was designed to be, pointing us to Jesus, then it's an idol, a diversion, and has gotten us off-track. If we have fallen out of love, let's repent, and renew vows with our First Love.

Love, grace, and peace …

♪Colossians 3:16,

---

91 Merriam-Webster dictionary | www.merriam-webster.com | www.learnersdictionary.com
92 Eph. 5:22–33 (27, 32); Isa. 61:10; 62:5; Jer. 33:11; Matt. 9:15; 22:37; 25:1–13; John 3:29; Rev. 18:23; 21:2, 9; 22:17
93 *Strong's Exhaustive Concordance of the Bible* | Blue Letter Bible | www.blueletterbible.org

Rodney

Take a moment to meditate, muse, and memorize God's word. What is the Holy Spirit saying to you right now?

_____

_____

_____

_____

_____

_____

_____

_____

_____

_____

_____

_____

_____

_____

_____

 LETTER #34 | ♪COL. 1:10 (NKJV)

DISCORD

[n. Discord: 1a) lack of agreement or harmony (as between persons, things, or ideas)
1b) active quarreling or conflict resulting from discord among persons or factions
2a) music: a combination of musical sounds that strikes the ear harshly; dissonance
2b) a harsh or unpleasant sound][94]

Galatians 5:19–21 (NKJV)[95]

**19 Now the works of the flesh are evident, which are: adultery, fornication, uncleanness, lewdness,
20 idolatry, sorcery, hatred, contentions, jealousies, outbursts of wrath, selfish ambitions, dissensions, heresies,[G139]
21 envy, murders, drunkenness, revelries, and the like; of which I tell you beforehand, just as I also told you in time past, that those who practice such things will not inherit the kingdom of God.**

[G139] αἵρεσις haíresis, hah'-ee-res-is; from G138; properly, a choice, i.e. (specially) a party or (abstractly) disunion:—heresy (which is the Greek word itself), sect.[96]

Dear Worship Leader,

Be on high alert for any of the devil's devices, what I call the Dirty Ds: discord, division, disunity, deceit, dissension, dispute, debate, disrespect, disagreement, disharmony, etc. James 3:16 (NKJV) says, "For where envy and self-seeking exist, confusion and every evil thing are there." First John 2:16 (NKJV) teaches, "For all that is in the world—the lust of the flesh, the lust of the eyes, and the pride of life—is not of the Father but is of the world."

These are methods and strategies from the kingdom of this world to steal, kill, and destroy God's people and His plan. Unfortunately, many are known to be pervasive and prevalent among music ministries, where musical elements of harmony, unison, and blending are needed most. Yet we have wars and fights within our choirs and teams that stem from "desires for pleasure that war in your members" as James 4:1 (NKJV) states.

We find the solution in Galatians 5:16 (NKJV), which says, "I say then: Walk in the Spirit, and you shall not fulfill the lust of the flesh." This exposes the *root*. Verses 22–23 go on to list the *fruit* of the Spirit: love, joy, peace, longsuffering, kindness, goodness, faithfulness, gentleness, and self-control.

It all comes down to which choice, or which tree: flesh or Spirit? With the flesh come death, bondage, pride, lies, hatred, and lust. With the Spirit come life, liberty, humility, truth, love, and service. We can follow the kingdom of darkness or the kingdom of light, which is righteousness, peace, and joy in the Holy Ghost (Romans 14:17). If we live, walk, and are led by the Spirit, our lives will produce fruit in harmony with heaven. As in Psalm 133, we will enjoy unity, anointing, and blessing. If not, we will eat the opposite.

---

[94] Merriam-Webster dictionary | www.merriam-webster.com | www.learnersdictionary.com
[95] Prov. 6:12–19; John 10:10; Eph. 6:11; Titus 3:9–11; 1 Cor. 1:10–17; 3:1–4; 6:1–11; 13; Rom. 16:17; Luke 11:17–18
[96] *Strong's Exhaustive Concordance of the Bible* | Blue Letter Bible | www.blueletterbible.org

Love, grace, and peace …

♪Colossians 3:16,

Rodney

Take a moment to meditate, muse, and memorize God's word. What is the Holy Spirit saying to you right now?

_____

_____

_____

_____

_____

_____

_____

_____

_____

_____

_____

_____

_____

_____

LETTER #35 | ♪COL. 1:10 (NKJV)

ELITISM

[a. Elitist: a) giving special treatment and advantages to wealthy or powerful people b) regarding other people as inferior because they lack power, wealth, or status][97]

―――∞∞∞―――

1 Corinthians 12:21–26 (NKJV)[98]

21 And the eye cannot say to the hand, "I have no need of you"; nor again the head to the feet, "I have no need of you."
22 No, much rather, those members of the body which seem to be weaker are necessary.
23 And those members of the body which we think to be less honorable, on these we bestow greater honor; and our unpresentable parts have greater modesty,
24 but our presentable parts have no need. But God composed the body, having given greater honor to that part which lacks it,
25 that there should be no schism in the body, but that the members should have the same care for one another.
26 And if one member suffers, all the members suffer with it; or if one member is honored,[G1392] all the members rejoice with it.

―――∞∞∞―――

[G1392] δοξάζω doxázō, dox-ad'-zo; from G1391; to render (or esteem) glorious (in a wide application):—(make) glorify(-ious), full of (have) glory, honour, magnify.[99]

Dear Worship Leader,

Along with musicianship and leadership come certain perks and privileges. We typically serve on a platform that's higher than others. We're usually holding a microphone that amplifies our voices louder than the next. It's normal for us to be front and center, with the crowd facing us. Sometimes we have lights and cameras pointing in our direction, not to mention our images magnified and projected on what looks like movie screens. On cue, when we enter the sanctuary, from backstage Green Rooms, many times the congregation is already seated, waiting for us to begin. And once we start, it's not uncommon for congregants to stand up clapping with raised hands—concert style—at our command. Furthermore, the bigger the church, the greater the likelihood that you'll meet people who know you by name that you've never met before. Even out in the community, we're recognized and regarded as if we're part of an elitist celebrity club. I've had unknown people ask for pictures.

Seems more like the life of a rock star than a foot washing servant. When service goes well, the entire church cheers for us. When it doesn't, we can feel like hiding in a back room somewhere because everyone saw what happened. Paid or unpaid, the church culture can be complicated to navigate.

As Proverbs 4:23 (NKJV) says, "Keep your heart with all diligence, For out of it spring the issues of life." In other words, *guard your heart*. Even if you're one that desires not to be in the limelight, preferential treatment can grow on you. *Guard your heart*. This celebrity culture

―――――――

[97] Merriam-Webster dictionary | www.merriam-webster.com | www.learnersdictionary.com
[98] Phil. 2:1–11; Isa. 14:12–14; 2 Chron. 26:5, 16; Judg. 16:18–20; Dan. 4:28–37; Matt. 23:5–7; 25:40, 45; John 13:1–17; James 2:1–13; 4:6; 1 Tim. 5:10; Heb. 6:10; 13:2–3, 16 | Matt. 21:12–17; Mark 11:15–19; Luke 19:45–48; John 2:13–22
[99] *Strong's Exhaustive Concordance of the Bible* | Blue Letter Bible | www.blueletterbible.org

can be like cancer to your spirit and soul. *Guard your heart.* This position and gifting attract a lot of glory, honor, and attention. *Guard your heart,* lest one day you have a change of heart, for the worse.

Love, grace, and peace …

♪Colossians 3:16,

Rodney

Take a moment to meditate, muse, and memorize God's word. What is the Holy Spirit saying to you right now?

_____

_____

_____

_____

_____

_____

_____

_____

_____

_____

_____

LETTER #36 | ♪COL. 1:12 (NKJV)

EXAMPLE

[n. Example: one that serves as a pattern to be imitated or not to be imitated][100]

1 Peter 5:2–4 (KJV)[101]

2 Feed the flock of God which is among you, taking the oversight thereof, not by constraint, but willingly; not for filthy lucre, but of a ready mind;
3 Neither as being lords over God's heritage, but being ensamples[G5179] **to the flock.**
4 And when the chief Shepherd shall appear, ye shall receive a crown of glory that fadeth not away.

[G5179] τύπος týpos, too'-pos; from G5180; a die (as struck), i.e. (by implication) a stamp or scar; by analogy, a shape, i.e. a statue, (figuratively) style or resemblance; specially, a sampler ("type"), i.e. a model (for imitation) or instance (for warning):—en-(ex-)ample, fashion, figure, form, manner, pattern, print.
[G5180] τύπτω týptō, toop'-to; a primary verb (in a strengthened form); to "thump", i.e. cudgel or pummel (properly, with a stick or bastinado), but in any case by repeated blows; by implication, to punish; figuratively, to offend (the conscience):—beat, smite, strike, wound.[102]

Dear Worship Leader,

I love to see worship leaders actually worship instead of just barking out orders to the congregation. I believe the church of today is saying to its leaders what the Greeks said to Philip in John 12:21 (KJV). "Sir, we would see Jesus." Show us Jesus. Show us what it looks like to be set on fire by the Holy Ghost. That's different from just talking about fire. Lead the way! Telling us to praise Him is one thing, but when you praise Him yourself, right in the middle of your worship set, the atmosphere changes. Not only that, but we also get to see you change. Yes, feed us, but sit down at the table yourself and dine with us. As God's sheep, let's all get full together.

Sometimes my family and I will go into a restaurant, order a sampler, and instantly know whether we will enjoy the rest of the meal or not. Yes, it's only a taste, but it's also a foreshadow of things to come. When you lead worship, give us a sampler of Jesus, of worship, of heaven. Help us hunger and thirst for more of Him and His presence. Declare with Psalm 34:8 (KJV), "O taste and see that the LORD is good …"

And please don't stop there. Be a sampler for Jesus when you leave the platform (Titus 2:7–8). Give us a taste of Him in the pew while the pastor is preaching and when others are leading in song or prayer. When the service is over, show us Jesus in word, in conduct, in love, in spirit, in faith, and in purity (1 Timothy 4:12 NKJV). Shepherds have been known to brand, or mark, their sheep so that others will know who they belong to. Show us whose sheep you are by the life you live.

---

[100] Merriam-Webster dictionary | www.merriam-webster.com | www.learnersdictionary.com
[101] Phil. 3:17; John 13:15; Heb. 4:11; 1 Cor. 10:6, 11; 1 Thess. 1:7; 2 Thess. 3:9; James 5:10; 1 Pet. 2:21; 2 Pet. 2:6
[102] *Strong's Exhaustive Concordance of the Bible* | Blue Letter Bible | www.blueletterbible.org

Jesus, the author and finisher of our faith, modeled service. He washed feet, resisted temptation, and endured an old rugged cross. He won His race and gave us the victory. Let's follow His footsteps and win our races the same way He did!

Love, grace, and peace …

♪Colossians 3:16,

Rodney

Take a moment to meditate, muse, and memorize God's word. What is the Holy Spirit saying to you right now?

_____

_____

_____

_____

_____

_____

_____

_____

_____

_____

_____

_____

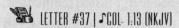 LETTER #37 | ♪COL. 1:13 (NKJV)

ENJOYMENT

[v. Enjoy: 1) to have a good time
2) to take pleasure or satisfaction in][103]

Psalm 16:11 (NKJV)[104]

**11 You will show me the path of life;
In Your presence is fullness**[H7648] **of joy;**[H8057]
At Your right hand are pleasures[H5273] **forevermore.**

[H7648] שֹׂבַע **sôba‘,** so'-bah; from H7646; satisfaction (of food or [figuratively] joy):—fill, full(-ness), satisfying, be satisfied.
[H8057] שִׂמְחָה **simchâh,** sim-khaw'; from H8056; blithesomeness or glee, (religious or festival):—× exceeding(-ly), gladness, joy(-fulness), mirth, pleasure, rejoice(-ing).
[H5273] נָעִים **nâ‘îym,** naw-eem'; from H5276; delightful (objective or subjective, literal or figurative):—pleasant(-ure), sweet.[105]

Dear Worship Leader,

There is no joy like the joy of being in the presence of Jesus. If I were to summarize my job as a worship leader, it would be this: to usher in the presence of God among His people. That is, His manifest presence, His Shekinah glory, where He fills the room and everyone in it! Everything else is secondary. Any success I've had over the years, in this role, has been because of His presence. I have one job: to get Jesus in the room. If I can help get people to Jesus, nothing is impossible.

God is recklessly and relentlessly passionate about being with His people. After aggressively snatching the children of Israel from the hand of Pharaoh, in Exodus 25:8 (NKJV), God says to Moses, "And let them make Me a sanctuary, that I may dwell among them." Exodus 29:46 (NKJV) elaborates. "And they shall know that I am the LORD their God, who brought them up out of the land of Egypt, that I may dwell among them. I am the LORD their God." The word "dwell" in Hebrew is [H7931] שָׁכַן shâkan, shaw-kan'—where we get Shekinah. It is also the word "rested" in Exodus 40:35 (NKJV). "And Moses was not able to enter the tabernacle of meeting, because the cloud rested above it, and the glory of the LORD filled the tabernacle." It's unfathomable to me that the God of all creation wants His glory to dwell, or rest, with us.

In return, when God's people become passionate about being with Him, electricity, excitement, and joy fill the room. I love how the sons of Korah put it in Psalm 84:10–11 (NKJV). "For a day in Your courts is better than a thousand. I would rather be a doorkeeper in the house of my God Than dwell in the tents of wickedness. For the LORD God is a sun and shield; The LORD will give grace and glory; No good thing will He withhold From those who walk uprightly."

Love, grace, and peace …

---

103 Merriam-Webster dictionary | www.merriam-webster.com | www.learnersdictionary.com
104 Ps. 4:7; 19:7–11; 21:6; 30:11; 43:4; 45:15; 51:8; 68:3; 97:11; 100:2; 106:5; 119:97, 103; 122:1; 137:3, 6; Gal. 5:22–23; Exod. 15:1–21; 24:16; 25:8; 29:45–46; 40:35; Mark 2:1–12; Neh. 8:10; Acts 2:28; 8:8; 13:52; 15:3; 20:24
105 *Strong's Exhaustive Concordance of the Bible* | Blue Letter Bible | www.blueletterbible.org

♪Colossians 3:16,

Rodney

Take a moment to meditate, muse, and memorize God's word. What is the Holy Spirit saying to you right now?

_____

_____

_____

_____

_____

_____

_____

_____

_____

_____

_____

_____

_____

_____

_____

 LETTER #38 | ♪COL. 1.14 (NKJV)

EMOTIONALISM

[n. Emotionalism: 1) a tendency to regard things emotionally
2) undue indulgence in or display of emotion][106]

———————

Ecclesiastes 3:1–4 (NKJV)[107]

**1 To everything there is a season,
A time[H6256] for every purpose under heaven:
2 A time[H6256] to be born,
And a time[H6256] to die;
A time[H6256] to plant,
And a time[H6256] to pluck what is planted;
3 A time[H6256] to kill,
And a time[H6256] to heal;
A time[H6256] to break down,
And a time[H6256] to build up;
4 A time[H6256] to weep,
And a time[H6256] to laugh;
A time[H6256] to mourn,
And a time[H6256] to dance;**

———————

[H6256] עֵת ʻêth, ayth; from H5703; time, especially (adverb with preposition) now, when, etc.:— after, (al-) ways, ✕ certain, continually, evening, long, (due) season, so (long) as, (even-, evening-, noon-) tide, (meal-), what) time, when.[108]

Dear Worship Leader,

Emotions are meant to flow through us but not rule over us; that's emotionalism. We are only ruled by the Holy Spirit. Everything has its season and every purpose has its time. A healthy church will experience periods of weeping, laughter, mourning, and dancing and allow freedom and space for it all. Just as relationships and families have a need for fluidity of expression, so do congregations. I weep for the church that only dances and never mourns, or vice versa. I pray for the worship leader that has to wear a mask or paint on a face to lead each week. Yes, we must learn to regulate and temper our emotions so that congregants aren't held hostage to our every whim, but we also need to be in a safe environment where we can freely emote and grow.

Lord, please make Your churches greenhouses. Give Your leaders and pastors the wisdom and grace to shepherd in all seasons. We need winter, spring, summer, and fall. We also need freedom for personal expression and ministerial care through it all. Let Your house of prayer serve as a shelter, a lighthouse, and a strong tower from the enemy. We need a place where both the sick and the strong can call on the name of the Lord. James 5:13 (NKJV) says, "Is anyone among you suffering? Let him pray. Is anyone cheerful? Let him sing psalms." That means You have room in Your house for both.

As led by the Spirit, let the people of God see you weep, mourn, laugh, and dance; it releases them to do the same. It also teaches them to worship God at all times. We weren't created

---

[106] Merriam-Webster dictionary | www.merriam-webster.com | www.learnersdictionary.com
[107] Matt. 21:13; Prov. 18:10; Ps. 18; 34; 61; Gal. 6:1–5; James 5:13–18; 1 Cor. 12; Rom. 12:3–21 (15); Acts 2:42–47; 9:39; 12:5–17; 20:37; 1 Sam. 1:1–18; John 11:33, 35; Luke 7:38; 1 Thess. 4:13–18; 2 Cor. 1:3–4; ♪Col. 4:18; Heb. 13:3
[108] *Strong's Exhaustive Concordance of the Bible* | Blue Letter Bible | www.blueletterbible.org

as robots or machines. God gave us feelings. As a living sacrifice, pour them out on the altar and give them to God. He wants it all. As Hannah did in need of a child, let your feelings flow through you in prayer and worship to God.

Love, grace, and peace …

♪Colossians 3:16,

Rodney

Take a moment to meditate, muse, and memorize God's word. What is the Holy Spirit saying to you right now?

_____

_____

_____

_____

_____

_____

_____

_____

_____

_____

_____

LETTER #39 | ♪COL. 1:15 (NKJV)

FILLED

[v. Fill: 1) to put into as much as can be held or conveniently contained
2) feed, satiate
3) to occupy the whole of][109]

Ephesians 5:17–21 (NKJV)[110]

17 Therefore do not be unwise, but understand what the will of the Lord is.
18 And do not be drunk with wine, in which is dissipation; but be filled[G4137] with the Spirit,
19 speaking to one another in psalms and hymns and spiritual songs, singing and making melody in your heart to the Lord,
20 giving thanks always for all things to God the Father in the name of our Lord Jesus Christ,
21 submitting to one another in the fear of God.

[G4137] πληρόω plēróō, play-ro'-o; from G4134; to make replete, i.e. (literally) to cram (a net), level up (a hollow), or (figuratively) to furnish (or imbue, diffuse, influence), satisfy, execute (an office), finish (a period or task), verify (or coincide with a prediction), etc.:— accomplish, ✕ after, (be) complete, end, expire, fill (up), fulfil, (be, make) full (come), fully preach, perfect, supply.[111]

Dear Worship Leader,

When the Spirit fills you, He takes over! Just as someone intoxicated with wine is controlled by that substance, someone filled, or "drunk," with the Spirit is under the Spirit's control. He, the Holy Spirit, God Himself, changes our walk.

Eight times Paul uses the Greek word for "walk" in Ephesians, [G4043] περιπατέω peripatéō, per-ee-pat-eh'-o. He discusses our past walk (2:2); walking in good works (2:10); walking worthy of our calling (4:1); not walking as other Gentiles (4:17) or in vanity (4:17); walking in love (5:2); walking as children of light (5:8); and walking circumspectly, in wisdom—not as fools (5:15). Afterward, he explains why this is so critical. In Ephesians 5:16 (NKJV) he says "redeeming the time, because the days are evil." As children of light, using time cautiously and wisely is essential since we live in a dark world. Thus, verses 17–18 state, "Therefore, do not be unwise, but understand what the will of the Lord is. And do not be drunk with wine, in which is dissipation, but be filled with the Spirit." And this imperative means a continual filling!

Whenever our walk is "off," it's comforting to know that we have an alternative, the Spirit's filling! With His filling comes good fruit—in all goodness, righteousness, and truth (5:9). With His filling also comes great freedom—in speaking, singing, and making melody (5:19); giving thanks (5:20); and submitting (5:21). And the more we practice them, the more we're filled. Spiritual "drunkenness" impairs our ability to walk in the flesh but heightens our sensitivity to the things of God. No more earthly AM/FM radio. Now we have access to

---

[109] Merriam-Webster dictionary | www.merriam-webster.com | www.learnersdictionary.com
[110] Acts 2:17; John 14:17; 15:26; 16:13; Luke 4:18; ♪Col. 4:5; 2 Cor. 3:17 | Matt. 23:32; Luke 2:40; 3:5; John 12:3; 16:6; Acts 2:2; 5:3, 28; 13:52; Rom. 1:29; 15:14; 2 Cor. 7:4; Eph. 1:23; 3:19; 4:10; 5:18; Phil. 1:11; ♪Col. 1:9; 2 Tim. 1:4
[111] *Strong's Exhaustive Concordance of the Bible* | Blue Letter Bible | www.blueletterbible.org

a heavenly satellite that enables us to receive God's divine SiriusXM radio, where we are empowered to move from the natural into the supernatural!

Love, grace, and peace …

♪Colossians 3:16,

Rodney

Take a moment to meditate, muse, and memorize God's word. What is the Holy Spirit saying to you right now?

_____

_____

_____

_____

_____

_____

_____

_____

_____

_____

_____

_____

 LETTER #40 | ♪COL. 1:16 (NKJV)

FIGHT

[v. Fight: 1) to contend against in or as if in a battle or physical combat
2) wage, carry on
3) to struggle or endure or surmount
4) to gain by struggle
5) to manage (a ship) in a battle or storm][112]

Ephesians 6:10–13 (NKJV)[113]

10 Finally, my brethren, be strong in the Lord and in the power of His might.
11 Put on the whole armor of God, that you may be able to stand against the wiles of the devil.
12 For we do not wrestle[G3823] against flesh and blood, but against principalities, against powers, against the rulers of the darkness of this age, against spiritual hosts of wickedness in the heavenly places.
13 Therefore take up the whole armor of God, that you may be able to withstand in the evil day, and having done all, to stand.

[G3823] πάλη pálē, pal'-ay; from πάλλω pállō (to vibrate; another form for G906); wrestling:—+ wrestle.[114]

Dear Worship Leader,

To be effective in ministry, we must learn to properly fight, wrestle, and wage war. I like to use the term *warship* [war + worship] because we are at war, fighting through our worship. But actually warship is defined in Merriam-Webster dictionary as a naval vessel or military ship that has many weapons and is used for fighting in wars. That's a perfect illustration for us.

Whether you know it or not, you and I were drafted into a war—signed up for battle. David said in Psalm 144:1 (NKJV), "Blessed be the LORD my Rock, Who trains my hands for war, And my fingers for battle." David is a great example of being both a worshipper and a warrior. We also need to be both.

We're battling a lot. And no, it's not easy. Paul said in 2 Corinthians 7:5 (KJV), "For, when we were come into Macedonia, our flesh had no rest, but we were troubled on every side; without were fightings, within were fears." We're fighting on the outside, inside, and every side. Sometimes it's a battle just to show up at rehearsal. It's a struggle to get the music correct; get the team on one accord; deal with personalities and mood swings; handle conflict, criticism, and controversy. We're wrestling to keep our heart and mind right. We're warring for strength, peace, and freedom—for lives, families, and generations. We're always in a fight.

Ephesians 6:12 makes clear who our fight is against and who it isn't against. It's *never* against a person, it's *always* against the enemy behind the scenes instigating, with evil schemes and strategies. And since the enemy is spiritual, our weapons must also be spiritual—and not carnal. *Worship and prayer are spiritual weapons!* We stand armored with the song of the Lord.

---

[112] Merriam-Webster dictionary | www.merriam-webster.com | www.learnersdictionary.com
[113] Eph. 6:14–20; 2 Cor. 10:3–6; 11:22–33; Exod. 15:2; Ps. 28:7; 118:14; Isa. 12:2; 1 Sam. 16:23; 2 Chron. 20:20–30
[114] *Strong's Exhaustive Concordance of the Bible* | Blue Letter Bible | www.blueletterbible.org

He's our strength, song, and salvation. May we never forget this—and never show up to a gunfight with only a knife!

Love, grace, and peace …

♪Colossians 3:16,

Rodney

Take a moment to meditate, muse, and memorize God's word. What is the Holy Spirit saying to you right now?

_____

_____

_____

_____

_____

_____

_____

_____

_____

_____

_____

_____

SPIRITUAL CHECKUP: INSPIRE

Review the last ten letters and record any key highlights. Has the Holy Spirit revealed any …

Instruction?

_____

_____

_____

_____

Needs?

_____

_____

_____

_____

Scripture?

_____

_____

_____

_____

Principles?

_____

_____

_____

_____

Interests?

_____

_____

_____

_____

Reproof?

_____

_____

_____

_____

Encouragement?

_____

_____

_____

_____

LETTER #41 | ♪COL. 1:17 (NKJV)

FAITH

[n. Faith: 1) allegiance to duty or a person: loyalty
2) belief and trust in and loyalty to God
3) something that is believed especially with strong conviction, especially: a system of religious beliefs][115]

Hebrews 11:6 (NKJV)[116]

6 But without faith[G4102] it is impossible to please Him, for he who comes to God must believe[G4100] that He is, and that He is a rewarder of those who diligently seek Him.

[G4100] πιστεύω pisteúō, pist-yoo'-o; from G4102; to have faith (in, upon, or with respect to, a person or thing), i.e. credit; by implication, to entrust (especially one's spiritual well-being to Christ):—believe(-r), commit (to trust), put in trust with.

[G4102] πίστις pístis, pis'-tis; from G3982; persuasion, i.e. credence; moral conviction (of religious truth, or the truthfulness of God or a religious teacher), especially reliance upon Christ for salvation; abstractly, constancy in such profession; by extension, the system of religious (Gospel) truth itself:—assurance, belief, believe, faith, fidelity.[117]

Dear Worship Leader,

In the apostle Paul's final letter to Timothy he declares, "I have fought a good fight, I have finished my course, I have kept the faith (2 Timothy 4:7 KJV)." That's a "drop the mic" moment. What a testimony! At the end of our work down here on earth, to be able to make such a statement is awe-inspiring.

This is a fight of faith (1 Timothy 6:12). And without faith, it is impossible to please God. Dr. Tony Evans says, "Faith is acting like it is so, even when it's not so, in order that it might be so, simply because God said so." God wants us to trust Him regardless. This is Peter-like, walking-on-water type of faith. It surpasses earthly reasoning and defies human logic. We walk by faith, not by sight (2 Corinthians 5:7). Faith is being sure of what we hope for, being convinced of what we do not see (Hebrews 11:1 NET). Through the Spirit, we have this capacity.

Hebrews 11 is known as the Hall of Faith. After encouraging us to draw near (10:22) and not draw back (10:38–39), for forty verses, the writer lists stirring examples of men and women who chose to trust God—who cannot lie (6:13–18)—based on His word, promise, credit, and track record!

Don't miss this: the just shall *live* by faith (10:38). It's how we see, think, hear, speak, pray, sing, and walk. "By faith we understand that the worlds were framed by the word of God, so that the things which are seen were not made of things which are visible" (Hebrews 11:3 NKJV). Our God spoke something into nothing and produced everything. And we're made in His image. I wonder what reward or

115 Merriam-Webster dictionary | www.merriam-webster.com | www.learnersdictionary.com
116 2 Pet. 1:16–21; Gen. 1:27; 18:14; Acts 6:5; 11:24; 14:9–10; Matt. 8:8–10; 9:28; 14:28–29; 19:26; Rom. 10:17; Titus 1:2; 1 Cor. 1:20–25; Mark 2:5; 9:23; 10:27; 14:36; Jer. 32:17, 27; Luke 17:5; 18:27; Rom. 8:3; 15:1; Heb. 6:4, 18; 10:4
117 *Strong's Exhaustive Concordance of the Bible* | Blue Letter Bible | www.blueletterbible.org

promise is awaiting our next step of faith (10:35–36). In Matthew 17:20, Jesus declares that if we have mustard seed faith, we can move mountains and nothing will be impossible for us!

Love, grace, and peace …

♪Colossians 3:16,

Rodney

Take a moment to meditate, muse, and memorize God's word. What is the Holy Spirit saying to you right now?

_____

_____

_____

_____

_____

_____

_____

_____

_____

_____

_____

_____

_____

LETTER #42 | ♪COL. 1:18 (NKJV)

FEAR

[n. Fear: 1) an unpleasant often strong emotion caused by anticipation or awareness of danger
2) anxious concern: solicitude
3) profound reverence and awe especially toward God
4) reason for alarm: danger][118]

2 Timothy 1:5–7 (NKJV)[119]

**5 when I call to remembrance the genuine faith that is in you, which dwelt first in your grandmother Lois and your mother Eunice, and I am persuaded is in you also.
6 Therefore I remind you to stir up the gift of God which is in you through the laying on of my hands.
7 For God has not given us a spirit of fear,[G1167] but of power and of love and of a sound mind.**

[G1167] δειλία deilía, di-lee'-ah; from G1169; timidity:—fear.
[G1169] δειλός deilós, di-los'; from δεός deós (dread); timid, i.e. (by implication) faithless:—fearful.[120]

Dear Worship Leader,

What are you afraid of? What comes to your mind first? For me today, in my flesh, my top three answers would be death, failure, and people—and under each are subcategories.

Paul wrote this letter to Timothy and me! I'm often attacked spiritually by negative, unhealthy, ungodly fear (1:7) that hinders me from firing up my gift on all cylinders (1:6). God has also blessed me by the laying on of hands (1:6) and a genuine faith inherited from my (grand)parents (1:5).

So why am I ever afraid? The world, the flesh, and the devil. Like finding mouse droppings in our home when we lived in Iowa, it was a way to expose and track down the "villain." Just as mice drop so many pellets per day, so does the enemy! Whenever we see, sense, or feel his fear-pellets, remember that fear *did not come from God.* It's the enemy's lie and spiritual attempt to steal, kill, and destroy (John 10:10).

To victoriously combat this, like Timothy, God did give to us a positive, healthy, and genuine faith that dwells in us. With this inheritance comes true spiritual *power,* spiritual *love,* and a spiritually *sound mind.* That means the enemy loses and is overpowered 3–1! This is life more abundantly (John 10:10).

(1) God gave us spiritual power! Walking in the Spirit immediately shuts down and incapacitates our flesh (Galatians 5:16–26).
(2) God gave us spiritual love! There's no fear in love. Perfect love casts out fear because fear involves torment (1 John 4:17–19).

---

118 Merriam-Webster dictionary | www.merriam-webster.com | www.learnersdictionary.com
119 Rom. 8:38–39; Ps. 23; 1 Cor. 15 | 2 Cor. 9:8; 2 Chron. 26:5; Eph. 1:3; 3:20; Jude 1:24 | Prov. 29:25; Heb. 13:6; Matt. 10:28; Rom. 8:31 | 2 Tim. 4:17–18; Rom. 12:1–2; James 1:21; 1 Pet. 1:13; 5:8; 1 Thess. 5:6, 8; Matt. 6:25–34; 10:19
120 *Strong's Exhaustive Concordance of the Bible* | Blue Letter Bible | www.blueletterbible.org

(3) God gave us a spiritually sound mind! In Him, our hearts/minds are now safe, sober, and self-controlled (1 Timothy 4:12–16).

In 1 Timothy 4:15–16, for a growing faith, Paul prescribes scriptural meditation, self-care, and sound doctrine— "vitamin S." *Take daily. Apply to fear. Use liberally. Unlimited refills. Share.*

Love, grace, and peace …

♪Colossians 3:16,

Rodney

Take a moment to meditate, muse, and memorize God's word. What is the Holy Spirit saying to you right now?

_____

_____

_____

_____

_____

_____

_____

_____

_____

_____

_____

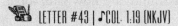 LETTER #43 | ♪ COL. 1:19 (NKJV)

FEELINGS

[n. Feeling: 1) an awareness by your body of something in it or on it: sensation
2) an emotional state or reaction
3) capacity to respond emotionally especially with the higher emotions][121]

Hebrews 4:14–16 (KJV)[122]

14 Seeing then that we have a great high priest, that is passed into the heavens, Jesus the Son of God, let us hold fast our profession.
15 For we have not an high priest which cannot be touched with the feeling[G4834] of our infirmities; but was in all points tempted like as we are, yet without sin.
16 Let us therefore come boldly unto the throne of grace, that we may obtain mercy, and find grace to help in time of need.

[G4834] συμπαθέω sympathéō, soom-path-eh'-o; from G4835; to feel "sympathy" with, i.e. (by implication) to commiserate:—have compassion, be touched with a feeling of.
[G4835] συμπαθής sympathḗs, soom-path-ace'; from G4841; having a fellow-feeling ("sympathetic"), i.e. (by implication) mutually commiserative:—having compassion one of another.[123]

Dear Worship Leader,

Great musicians have the capacity to express a myriad of feelings and emotions through the medium of music. Any instrumentalist or singer unable to connect emotionally is probably not a good artist. Music is communication. It's therapy for the soul. Somehow, feelings I could not express through words as a child, I learned to emote freely through music. Music became sort of a teacher and counselor for me.

But what happens when the music stops? Am I still in touch emotionally outside the musical performance or event? Am I still in the driver's seat, or are my feelings taking me for a ride I cannot control? For me, it was the latter. After the song ended, I needed counseling—as a child, teenager, and an adult. My musical gift opened doors for me that my personal immaturity and insecurity could not handle. Along with my musical chart, I needed a feelings chart for self-evaluation and self-care. How fluent are you in the language and world of emotional intelligence (EQ)? Do emotions freely flow through you? Are you in control, are they in control, or are you unsure?

We're comprised of spirit, soul, and body (1 Thessalonians 5:23). As a believer, the spirit (governed by the Holy Spirit) is to lead the soul (mind, will, and emotions) and body. Whenever the reverse happens we're in trouble. If the body or soul is running the ship, then we're in the flesh and thus out of control (Proverbs 25:28). We're all in need of spiritual self-control.

Jesus sympathizes with us. He was in touch emotionally, but feelings didn't rule Him. Even through temptation, the Holy Spirit led Him (Matthew 4:1–11). He was without sin and only did the will of the Father (John 5:30). If your ship is in danger of mutiny, come boldly to the throne of grace to obtain mercy and find grace to help in time of need (Hebrews 4:16).

---

[121] Merriam-Webster dictionary | www.merriam-webster.com | www.learnersdictionary.com
[122] Matt. 9:36; 14:14; 15:32; 18:27, 33; 20:34; Mark 1:41; 5:19; 6:34; 8:2; 9:22; Luke 7:13; 10:33; 15:20; John 11:35
[123] *Strong's Exhaustive Concordance of the Bible* | Blue Letter Bible | www.blueletterbible.org

Love, grace, and peace …

♪Colossians 3:16,

Rodney

Take a moment to meditate, muse, and memorize God's word. What is the Holy Spirit saying to you right now?

_____

_____

_____

_____

_____

_____

_____

_____

_____

_____

_____

_____

_____

_____

 LETTER #44 | ♪COL. 1:20 (NKJV)

FRIENDS

[n. Friend: 1) one attached to another by affection or esteem
2) a favored companion
3) a person who you like and enjoy being with][124]

Acts 27:3 (KJV)[125]

3 And the next day we touched at Sidon. And Julius courteously[G5364] **entreated Paul, and gave him liberty to go unto his friends**[G5384] **to refresh himself.**

[G5364] φιλανθρώπως philanthrŏpōs, fil-an-thro'-poce; adverb from a compound of G5384 and G444; fondly to man ("philanthropically"), i.e. humanely:—courteously.

[G5384] φίλος phílos, fee'-los; properly, dear, i.e. a friend; actively, fond, i.e. friendly (still as a noun, an associate, neighbor, etc.):—friend.[126]

Dear Worship Leader,

The journey, at times, can feel very lonely. So when God places friends in your path, it's so refreshing. Friends are like flowers along the dusty road of life. They are as rejuvenating as a cold glass of ice water after a long hot summer's day. Like watching your favorite movie or television show with a basketful of yummy snacks, they bring a smile to your face, warmth to your heart, and lots of good belly laughs.

I'm learning to make time for true friends. Even if the call or visit makes the day or weekend a little longer, it's usually worth it in the end. Yes, you're busy, but please don't get too busy for a little break with a loving friend every now and then. Some relationships only make withdrawals from your life, but good friendships overflow from deposits.

Proverbs 18:24 (NKJV) says, "A man who has friends must himself be friendly, But there is a friend who sticks closer than a brother."

Friendships, as beneficial as they are, still require investment, maintenance, and plenty of grace. Similar to the vehicles we treasure and enjoy, they need gas, oil changes, and a good wash from time to time. Personally, I don't do well with friendships that are guilt-driven and high-maintenance. My family and ministry life won't allow much room or space for that. But over time, relationships without their share of care and cultivation do not survive. In order to have thriving friendships, there must be reciprocity. One-sided giving leads to debt, bankruptcy, and closure.

In John 15:13–15, Jesus calls us friends. He is the friend that sticks closer than a brother. Grace and truth came through Him (John 1:14, 17). Thank God for His example. May all our friendships flourish as a result. There will come a day in time that we ourselves will need ROI, a return on investment.

Love, grace, and peace …

---

[124] Merriam-Webster dictionary | www.merriam-webster.com | www.learnersdictionary.com
[125] Matt. 26:37; 2 Tim. 4:16; 2 Cor. 11:22–33; Exod. 4:14; 1 Sam. 18:1–4; Prov. 17:17, 22; 25:11; 27:6, 17; 3 John 1:14
[126] *Strong's Exhaustive Concordance of the Bible* | Blue Letter Bible | www.blueletterbible.org

♪Colossians 3:16,

Rodney

Take a moment to meditate, muse, and memorize God's word. What is the Holy Spirit saying to you right now?

_____

_____

_____

_____

_____

_____

_____

_____

_____

_____

_____

_____

_____

_____

_____

 LETTER #45 | ♪COL. 1:21 (NKJV)

FORGIVENESS

[v. Forgive: 1) to cease to feel resentment against (an offender): pardon
2a) to give up resentment of or claim to requital for
2b) to grant relief from payment of][127]

Matthew 18:27 (NKJV)

27 "Then the master of that servant was moved with compassion,[G4697] released[G630] him, and forgave[G863] him the debt.

[G4697] σπλαγχνίζομαι splanchnízomai, splangkh-nid'-zom-ahee; middle voice from G4698; to have the bowels yearn, i.e. (figuratively) feel sympathy, to pity:—have (be moved with) compassion.

[G630] ἀπολύω apolýō, ap-ol-oo'-o; from G575 and G3089; to free fully, i.e. (literally) relieve, release, dismiss (reflexively, depart), or (figuratively) let die, pardon or (specially) divorce:—(let) depart, dismiss, divorce, forgive, let go, loose, put (send) away, release, set at liberty.

[G863] ἀφίημι aphíēmi, af-ee'-ay-mee; from G575 and ἵημι híēmi (to send; an intensive form of εἶμι eîmi, to go); to send forth, in various applications (as follow):—cry, forgive, forsake, lay aside, leave, let (alone, be, go, have), omit, put (send) away, remit, suffer, yield up.[128]

Dear Worship Leader,

If you've ever experienced forgiveness, you've been the recipient of a miracle. As believers, we're all walking miracles. Forgiveness is a divine gift graciously offered to us only by the love, mercy, and unmerited favor of God. I cannot think of any long-term relationship that does not, at some point, beg for mercy. Humans sin, miss the mark, fall short, make mistakes, misjudge, miscalculate, and are pretty messy (Romans 3:23). Unforgiveness is a dangerous, divisive and destructive Satanic device (2 Corinthians 2:10–11). Like oxygen to our souls, we all need forgiveness and grace, lest a root of bitterness spring up, cause trouble, and defile many (Hebrews 12:15). Jesus gives us the only real solution: a life of forgiveness and grace, or seventy times seven (Matthew 18:22). I know reconciliation is not always safe or possible, but forgive everyone in your heart. As Jesus taught, forgive us our debts as we forgive our debtors (Matthew 6:12).

Love, grace, and peace …

♪Colossians 3:16,

Rodney

The King models Forgiveness in Five ways (Matthew 18:21–35)

1. Recognize the offense (cost/debt) (v. 24).
    - Assess the hurt or damage caused. Count the cost.
2. Realize the offender's inability to pay (vv. 25–26).
    - Accept human limitations—bill too high, debt too great.
3. Relate to the offender (v. 27). (See chart below.)
    - Allow compassion to change you—as relatives of grace.

---

[127] Merriam-Webster dictionary | www.merriam-webster.com | www.learnersdictionary.com
[128] *Strong's Exhaustive Concordance of the Bible* | Blue Letter Bible | www.blueletterbible.org

4. Release the offender (v. 27).
   ◆ Agree that unforgiveness binds us all. Release them to God.
5. Remit (forgive) the offense (debt) (v. 27).
   ◆ Apply Christ's finished work/payment. Expunge the records.

Your offenses/sins toward God	Their offenses/ sins toward you
God's goodness/ kindness toward you	Your goodness/kindness toward them

Take a moment to meditate, muse, and memorize God's word. What is the Holy Spirit saying to you right now?

_____

_____

_____

_____

_____

_____

_____

_____

_____

_____

_____

_____

_____

LETTER #46 | ♪COL. 1:22 (NKJV)

GRACE

[n. Grace: 1a) unmerited divine assistance given to humans for their regeneration or sanctification
1b) a virtue coming from God
1c) a state of sanctification enjoyed through divine assistance
2) approval, favor
3) a charming or attractive trait or characteristic][129]

♪Colossians 3:16 (NKJV)

16 Let the word of Christ dwell in you richly in all wisdom, teaching and admonishing one another in psalms and hymns and spiritual songs, singing with grace[G5485] in your hearts to the Lord.

[G5485] χάρις cháris, khar'-ece; from G5463; graciousness (as gratifying), of manner or act (abstract or concrete; literal, figurative or spiritual; especially the divine influence upon the heart, and its reflection in the life; including gratitude):—acceptable, benefit, favour, gift, grace(- ious), joy, liberality, pleasure, thank(-s, -worthy).
[G5463] χαίρω chaírō, khah'-ee-ro; a primary verb; to be "cheer"ful, i.e. calmly happy or well-off; impersonally, especially as salutation (on meeting or parting), be well:—farewell, be glad, God speed, greeting, hail, joy(- fully), rejoice.[130]

Dear Worship Leader,

One of the biggest challenges I have with singers is to get them to smile while singing. Really, it's what Paul is asking for in ♪Colossians 3:16. Singing with grace is *the smile on our faces, illuminated from the smile in our hearts, generated from the God of all grace smiling on us.* He's not requesting phony, plastic, painted-on faces masking disconnected and displeased dispositions. Our churches don't need a façade, a fashion show, or feigned faith. What blesses the people is us dwelling with God in true spiritual worship that touches heaven, brings glory down, and lights up the house—with every heart in it!

In Exodus 34:29–35, Moses, after spending one-on-one face time with God on the mountain, had to put a veil over his face because he was shining so brightly. The very presence of God so illuminated Moses, it was hard for the children of Israel to look at him! Second Corinthians 3:12–18 enlightens us further. Yes, Moses was bright, but the children of Israel were also dark. Their minds were blinded and they had a veil on their heart (3:14–15). When we turn to the Lord, that veil is taken away (3:16). Where the Spirit of the Lord is, there is liberty—no more veil on the heart/mind (3:17). Second Corinthians 3:18 (NKJV) says, "But we all, with unveiled face, beholding as in a mirror the glory of the Lord, are being transformed into the same image from glory to glory, just as by the Spirit of the Lord." As believers, we have no more veil, only light (4:3–4)! We now sing as children of light, with glory and grace lit in our hearts.

Grace is gratitude. It's Thanksgiving every day. It's unmerited, unearned, undeserved favor. It's God's riches at Christ's expense. It's God doing for us what we could never do for ourselves. It's

---

[129] Merriam-Webster dictionary | www.merriam-webster.com | www.learnersdictionary.com
[130] *Strong's Exhaustive Concordance of the Bible* | Blue Letter Bible | www.blueletterbible.org

abounding grace, sufficient grace, glorious and amazing grace. Doesn't that bring joy to your heart and a smile to your face? Light up the world for Christ. God has graciously smiled on us.

Ἀγάπη, χάρις, and εἰρήνη …

♪Colossians 3:16,

Rodney

Take a moment to meditate, muse, and memorize God's word. What is the Holy Spirit saying to you right now?

_____

_____

_____

_____

_____

_____

_____

_____

_____

_____

_____

_____

_____

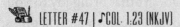 LETTER #47 | ♪COL. 1:23 (NKJV)

GLORY

[n. Glory: 1) praise, honor, or distinction extended by common consent: renown 2) something that secures praise or renown 3) a state of great gratification or exaltation 4) great beauty and splendor: magnificence][131]

2 Chronicles 5:13–14 (NKJV)

13 indeed it came to pass, when the trumpeters and singers were as one, to make one sound to be heard in praising and thanking the LORD, and when they lifted up their voice with the trumpets and cymbals and instruments of music, and praised the LORD, saying:

"For He is good,
For His mercy endures forever," that the house, the house of the Lord, was filled with a cloud,
14 so that the priests could not continue ministering because of the cloud; for the glory[H3519] of the LORD filled the house of God.

[H3519] כָּבוֹד kâbôwd, kaw-bode'; rarely כָּבֹד kâbôd; from H3513; properly, weight, but only figuratively in a good sense, splendor or copiousness:—glorious(-ly), glory, honour(-able).[132]

Dear Worship Leader,

We long for moments like 2 Chronicles 5, when the glory of God is so thick it's hard for the minister to move on. But what about other times when there's no smoke and no cloud? Have we become spiritual junkies waiting in line for the next roller-coaster high, the next glory fix, the next miracle, the next creative idea—the next adrenaline rush? If so, that sounds more like a chemical addiction than true worship.

In John 4:23–24, Jesus makes clear to the Samaritan woman that true spiritual worship is about worshipping the Father. We're not worshipping an experience or cool moment. The Father is a Person and we're in a relationship with Him. Glorifying the Father sometimes leads to His glory cloud being manifested in the house, or a Mount of Transfiguration experience, as in Matthew 17:1–8. In these moments, like Peter, it's tempting to want to stay or "tabernacle" there (17:4). But on the Mount of Transfiguration, the Father was spotlighting a relationship between Him and His Son in whom He was well pleased (17:5). Afterward, Jesus came down from the mountain, and the journey with Him continued (17:9).

We will all have mountains and valleys, highs and lows, but let's not idolize either. The spouse that lives only for the next bedroom high needs to reprogram their mind for enjoying the many little moments of intimacy that happen throughout the day. Whether we run, walk, or stand still, it's all to the *glory* of God. I love how 1 Corinthians 10:31 (NKJV; emphasis mine) says, "Therefore, whether you eat or drink, or whatever you do, do all to the *glory* of God." Romans 11:36 (NKJV; emphasis mine) declares, "For of Him and through Him and to Him are all things, to whom be *glory* forever. Amen." So enjoy Him through it all. Give Him great glory in it all. That's the abiding life in John 15—when He gloriously fills our hearts in moments great and small.

---

131 Merriam-Webster dictionary | www.merriam-webster.com | www.learnersdictionary.com
132 *Strong's Exhaustive Concordance of the Bible* | Blue Letter Bible | www.blueletterbible.org

Love, grace, and peace …

♪Colossians 3:16,

Rodney

Take a moment to meditate, muse, and memorize God's word. What is the Holy Spirit saying to you right now?

_____

_____

_____

_____

_____

_____

_____

_____

_____

_____

_____

_____

_____

_____

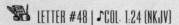 LETTER #48 | ♪COL. 1:24 (NKJV)

GROWTH

[v. Grow: 1) to become larger: to increase in size, amount, etc.
2) to become better or improved in some way: to become more developed, mature, etc.
3) to become larger and change from being a child to being an adult as time passes: to pass from childhood to adulthood][133]

———∞———

Hebrews 5:12–14 (NKJV)[134]

**12 For though by this time you ought to be teachers, you need someone to teach you again the first principles of the oracles of God; and you have come to need milk and not solid food.
13 For everyone who partakes only of milk is unskilled in the word of righteousness, for he is a babe.
14 But solid food belongs to those who are of full age,[G5046] that is, those who by reason of use have their senses exercised to discern both good and evil.**

———∞———

[G5046] τέλειος *teleios*, tel'-i-os; from G5056; complete (in various applications of labor, growth, mental and moral character, etc.); neuter (as noun, with G3588) completeness:— of full age, man, perfect.[135]

Dear Worship Leader,

Here's a sobering truth: Showing up to church and serving in ministry does not mean that you are actually growing. Selah. Furthermore, promotion and increase in one's leadership roles and responsibilities within the church do not equate to spiritual growth. I know it's possible to be at the highest pastoral or executive level and still be a babe, or stagnant in your walk, as it relates to spiritual maturity and development.

The process of spiritual growth and maturity is similar to the physical process of moving from childhood into adulthood in that it requires us having teachers and remaining teachable. This process necessitates love, grace, patience, feeding (from milk to meat), strength, skill, scripture, righteousness, character, hope, wisdom, perception, judgment, understanding, discipline, training, testing, correction, exercise, practice, transparency, joy, vulnerability, discernment, and so on. None of this simply happens overnight but in the process of time intentional, deliberate, consistency over time. This is true discipleship.

As musicians and singers, sometimes your musical gifting and commitment can camouflage your true need for discipling. Spiritually, are we dying while leading? The ministry can be flourishing all around us while we suffer from malnutrition and anorexia. Close proximity to good food religiously looks good, feels good, and can be helpful, but that doesn't mean there's proper digestion and fruitfulness (Matthew 13:1–23).

How's your spiritual health these days? Are you eating well and exercising regularly? Who's teaching you and walking with you? Are you growing and making wise decisions? Do you

---

133 Merriam-Webster dictionary | www.merriam-webster.com | www.learnersdictionary.com
134 2 Tim. 3:14–17; 4:2–5; Eph. 4:11–16; 1 Pet. 2:2; 2 Pet. 1:5–11; 3:18; Luke 2:40, 52; Acts 13:46; 1 Tim. 2:1–2; 3; ♪Col. 1:10–11, 28; 2:19; Matt. 13:23; 28:16–20; James 1:21–25; Rom. 10:17; 1 Thess. 3:12; 4:9–12; Heb. 4:12; Prov. 22:6
135 *Strong's Exhaustive Concordance of the Bible* | Blue Letter Bible | www.blueletterbible.org

have a personal community of believers that you are doing life with and accountable to? Who are you teaching and helping to grow up?

Love, grace, and peace …

♪Colossians 3:16,

Rodney

Take a moment to meditate, muse, and memorize God's word. What is the Holy Spirit saying to you right now?

_____

_____

_____

_____

_____

_____

_____

_____

_____

_____

_____

_____

_____

LETTER #49 | ♪COL. 1:25 (NKJV)

GOSPEL

[n. Gospel: 1a) the message concerning Christ, the kingdom of God, and salvation 1b) one of the first four New Testament books telling of the life, death, and resurrection of Jesus Christ 2) gospel music][136]

1 Corinthians 15:1–4 (NKJV)

1 Moreover, brethren, I declare to you the gospel[G2098] which I preached to you, which also you received and in which you stand,
2 by which also you are saved, if you hold fast that word which I preached to you—unless you believed in vain.
3 For I delivered to you first of all that which I also received: that Christ died for our sins according to the Scriptures,
4 and that He was buried, and that He rose again the third day according to the Scriptures,

[G2098] εὐαγγέλιον euangélion, yoo-ang-ghel'-ee-on; from the same as G2097; a good message, i.e. the gospel:—gospel.
[G2097] εὐαγγελίζω euangelízō, yoo-ang-ghel-id'-zo; from G2095 and G32; to announce good news ("evangelize") especially the gospel:—declare, bring (declare, show) glad (good) tidings, preach (the gospel).[137]

Dear Worship Leader,

One of the greatest experiences you and I will have in this life is sharing the gospel. It is good news—the death, burial, and resurrection of our Lord and Savior Jesus Christ. It's good news because Christ Jesus came into the world to save sinners (1 Timothy 1:15)—by *grace* alone, through *faith* alone, in *Christ* alone (John 3:15–18). Memorize verses like these for your own confirmation, affirmation, and edification but also so you can share your faith with anyone at any time (1 Peter 3:15). Our worship teams need to be equipped for winning souls. He that winneth souls is wise (Proverbs 11:30)!

Love, grace, and peace …

♪Colossians 3:16,

Rodney

The Romans Road and Other Helpful Verses for Sharing the Gospel

* ★ Romans 3:23 (NKJV)
  * ○ for all have sinned and fall short of the glory of God,
* ★ Romans 6:23 (NKJV)
  * ○ For the wages of sin is death, but the gift of God is eternal life in Christ Jesus our Lord.
* ★ Romans 5:8 (NKJV)
  * ○ But God demonstrates His own love toward us, in that while we were still sinners, Christ died for us.
* ★ Romans 10:9–10 (NKJV)
  * ○ that if you confess with your mouth the Lord Jesus and believe in your heart that God has raised Him from the dead, you will be saved.

---

[136] Merriam-Webster dictionary | www.merriam-webster.com | www.learnersdictionary.com
[137] *Strong's Exhaustive Concordance of the Bible* | Blue Letter Bible | www.blueletterbible.org

- o For with the heart one believes unto righteousness, and with the mouth confession is made unto salvation.
- ★ Ephesians 2:8–9 (NKJV)
  - o For by grace you have been saved through faith, and that not of yourselves; it is the gift of God,
  - o not of works, lest anyone should boast.
- ★ 1 John 5:13 (NKJV)
  - o These things I have written to you who believe in the name of the Son of God, that you may know that you have eternal life, and that you may continue to believe in the name of the Son of God.

Take a moment to meditate, muse, and memorize God's word. What is the Holy Spirit saying to you right now?

_____

_____

_____

_____

_____

_____

_____

_____

_____

_____

_____

LETTER #50 | ♪COL. 1:26 (NKJV)

GIFTS

[n. Gift: 1) a notable capacity, talent, or endowment
2) a special ability
3) something voluntarily transferred by one person to another without compensation][138]

Ephesians 4:11–16 (NKJV)

11 And He Himself gave some to be apostles, some prophets, some evangelists, and some pastors and teachers,
12 for the equipping of the saints for the work of ministry, for the edifying of the body of Christ,
13 till we all come to the unity of the faith and of the knowledge of the Son of God, to a perfect man, to the measure of the stature of the fullness of Christ;
14 that we should no longer be children, tossed to and fro and carried about with every wind of doctrine, by the trickery of men, in the cunning craftiness of deceitful plotting,
15 but, speaking the truth in love, may grow up in all things into Him who is the head—Christ—
16 from whom the whole body, joined and knit together by what every joint supplies, [G2024] according to the effective working by which every part does its share, causes growth of the body for the edifying of itself in love.

[G2024] ἐπιχορηγία epichorēgía, ep-ee-khor-ayg-ee'-ah; from G2023; contribution:—supply.[139]

Dear Worship Leader,

We have all been spiritually gifted in the body of Christ to make a contribution, without exception (Ephesians 4:16; ♪Colossians 2:19). None of us has everything; all of us have something. As recipients and dispensers of God's grace, we have all been strategically positioned to serve as it has pleased the Lord (1 Corinthians 12:18). We are one body, connected through one Spirit endowed with divine gifts that are designed to complement each other, not compete. As a team, our Head Coach wants us all engaged. All members, positions, and giftings are significant for maximal impact.

While we personally benefit from our own gifts, like fruit on a tree, they are not simply to serve ourselves but are also for the benefit of others. Ephesians 4:7–12 says that Christ Himself gave gifts for the saint's *equipping* [restoring and complete furnishing], the ministry's *work*, [labor and toil], and the body's *edifying* [building, architecture, and structure]. All of this requires resources and tools! Well, we are God's human resources and our spiritual gifts are tools from His divine toolbox—under the ownership and employment of His kingdom construction service, contracted to "build" and "grow up" His church (4:12–16). Jesus, a carpenter-builder by trade, told Peter in Matthew 16:18 (NKJV), "I will build My church, and the gates of Hades shall not prevail against it."

No matter the gift, the same goal is on our job descriptions: to build and grow up the church. Once you discover your particular gifts, rejoice—but use them to build and grow up the church. They're not for boasting or belittling. That's from the opposing team! To the contrary, we join the Spirit's work of building and

---

[138] Merriam-Webster dictionary | www.merriam-webster.com | www.learnersdictionary.com
[139] *Strong's Exhaustive Concordance of the Bible* | Blue Letter Bible | www.blueletterbible.org

growing up God's people. How can you use your gifts now to love, support, and serve others in need? May we all, with one accord, build and grow up together—till He comes.

Love, grace, and peace …

♪Colossians 3:16,

Rodney

Take a moment to meditate, muse, and memorize God's word. What is the Holy Spirit saying to you right now?

_____

_____

_____

_____

_____

_____

_____

_____

_____

_____

_____

_____

_____

SPIRITUAL CHECKUP: INSPIRE

Review the last ten letters and record any key highlights. Has the Holy Spirit revealed any ...

Instruction?

_____

_____

_____

_____

Needs?

_____

_____

_____

_____

Scripture?

_____

_____

_____

_____

Principles?

_____

_____

_____

_____

Interests?

_____

_____

_____

_____

Reproof?

_____

_____

_____

_____

Encouragement?

_____

_____

_____

_____

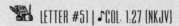 LETTER #51 | ♪COL. 1:27 (NKJV)

GUARD

[n. Guard: 1) one assigned to protect or oversee another
2) a defensive state or attitude
3) the act or duty of protecting or defending][140]

Proverbs 4:20–23 (NKJV)[141]

20 My son, give attention to my words; Incline your ear to my sayings. 21 Do not let them depart from your eyes; Keep[H8104] **them in the midst of your heart; 22 For they are life to those who find them, And health to all their flesh. 23 Keep**[H5341] **your heart with all diligence, For out of it spring the issues of life.**

[H8104] שָׁמַר **shâmar,** shaw-mar'; a primitive root; properly, to hedge about (as with thorns), i.e. guard; generally, to protect, attend to, etc.:—beward, be circumspect, take heed (to self), keep(-er, self), mark, look narrowly, observe, preserve, regard, reserve, save (self), sure, (that lay) wait (for), watch(-man).
[H5341] נָצַר **nâtsar,** naw-tsar'; a primitive root; to guard, in a good sense (to protect, maintain, obey, etc.) or a bad one (to conceal, etc.):—besieged, hidden thing, keep(-er, -ing), monument, observe, preserve(-r), subtil, watcher(-man).[142]

Dear Worship Leader,

I wish we were face-to-face for this letter; it's that important. *Never let your guard down.* As long as we have this earth suit on, there is an enemy waiting for us to go out on the battlefield without our armor (1 Peter 5:8). We need to put on the whole armor of God, as Paul commanded in Ephesians 6:11–13! With it, we're warriors. Without it, we're wheat.

Of utmost importance is guarding our hearts and minds (Philippians 4:7). That's why we all live in a gated community. God placed four types of gates around our brains (gateway to hearts/minds): ear gate, eye gate, mouth gate, and nose gate. Why? He wants to help protect our most prized possession—how we think and feel, from unwanted guests. [Insert song here: "O Be Careful Little Eyes"] Yes, the battle is for your heart/mind!

As musicians and singers, we heavily minister from our hearts. So imagine how devastating it is for us to suffer from heart disease (the leading cause of death in the USA). Not only does that affect our hearts, but also it corrupts our music, our songs, and our ministries. We die. If the enemy can persuade us to keep all that's helpful out and keep all that's harmful in, he can take us out and our ministries with one blow to the heart.

The solution is nothing new. How's our spiritual eating and exercise, our input and output? That's why James 1:27 says for us to keep ourselves unspotted from this evil world. Whoever we fall in love with will take over our gates and overthrow our kingdoms. With love always

---

140 Merriam-Webster dictionary | www.merriam-webster.com | www.learnersdictionary.com
141 Prov. 5–7; 2 Chron. 26:5, 16; Judg. 16:4, 20; 2 Sam. 11; 1 Cor. 10:1–13; Eccles. 4:9–12; 12:13; Ps. 19:7–14; 141:3–4, 9; Eph. 6:10–20; Jude 1:20–25; Isa. 14:12–14; 2 Cor. 2:5–11; Heb. 4:12; 1 Sam. 15:11, 17; Phil. 4:6–9; 1 John 5:21; John 10:10; 14:15; James 1:27; Josh. 22:5; 23; Deut. 8; Exod. 15:26; Gen. 2:15; Job 31:1; 1 Pet. 5:8–9; 1 Thess. 5 | ♪Col. 1:4, 10, 17, 18, 20, 23, 25, 28; 2:1–3, 16–17, 18, 23; 3:1–3, 5, 8–9, 10, 12–13, 14, 16, 19, 21, 22, 23–24; 4:13–15, 17 (https://soundcloud.com/col316/sets/favs-from-colossians-project)
142 *Strong's Exhaustive Concordance of the Bible* | Blue Letter Bible | www.blueletterbible.org

come keys and access. Let's completely give our hearts to Christ! We then benefit from His *community* and His *counseling*. Together we fight and sing, we watch and pray, and we worship and win!

Love, grace, and peace …

♪Colossians 3:16,

Rodney

Take a moment to meditate, muse, and memorize God's word. What is the Holy Spirit saying to you right now?

_____

_____

_____

_____

_____

_____

_____

_____

_____

_____

_____

LETTER #52 | ♪COL. 1:28 (NKJV)

GOODNESS

[n. Goodness: the quality or state of being good][143]

Psalm 23:1–6 (KJV)[144]

[[A Psalm of David.]] 1 The Lord is my shepherd; I shall not want. 2 He maketh me to lie down in green pastures: he leadeth me beside the still waters. 3 He restoreth my soul: he leadeth me in the paths of righteousness for his name's sake. 4 Yea, though I walk through the valley of the shadow of death, I will fear no evil: for thou art with me; thy rod and thy staff they comfort me. 5 Thou preparest a table before me in the presence of mine enemies: thou anointest my head with oil; my cup runneth over. 6 Surely goodness[H2896] and mercy shall follow me all the days of my life: and I will dwell in the house of the Lord for ever.

[H2896] טוֹב ṭôwb, tobe; from H2895; good (as an adjective) in the widest sense; used likewise as a noun, both in the masculine and the feminine, the singular and the plural (good, a good or good thing, a good man or woman; the good, goods or good things, good men or women), also as an adverb (well):—beautiful, best, better, bountiful, cheerful, at ease, × fair (word), (be in) favour, fine, glad, good (deed, -lier, -liest, -ly, -ness, -s), graciously, joyful, kindly, kindness, liketh (best), loving, merry, × most, pleasant, pleaseth, pleasure, precious, prosperity, ready, sweet, wealth, welfare, (be) well(-favoured).[145]

Dear Worship Leader,

You and I have a good shepherd (John 10:11, 14). If you carefully examine your life, you'll see that He's always been there. His fingerprints and footprints are everywhere. Just as Psalm 23 begins and ends with the Lord, so does your earthly life, and beyond. This well-loved psalm has been a favorite of mine as far back as I can remember. My grandfather taught it to me. As I grow older, it becomes even more dear to me. It's filled with rich benefits from dwelling with the good Shepherd.

❖ Benefit #1–Daily Needs (v. 1)—>His Provision
   ➤ All sheep really require is the Shepherd. In Him is access to everything they need and want. Their bond is unbreakable.
❖ Benefit #2–Direction (v. 2)—>His Peace
   ➤ Without the Shepherd, sheep would be lost. He orders and directs their steps, prepares the way, and knows what's best.
❖ Benefit #3–Deliverance (v. 3)—>His Protection
   ➤ Sheep often need repair, restoration, and refuge. They go astray and need the Shepherd's gentle but firm touch.
❖ Benefit #4–Defense (v. 4)—>His Presence
   ➤ The Shepherd never leaves them. They have no reason to fear. His rod and staff guide, protect, and comfort them.

---

[143] Merriam-Webster dictionary | www.merriam-webster.com | www.learnersdictionary.com
[144] Matt. 6:8, 32; Luke 9:11; 12:30; 15:6; Acts 2:45; 4:35; Rom. 16:2; 2 Cor. 11:9; Eph. 4:28; Phil. 4:11–19; Heb. 4:16
[145] *Strong's Exhaustive Concordance of the Bible* | Blue Letter Bible | www.blueletterbible.org

❖ Benefit #5–Delight (v. 5)—>His Prosperity
   ➤ Even amid enemies, the Shepherd feeds, leads, and provides blessing, oil, and favor. Their cup is abundantly overflowing.
❖ Benefit #6–Destiny (v. 6)—>His Promises
   ➤ Goodness and mercy chase them down. It's their destiny to forever enjoy and dwell with the good Shepherd.

On his deathbed, my grandfather, as usual, led us in quoting this psalm. What comfort in knowing we will never be separated from the good Shepherd. Romans 8:38–39 (KJV) says, "For I am persuaded, that neither death, nor life, nor angels, nor principalities, nor powers, nor things present, nor things to come, Nor height, nor depth, nor any other creature, shall be able to separate us from the love of God, which is in Christ Jesus our Lord." Amen to forever together with Him!

Love, grace, and peace …

♪Colossians 3:16,

Rodney

Take a moment to meditate, muse, and memorize God's word. What is the Holy Spirit saying to you right now?

_____

_____

_____

_____

_____

_____

_____

_____

Him we preach, warning every man and teaching every man in all wisdom, that we may present every man perfect in Christ Jesus.

(♪Colossians 1:28 NKJV)

PART 2
LETTERS H TO Z

LETTER #53 | ♪COL. 1:29 (NKJV)

HONOR

[v. Honor: 1a) to regard or treat (someone) with respect and admiration: to show or give honor to (someone)
1b) to show admiration for (someone or something) in a public way: to give a public honor to (someone or something)][146]

〰〰〰

1 Peter 2:13–17 (NKJV)[147]

13 Therefore submit yourselves to every ordinance of man for the Lord's sake, whether to the king as supreme, 14 or to governors, as to those who are sent by him for the punishment of evildoers and for the praise of those who do good. 15 For this is the will of God, that by doing good you may put to silence the ignorance of foolish men— 16 as free, yet not using liberty as a cloak for vice, but as bondservants of God. 17 Honor[G5091] **all people. Love the brotherhood. Fear God. Honor**[G5091] **the king.**

〰〰〰

[G5091] τιμάω timáō, tim-ah'-o; from G5093; to prize, i.e. fix a valuation upon; by implication, to revere:—honour, value.
[G5093] τίμιος tímios, tim'-ee-os; from G5092; valuable, i.e. (objectively) costly, or (subjectively) honored, esteemed, or (figuratively) beloved:—dear, honourable, (more, most) precious, had in reputation.[148]

Dear Worship Leader,

Honoring others is a precious life principle. Great leadership first requires becoming a great follower. If we want others to honor us in positions of authority, it pays for us to humbly do the same. The people you lead are closely watching how you treat others, particularly those above you—that you follow.

I love that 1 Peter 2:17 uses the same Greek word for "honor" when commanding us to honor all people and honor the king. This word is used in reference to how we esteem our fathers and mothers as well as widows (Ephesians 6:2; 1 Timothy 5:3). It covers those in authority and those without it. This includes bosses, coworkers, vendors, employees, and customers. It's honoring people in the community of great clout and notoriety as well as those with none. In church, it means that we honor everyone from the senior pastor on down. Depending on your upbringing, this may or may not be challenging for you, but *everyone has value in God's eyes.* Christ died for us all. When we dishonor God's people, we dishonor Him. But whenever we love, honor, respect, and submit to legitimate authority—that's good worship leading!

Honoring others doesn't mean we can't be honest. Christ was full of grace and truth. In Him, we can be loving, gracious, kind, and respectful—even during difficult conversations, meetings, and rehearsals. We can speak the truth in love (Ephesians 4:15). We can communicate with grace, seasoned with salt (♪Colossians 4:6). We can minister words of edification and grace without using corrupt communication (Ephesians 4:29). People matter. Let's not step on others in the name of promoting God's

---

[146] Merriam-Webster dictionary | www.merriam-webster.com | www.learnersdictionary.com
[147] Matt. 8:8–10; 10:42; 11:11; 18:10; 25:37–40; Luke 1:52; 7:28; 9:48; 1 Sam. 24:1–7; Exod. 20:12; 1 Tim. 5:10, 17; 2 Cor. 5:14–15; John 1:14; Phil. 2:1–11; 1 Thess. 5:12–13; 1 Cor. 12:12–26; Rom. 12:3–16 (10, 16); James 4:6; 1 Pet. 5:5
[148] *Strong's Exhaustive Concordance of the Bible* | Blue Letter Bible | www.blueletterbible.org

program and agenda. We want to represent the family of God well by loving all those made in His image—esteeming them with dignity, worth, value, and honor.

Love, grace, and peace …

♪Colossians 3:16,

Rodney

Take a moment to meditate, muse, and memorize God's word. What is the Holy Spirit saying to you right now?

_____

_____

_____

_____

_____

_____

_____

_____

_____

_____

_____

_____

_____

LETTER #54 | ♪COL. 2.1–3 (NKJV)

HEALTH

[n. Health: 1a) the condition of being sound in body, mind, or spirit
1b) the general condition of the body
2a) a condition in which someone or something is thriving or doing well: well-being
2b) general condition or state
3) a toast to someone's health or prosperity][149]

3 John 1:2–4 (NKJV)[150]

2 Beloved, I pray that you may prosper in all things and be in health,[G5198] just as your soul prospers. 3 For I rejoiced greatly when brethren came and testified of the truth that is in you, just as you walk in the truth. 4 I have no greater joy than to hear that my children walk in truth.

[G5198] ὑγιαίνω hugiainō, hoog-ee-ah'-ee-no; from G5199; to have sound health, i.e. be well (in body); figuratively, to be uncorrupt (true in doctrine):—be in health, (be safe and) sound, (be) whole(-some).
[G5199] ὑγιής hugiēs, hoog-ee-ace'; from the base of G837; healthy, i.e. well (in body); figuratively, true (in doctrine):—sound, whole.
[G837] αὐξάνω auxánō, owx-an'-o; a prolonged form of a primary verb; to grow ("wax"), i.e. enlarge (literal or figurative, active or passive):—grow (up), (give the) increase.[151]

Dear Worship Leader,

Our health is extremely important. On earth, we only get one body. And as much as others can do for us, no one can replace us in offering self-care to ourselves. We have all been given the gift of life. As stewards of God, it is required that we are found faithful—faithful managers over all that God has graciously entrusted to our hands (1 Corinthians 4:1–2). At the end of this life, we want God to say, "Well done, good and faithful servant," like He did to the servants who gained Him talents and did not waste them (Matthew 25:21, 23). In gratitude, we want to offer Him a return on His investment. We want His kingdom to be better, wiser, stronger, richer, and further—as a result of our living, growing, and sowing.

Jesus commands us to love our neighbors as ourselves. Unfortunately, many of us have spent years trying to love our neighbors instead of ourselves. It's not good stewardship to neglect self-care. It doesn't make the kingdom of God look more appealing for everyone around us to be flourishing instead of us. We are the temple of God! First Corinthians 6:20 (NKJV) says, "For you were bought at a price; therefore glorify God in your body and in your spirit, which are God's."

As His children, God wants us to be prosperous in all things and be in health, just as our souls prosper (3 John 1:2). A prosperous soul living in a poor body will be hindered and halted in its impact. He wants us to be a growing tree fruitful in all things—spiritually, physically, mentally, emotionally, financially, etc. This takes divine self-love, self-leadership, self-evaluation, self-awareness, self-investment, self-work,

---

[149] Merriam-Webster dictionary | www.merriam-webster.com | www.learnersdictionary.com

[150] 1 Thess. 5:23; 1 Cor. 6:19; 9:27; 1 Tim. 4:7–8; Matt. 21:18–22; 22:39; 25:14–30; Eccles. 4:9; 12; Ps. 1:3; 90:10–12; James 1:26–27; 4:14; Rom. 12:1; Luke 9:23; 2 Cor. 9:8; Eph. 3:20; 4:16; Gal. 6:8–9; Prov. 6:6–11; 18:9; 23:20–21; 28:7

[151] *Strong's Exhaustive Concordance of the Bible* | Blue Letter Bible | www.blueletterbible.org

self-discipline, self-control, self-development, and self-care. Let's ask God to send others who are stronger to help us in any areas of need so we're all growing healthy, wealthy, and wise.

Love, grace, and peace …

♪Colossians 3:16,

Rodney

Take a moment to meditate, muse, and memorize God's word. What is the Holy Spirit saying to you right now?

_____

_____

_____

_____

_____

_____

_____

_____

_____

_____

_____

_____

_____

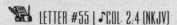 LETTER #55 | ♪COL. 2:4 (NKJV)

HYMNS

[n. Hymn: 1) a song of praise to God
2) a song of praise or joy
3) something resembling a song of praise][152]

♪Colossians 3:16 (NKJV)

16 Let the word of Christ dwell in you richly in all wisdom, teaching and admonishing one another in psalms and hymns[G5215] and spiritual songs, singing with grace in your hearts to the Lord.

[G5215] ὕμνος humnŏs, hoom'-nos; apparently from a simpler (obsolete) form of ὑδέω hudĕō (to celebrate; probably akin to G103; compare H5667); a "hymn" or religious ode (one of the Psalms):—hymn.
[G103] ᾄδω áidō, ad'-o; a primary verb; to sing:—sing.[153]

Matthew 26:30 (NKJV)

30 And when they had sung a hymn,[G5214] they went out to the Mount of Olives.

Acts 16:25 (NKJV)

25 But at midnight Paul and Silas were praying and singing hymns[G5214] to God, and the prisoners were listening to them.

[G5214] ὑμνέω humnĕō, hoom-neh'-o; from G5215; to hymn, i.e. sing a religious ode; by implication, to celebrate (God) in song:—sing a hymn (praise unto).

Dear Worship Leader,

If hymns aren't already an integral part of your repertoire and worship diet, I hope they will become so. Some of the more familiar ones are regularly requested at funerals and special events because they are well-loved and often filled with great foundational truth. Although there are some exceptions, I have found these songs to be very useful for congregational singing as well as teaching biblical truth and sound doctrine. The hymnodist Martin Luther, commonly known as the father of the Protestant Reformation, wrote hymns for the very purpose of scriptural and theological indoctrination. As a child, the church we attended sang out of a red book called *The New National Baptist Hymnal* every week. I didn't understand the depth of the verses and choruses back then, but as I have matured in the faith, I have come to cherish them—and sing them for my own edification and growth. I still use that old red hymnal. It's priceless to me.

Many of the hymns have powerful stories behind them. I enjoy reading and researching the events that led to the author's composition. Numerous songs were born out of trial and triumph. We see this pattern prevalent all throughout scripture. Somehow, suffering and salvation stir God's people to sing. In Psalm 40:1–3, David says that God put a new song in his mouth after rescuing him from his crying and miry clay experience. In Matthew 26:30, Jesus and His disciples sang a hymn prior to Him suffering on the cross. At midnight, Paul and Silas sang hymns to God while in prison. As a result, revival broke out and heaven set everyone free!

---

[152] Merriam-Webster dictionary | www.merriam-webster.com | www.learnersdictionary.com
[153] *Strong's Exhaustive Concordance of the Bible* | Blue Letter Bible | www.blueletterbible.org

There's nothing like a hymn or spiritual to soothe your heart and soul in times of hardship. May we always have hymns of prayer and praise on our lips and songs in our hearts. Abound or abased, high or low, the Lord is our joy, strength, and song.

Love, grace, and peace …

♪Colossians 3:16,

Rodney

Take a moment to meditate, muse, and memorize God's word. What is the Holy Spirit saying to you right now?

_____

_____

_____

_____

_____

_____

_____

_____

_____

_____

_____

_____

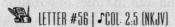

LETTER #56 | ♪COL. 2:5 (NKJV)

INVESTMENT

[v. Invest: 1) to commit (money) in order to earn a financial return
2) to make use of for future benefits or advantages
3) to involve or engage especially emotionally][154]

Galatians 6:6–10 (NKJV)[155]

6 Let him who is taught the word share in all good things with him who teaches. 7 Do not be deceived, God is not mocked; for whatever a man sows, that he will also reap. [G2325] **8 For he who sows to his flesh will of the flesh reap**[G2325] **corruption, but he who sows to the Spirit will of the Spirit reap**[G2325] **everlasting life. 9 And let us not grow weary while doing good, for in due season we shall reap**[G2325] **if we do not lose heart. 10 Therefore, as we have opportunity, let us do good to all, especially to those who are of the household of faith.**

[G2325] θερίζω **therízō,** ther-id'-zo; from G2330 (in the sense of the crop); to harvest:—reap.
[G2330] θέρος **théros,** ther'-os; from a primary θέρω **thérō** (to heat); properly, heat, i.e. summer:—summer.[156]

Dear Worship Leader,

Can I encourage you to *never give up* doing good or sowing good? I know how weariness can grow on you. Life is not easy. The nouns of life can make us weary. People, places, things, events, ideas, etc. have their way of depleting our strength and weighing us down. The verbs of life can do the same. We're always being called on to do, to be, to go, to pay, to wait, and the list goes on and on. The seasons of life can also become wearisome. Sometimes the hard ones seem to have no end in sight. But now the room's growing darker, you're starting to see it spin, and your heart is feeling faint.

Well, drink this truth from Galatians 6:6–10! It's from a God who is not mocked (6:7) and cannot lie (Numbers 23:19). All His promises are yes and amen (2 Corinthians 1:20). Heaven and earth will pass away, but not His word (Luke 21:33). He says that if you do not faint or lose heart, *you will reap* in due season! Every farmer knows that you don't reap in the same season that you sow, but faithfulness now will produce fruitfulness later. God's fifth season is on the way—due season!

The word for "season" (6:9) in the Greek is [G2540] καιρός kairós, kahee-ros', which means an occasion; a set or proper time. It's God's time clock. The same Greek word is used again when translated "opportunity" (6:10). In other words, if we sow in καιρός, we'll reap in καιρός. If we sow in the Spirit, we'll reap in the Spirit. If we sow in epic, we'll reap in epic (2 Corinthians 9:6). Kingdom investment is amazing because God Himself faithfully matches our sowing! Do you want to reap Luke 6:38—good measure, pressed down, shaken

---

[154] Merriam-Webster dictionary | www.merriam-webster.com | www.learnersdictionary.com
[155] Luke 18:1; 2 Cor. 4:1, 16; Eph. 3:13; 2 Thess. 3:13 | Matt. 9:36; 15:32; Mark 8:3; Heb. 12:3, 5 | 1 Tim. 5:9–10; Mark 9:41; Heb. 6:10, 18; 10:35; 11:26; Luke 6:23, 38; 19:17; 1 Cor. 3:8; 9:24–27; ♪Col. 2:18; 3:24; 2 John 1:8; 2 Tim. 4:8; 1 Thess. 2:19–20; James 1:12; 1 Pet. 5:4; Phil. 3:14; Matt. 25:21, 23; 2 Cor. 9:6–15; Num. 23:19; Titus 1:2; Isa. 40:21–31
[156] *Strong's Exhaustive Concordance of the Bible* | Blue Letter Bible | www.blueletterbible.org

together, and running over? Then keep giving in faith. In due season, you'll see that God exceeds and multiplies your investment!

Love, grace, and peace …

♪Colossians 3:16,

Rodney

Take a moment to meditate, muse, and memorize God's word. What is the Holy Spirit saying to you right now?

_____

_____

_____

_____

_____

_____

_____

_____

_____

_____

_____

_____

LETTER #57 | ♪COL. 2:6 (NKJV)

INSPIRATION

[v. Inspire: 1) to spur on: impel, motivate 2a) to breathe or blow into or upon 2b) to infuse (something, such as life) by breathing][157]

⎯⎯⎯∞∞∞⎯⎯⎯

Genesis 2:1–7 (NKJV)[158]

1 Thus the heavens and the earth, and all the host of them, were finished. 2 And on the seventh day God ended His work which He had done, and He rested on the seventh day from all His work which He had done. 3 Then God blessed the seventh day and sanctified it, because in it He rested from all His work which God had created and made. 4 This is the history of the heavens and the earth when they were created, in the day that the LORD God made the earth and the heavens, 5 before any plant of the field was in the earth and before any herb of the field had grown. For the LORD God had not caused it to rain on the earth, and there was no man to till the ground; 6 but a mist went up from the earth and watered the whole face of the ground. 7 And the LORD God formed man of the dust of the ground, and breathed into his nostrils the breath[H5397] of life; and man became a living being.

⎯⎯⎯∞∞∞⎯⎯⎯

[H5397] נְשָׁמָה neshâmâh, nesh-aw-maw'; from H5395; a puff, i.e. wind, angry or vital breath, divine inspiration, intellect. or (concretely) an animal:—blast, (that) breath(-eth), inspiration, soul, spirit.[159]

Dear Worship Leader,

We know that inspiration originates from the very breath of our Creator, God (Genesis 2:7; 2 Timothy 3:16). In Him we live, move, and have our being (Acts 17:28). Who else or what else inspires you, breathes life into you, and makes you feel revived, recharged, reenergized, replenished, and refreshed?

For me, lots of things fill my cup: quality time with family and friends; good food, folks, fun, and fellowship; films that are funny and filled with fantastic love stories; fine arts, such as plays, performances, and photography; old-fashioned antique shops; fondue with my wife at a weekend bed-and-breakfast; friendly banter; playful fighting with my son; having my feet in sand on a beach; field and nature walks in the morning while listening to sermons and music; a family staycation or vacation away; floating in a swimming pool; and so much more.

In ministry, this is imperative! Just as God rested on the seventh day from all His work, we're to follow His example (Genesis 2:2). We need time to dream, journal, write, and reflect. We require space to create and think outside the box. Without inspiration the creative dies. We have to unplug and hit the reset button in life. Working in a fallen world can get you out of alignment and have you behaving outside your "best self." It's necessary to revisit vision, values, mission, calling, and purpose. Readjustment is required; it's just what Dr. Jesus ordered. We resuscitate by scriptural meditation and prayer, a mind renewal (Romans 12:1–2).

---

157 Merriam-Webster dictionary | www.merriam-webster.com | www.learnersdictionary.com
158 Exod. 23:12; 31:17; 1 Sam. 16:23; 2 Sam. 16:14; Rom. 15:32; 1 Cor. 16:18; 2 Cor. 7:13; 2 Tim. 1:16; Philem. 1:7, 20
159 *Strong's Exhaustive Concordance of the Bible* | Blue Letter Bible | www.blueletterbible.org

We can crash life's vehicle by slamming on the brake or on the accelerator. Living too long at either extreme loses cadence and doesn't naturally flow with God's model of what is best for us. Pace yourself. Plan to regularly do something out of the ordinary. We get new mercies every day. Now take in a deep breath of fresh air. Inhale the good, and exhale the bad. *Restart!*

Love, grace, and peace …

♪Colossians 3:16,

Rodney

Take a moment to meditate, muse, and memorize God's word. What is the Holy Spirit saying to you right now?

_____

_____

_____

_____

_____

_____

_____

_____

_____

_____

_____

_____

_____

LETTER #58 | ♪COL. 2:7 (NKJV)

ILLITERACY

[a. Illiterate: 1) having little or no education, especially: unable to read or write
2) showing or marked by a lack of acquaintance with the fundamentals of a particular field of knowledge][160]

1 Timothy 4:12–16 (NKJV)[161]

12 Let no one despise your youth, but be an example to the believers in word, in conduct, in love, in spirit, in faith, in purity. 13 Till I come, give attention to reading,[G320] to exhortation, to doctrine. 14 Do not neglect the gift that is in you, which was given to you by prophecy with the laying on of the hands of the eldership. 15 Meditate on these things; give yourself entirely to them, that your progress may be evident to all. 16 Take heed to yourself and to the doctrine. Continue in them, for in doing this you will save both yourself and those who hear you.

[G320] ἀνάγνωσις anágnōsis, an-ag'-no-sis; from G314; (the act of) reading:—reading.[162]

Dear Worship Leader,

I believe biblical illiteracy is a problem we must face within the church and within our worship/music ministries. We may know the words to the songs we sing, but that usually doesn't equate to knowing the scriptures they're based on or the word of God itself. From my experience, in many ways the church of today seems to be biblically illiterate, liturgically anemic, doctrinally unsound, spiritually irreverent, and culturally irrelevant. God, help us!

This is in direct opposition to what God intends for His people. In Ephesians 1:17–23 (NKJV), Paul prays for the church of Ephesus to have God's wisdom, revelation, knowledge, and understanding. He wants them to know "what is the hope of His calling, what are the riches of the glory of His inheritance in the saints, and what is the exceeding greatness of His power toward us who believe." None of this is possible without us abiding in His word, and His word abiding in us (John 15:7). The same enrichment Paul wanted for the Ephesians, he wanted for Timothy, his disciple and spiritual son (1 Timothy 4:12–16). And God wants the same for us.

❖ Enriched in the Word vs. Biblically Illiterate (4:13, 15, 16)
  ➤ Personally read, study, meditate/muse, memorize, manifest, and minister God's rich word—as lifelong students.
❖ Enriched in Worship vs. Liturgically Anemic (4:12–16)
  ➤ Practice a healthy diet of richly singing psalms, hymns, and spiritual songs at home. Serving and sharing in corporate worship.
❖ Enriched in Wisdom vs. Doctrinally Unsound (4:13, 16)
  ➤ Pursue sound theology and rich doctrinal truth. Apply practical wisdom. Exercise spiritual self-care and leadership.
❖ Enriched in our Walk vs. Spiritually Irreverent (4:12, 15)

---

[160] Merriam-Webster dictionary | www.merriam-webster.com | www.learnersdictionary.com
[161] 1 Tim. 6:11; 2 Tim. 3:16–17; 4:2; Ps. 19:7–11; 119:1–176; Hosea 4:6; Matt. 13:18–23; James 1:21–27; Acts 17:11
[162] *Strong's Exhaustive Concordance of the Bible* | Blue Letter Bible | www.blueletterbible.org

➢ Pattern a rich life filled with the Spirit. One of righteousness, godliness, faith, love, patience, and gentleness.

❖ Enriched for the World vs. Culturally Irrelevant (4:15–16)
  ➢ Present the rich gospel of Christ to a lost, dark world—as salt and light. Fight offensively and defensively for His kingdom.

Love, grace, and peace …

♪Colossians 3:16,

Rodney

Take a moment to meditate, muse, and memorize God's word. What is the Holy Spirit saying to you right now?

_____

_____

_____

_____

_____

_____

_____

_____

_____

_____

_____

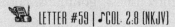 LETTER #59 | ♪COL. 2:8 (NKJV)

INTIMACY

[n. Intimacy: 1) the state of being intimate: familiarity
2) something of a personal or private nature][163]

⸺⚬⚬⚬⚬⸺

Genesis 2:18–25 (NKJV)

18 And the LORD God said, "It is not good that man should be alone; I will make him a helper comparable to him." 19 Out of the ground the LORD God formed every beast of the field and every bird of the air, and brought them to Adam to see what he would call them. And whatever Adam called each living creature, that was its name. 20 So Adam gave names to all cattle, to the birds of the air, and to every beast of the field. But for Adam there was not found a helper comparable to him. 21 And the LORD God caused a deep sleep to fall on Adam, and he slept; and He took one of his ribs, and closed up the flesh in its place. 22 Then the rib which the LORD God had taken from man He made into a woman, and He brought her to the man. 23 And Adam said: "This is now bone of my bones And flesh of my flesh; She shall be called Woman, Because she was taken out of Man." 24 Therefore a man shall leave his father and mother and be joined to his wife, and they shall become one flesh. 25 And they were both naked,[H6174] the man and his wife, and were not ashamed.

⸺⚬⚬⚬⚬⸺

[H6174] עָרוֹם 'ârôwm, aw-rome'; or עָרֹם 'ârôm; from H6191 (in its original sense); nude, either partially or totally:—naked.[164]

Dear Worship Leader,

You and I weren't meant to walk through life alone, isolated, and unknown. We were built for true intimacy with God, self, and others. Intimacy ("into me, see") is the gift of being fully known and fully loved. Genesis 2:25 is the epitome of this. In the Garden of Eden, Adam and Eve dwelt together in unity, oneness, order, transparency, vulnerability, trust, freedom, access, and confidence. Prior to Genesis 3, before the serpent and sin entered the scene, there was no division, no disorder, no covering up, no hiding, no shame, and no isolation. That's a perfect portrait of what it means to walk in true intimacy.

Just as it wasn't good for Adam to be all alone in life, the same is true for you and me. Married or single, we need one another. We all need helpers in this life. Where would we be without a community or village of family, friends, pastors, teachers, doctors, nurses, first responders, and so many others? We're a body of Christ. If the serpent can isolate us, we're left handicap and helpless—siphoned off from our support.

We all need a safe place where we can be naked and not ashamed—without fig leaves (Genesis 3:7). A place free from rejection, blame, chaos, secrecy, fear, masks, bondage, pride, and self-hatred. It wouldn't surprise me if the materials Adam and Eve used for the coverings they made were somehow connected to the tree of the knowledge of good and evil they had just sinfully eaten from. After eating its fruit, they hid in fear and shame. I wish they had never disobeyed God. But after sinning, I wish they had immediately run to safety confessing—naked and all. That's what godly sorrow does (2 Corinthians 7:10–11). It runs to the Father,

---

163 Merriam-Webster dictionary | www.merriam-webster.com | www.learnersdictionary.com
164 *Strong's Exhaustive Concordance of the Bible* | Blue Letter Bible | www.blueletterbible.org

falls toward the cross, chases after Christ, and pursues godly community and counseling. Intimacy is experiencing the unconditional love, acceptance, significance, and security of Christ on our best days—and on our worst.

Love, grace, and peace …

♪Colossians 3:16,

Rodney

Take a moment to meditate, muse, and memorize God's word. What is the Holy Spirit saying to you right now?

_____

_____

_____

_____

_____

_____

_____

_____

_____

_____

_____

LETTER #60 | ♪COL. 2:9 (NKJV)

IDENTITY

[n. Identity: 1a) the distinguishing character or personality of an individual: individuality
1b) the relation established by psychological identification
2) the condition of being the same with something described or asserted
3a) sameness of essential or generic character in different instances
3b) sameness in all that constitutes the objective reality of a thing: oneness][165]

Genesis 2:25; 3:7, 21 (NKJV)[166]

25 And they were both naked, the man and his wife, and were not ashamed.[H954]

7 Then the eyes of both of them were opened, and they knew that they were naked; and they sewed fig leaves together and made themselves coverings.

21 Also for Adam and his wife the LORD God made tunics of skin, and clothed them.

[H954] בּוּשׁ **bûwsh,** boosh; a primitive root; properly, to pale, i.e. by implication to be ashamed; also (by implication) to be disappointed or delayed:—(be, make, bring to, cause, put to, with, a-) shamed(-d), be (put to) confounded(-fusion), become dry, delay, be long.[167]

Dear Worship Leader,

As believers, you and I are unconditionally loved, accepted, significant, and secure in Christ. There's no "scarlet letter" or condemnation for us. That was settled on the cross. Our identity is forever found in Christ. Nothing can shake or change that, not even our sin. That's what the good-news gospel is all about. After receiving Jesus Christ as our Lord and Savior, we now have a forever home because He adopted us as sons and daughters. Period. Even if we get off course, like the parable of the prodigal son in Luke 15:11–32, we can always repent and come home. Our Father hates sin but loves us. He gladly forgives us, receives us, and celebrates our return.

Feeling sorry for our sin is godly. But instead, Adam and Eve sewed fig leaves together, covered themselves, and hid from the Lord (Genesis 3:7–8). That's what we call toxic shame. It causes us to hide our sin and ourselves. It's a destructive and dangerous lie because it illegitimately attaches poor behavior to your rich identity—a "scarlet letter." See if you can relate.

Godly sorrow says we've failed, we've done bad, we've done evil, and we've made a mess. Toxic shame says we *are* a failure, we *are* bad, we *are* evil, and we *are* a mess. Godly sorrow leads to repentance, changing our minds. Toxic shame leads to fig leaves, fear, hiding, isolation, image, blame, selfishness, false intimacy, self-loathing, self-righteousness, worldly sorrow, and death. Toxic shame is a deflection from the serpent that we are the problem, not him. It causes us to run away from safety to worldly, ungodly, unhealthy coping.

---

[165] Merriam-Webster dictionary | www.merriam-webster.com | www.learnersdictionary.com
[166] Rom. 8:1–39; 9:33; 10:11; 2 Cor. 7:8–12; Eph. 1–2; Heb. 12:2; 1 Pet. 2:4–10; ♪Col. 2:11–15; Matt. 18:10–14; Luke 15
[167] *Strong's Exhaustive Concordance of the Bible* | Blue Letter Bible | www.blueletterbible.org

Genesis 3:21 is such a glimpse of grace. After Adam and Eve's fall, amid consequences, the Lord God covered and clothed them Himself. He took tunics of skin, probably from a bloody animal He sacrificed, and with the protection of a Father, He wrapped Adam and Eve in love. That's the beginning of your love story with the Father. He's a good, *good* Father. That's who He is. And as a result of who He is, that's who we are in Christ!

Love, grace, and peace ...

♪Colossians 3:16,

Rodney

Take a moment to meditate, muse, and memorize God's word. What is the Holy Spirit saying to you right now?

_____

_____

_____

_____

_____

_____

_____

_____

_____

_____

_____

SPIRITUAL CHECKUP: INSPIRE

Review the last ten letters and record any key highlights. Has the Holy Spirit revealed any …

Instruction?

_____

_____

_____

_____

Needs?

_____

_____

_____

_____

Scripture?

_____

_____

_____

_____

Principles?

_____

_____

_____

_____

Interests?

_____

_____

_____

_____

Reproof?

_____

_____

_____

_____

Encouragement?

_____

_____

_____

_____

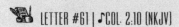 LETTER #61 | ♪COL. 2:10 (NKJV)

INTEGRITY

[n. Integrity: firm adherence to a code of especially moral or artistic values: incorruptibility
2) an unimpaired condition: soundness
3) the quality or state of being complete or undivided: completeness][168]

Psalm 78:70–72 (NKJV)[169]

70 He also chose David His servant, And took him from the sheepfolds; 71 From following the ewes that had young He brought him, To shepherd Jacob His people, And Israel His inheritance. 72 So he shepherded them according to the integrity[H8537] of his heart, And guided them by the skillfulness of his hands.

[H8537] תֹּם **tôm,** tome; from H8552; completeness; figuratively, prosperity; usually (morally) innocence:—full, integrity, perfect(-ion), simplicity, upright(-ly, -ness), at a venture. See H8550.[170]

Dear Worship Leader,

Integrity is a value worth possessing as a believer and a leader. King David shepherded God's people according to the integrity of his heart and guided them by the skillfulness of his hands (Psalm 78:72). Notice that the anatomy of a great leader requires both integrity and skill, both hand and heart. Empowering someone to lead with the absence of either could be tragic. But if you have to put more weight in one over the other, start with integrity. We can always attempt to teach or sharpen a skill, but only God can change the heart.

In recent years, I learned that walking in integrity is the polar opposite of living a compartmentalized life. To have integrity is to have a whole (integer) heart—not one that's divided and changing, catering to its current crowd or condition as would a chameleon. No, it's being the same person everywhere. One heart, soul, and mind. Not double-minded (James 1:8; 4:8).

Here is a personal declaration that I have come to hold dear: "As a follower of Jesus Christ, I am a man of faith who values **f**aithfulness, **a**uthenticity, **i**ntegrity, **t**ransparency, and **h**umility." I repeat that often. I penned it after personal failure. Some of my greatest lessons were learned through suffering. Honestly, it was good for me that I had been afflicted (Psalm 119:67, 71).

What are some of the core values you want to live by? These are characteristics you hope to be known for everywhere, whenever anyone mentions your name. Proverbs 22:1 (NKJV) says, "A good name is to be chosen rather than great riches, Loving favor than silver and gold." Ecclesiastes 7:1 (NKJV) also proclaims, "A good name is better than precious ointment, And the day of death than the day of one's birth." What do you want said at your funeral?

---

[168] Merriam-Webster dictionary | www.merriam-webster.com | www.learnersdictionary.com
[169] Ps. 19:14; 25:21; 26:1, 11; Prov. 10:9; 11:3: 19:1; 20:7; 28:6; Acts 13:22; 1 Kings 9:4; 1 Tim. 2:2; 3; Titus 1:5–9; 2
[170] *Strong's Exhaustive Concordance of the Bible* | Blue Letter Bible | www.blueletterbible.org

One hundred years from now, what name or legacy will you want passed on to your great grandchildren?

Love, grace, and peace …

♪Colossians 3:16,

Rodney

Take a moment to meditate, muse, and memorize God's word. What is the Holy Spirit saying to you right now?

_____

_____

_____

_____

_____

_____

_____

_____

_____

_____

_____

_____

_____

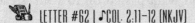 LETTER #62 | ♪COL. 2:11–12 [NKJV]

JESUS

[n. Jesus: 1) the Jewish religious teacher whose life, death, and resurrection as reported by the Evangelists are the basis of the Christian message of salvation — called also Jesus Christ
2) circa 6 b.c.–circa a.d. 30 Jesus of Nazareth; the Son of Mary source of the Christian religion and Savior in the Christian faith][171]

Mark 2:1–5 (NKJV)[172]

1 And again He entered Capernaum after some days, and it was heard that He was in the house. 2 Immediately many gathered together, so that there was no longer room to receive them, not even near the door. And He preached the word to them. 3 Then they came to Him, bringing a paralytic who was carried by four men. 4 And when they could not come near Him because of the crowd, they uncovered the roof where He was. So when they had broken through, they let down the bed on which the paralytic was lying. 5 When Jesus[G2424] saw their faith, He said to the paralytic, "Son, your sins are forgiven you."

[G2424] Ἰησοῦς Iēsoûs, ee-ay-sooce'; of Hebrew origin (H3091); Jesus (i.e. Jehoshua), the name of our Lord and two (three) other Israelites:—Jesus.[173]

Dear Worship Leader,

One of the greatest ways we can serve others is help them get to Jesus. No matter the need, Jesus is the answer! Christ, the Messiah. I AM THAT I AM. Lord and Savior. Prophet, Priest, and King. King of kings and Lord of lords. Alpha and Omega. In the Old Testament, Isaiah prophesied that His name shall be called Wonderful, Counselor, Mighty God, Everlasting Father, Prince of Peace. The New Testament teaches us that His name is above every name—that at the name of Jesus every knee should bow, of things in heaven, of those on earth, and of those under the earth, and that every tongue should confess that Jesus Christ is Lord, to the glory of God the Father.

We learn who Jesus is in the Gospel of John through Jesus's seven "I Am" statements.

1. I Am the Bread of life.
2. I Am the Light of the world.
3. I Am the Door.
4. I Am the Good Shepherd.
5. I Am the Resurrection and the Life.
6. I Am the Way, the Truth, and the Life.
7. I Am the True Vine.

Ephesians 1:20–23 (NKJV) says that after Jesus was raised from the dead, the Father "seated Him at His right hand in heavenly places, far above all principality and power and might and dominion, and every name that is named, not only in this age but also in that which is to come. And He put all things under His feet, and gave Him to be head over all things to the church, which is His body, the fullness of Him who fills all in all."

---

[171] Merriam-Webster dictionary | www.merriam-webster.com | www.learnersdictionary.com
[172] Mark 2:1–12, 17; Matt. 9:2–8; Luke 5:17–26; Exod. 3:14; Rev. 1:8; 19:16; Isa. 9:6; Phil. 2:9–10 | John 6:35, 41, 48, 51; 8:12, 58; 9:5; 10:7, 9, 11, 14; 11:25; 14:6; 15:1, 5; 18:5–6 | Gal. 6:1; James 5:14; Isa. 58:12; 1 Cor. 12; 2 Cor. 5:18
[173] *Strong's Exhaustive Concordance of the Bible* | Blue Letter Bible | www.blueletterbible.org

Time would fail me to tell of the many things that Jesus Himself did (John 21:25)! In 2014, I needed someone to uncover the roof and get me to Jesus Christ—through community and counseling. I hope you and I never get too high or too big to allow others to help. We all need the body of Christ! Four men carried the paralytic in Mark 2. Thirty courageous men and women carried me and my family. *They were Jesus to me!*

Love, grace, and peace …

♪Colossians 3:16,

Rodney

Take a moment to meditate, muse, and memorize God's word. What is the Holy Spirit saying to you right now?

_____

_____

_____

_____

_____

_____

_____

_____

_____

_____

_____

_____

 LETTER #63 | ♪ COL. 2:13 (NKJV)

KINGDOM

[n. Kingdom: 1) a politically organized community or major territorial unit having a monarchical form of government headed by a king or queen
2a) the eternal kingship of God
2b) the realm in which God's will is fulfilled
3a) a realm or region in which something is dominant
3b) an area or sphere in which one holds a preeminent position][174]

Matthew 4:23–25 (NKJV)

23 And Jesus went about all Galilee, teaching in their synagogues, preaching the gospel of the kingdom,[G932] and healing all kinds of sickness and all kinds of disease among the people. 24 Then His fame went throughout all Syria; and they brought to Him all sick people who were afflicted with various diseases and torments, and those who were demon-possessed, epileptics, and paralytics; and He healed them. 25 Great multitudes followed Him—from Galilee, and from Decapolis, Jerusalem, Judea, and beyond the Jordan.

[G932] βασιλεία **basileía**, bas-il-i'-ah; from G935; properly, royalty, i.e. (abstractly) rule, or (concretely) a realm (literally or figuratively):—kingdom, + reign.
[G935] βασιλεύς **basileús**, bas-il-yooce'; probably from G939 (through the notion of a foundation of power); a sovereign (abstractly, relatively, or figuratively):—king.[175]

Dear Worship Leader,

Prior to working for Dr. Tony Evans, senior pastor at Oak Cliff Bible Fellowship (OCBF), the kingdom agenda was basically a foreign concept to me. But Pastor Evans faithfully drilled it in us year after year. We served as members there for ten years. He defines the kingdom agenda as the visible demonstration of the comprehensive rule of God over every area of life. It's reflected through the four divinely ordained spheres of the individual, family, church, and government.

Based on Acts 2:42–47, he organized OCBF around four vital experiences: worship, fellowship, education, and outreach. I was promoted to be his associate pastor of worship. It was an experience of a lifetime. Just sitting at his feet watching him lead at such a high level far exceeded any dreams I had growing up on the South Side of Chicago. When he hired me, at age thirty, he told me the position was too big for me at the time but that one day I would outgrow it and it would become too small. What a fathering statement to make! His family became my family. His friends became my friends. His support became my support. This was a life–defining moment.

In 2014, when I fell into sin, it hurt everyone around me. But outside my wife, professionally speaking, it probably hurt Pastor Evans the most. I will never forget the tears we shed together. Under his leadership and care, my wife and I were nursed back into good health. Actually, better health than we had before. After more than a year of intense counseling and accountability, Pastor Evans restored and recommissioned me back into ministry. That's the kingdom agenda at work. That's the heart of a shepherd. We've been given the ministry of

---

174 Merriam-Webster dictionary | www.merriam-webster.com | www.learnersdictionary.com
175 *Strong's Exhaustive Concordance of the Bible* | Blue Letter Bible | www.blueletterbible.org

reconciliation! Ambassadors for Christ. Kingdom representatives. Although I fell, the church leaders didn't let me stay down. They took me to the King. King Jesus is still healing today.

Love, grace, and peace …

♪Colossians 3:16,

Rodney

Take a moment to meditate, muse, and memorize God's word. What is the Holy Spirit saying to you right now?

_____

_____

_____

_____

_____

_____

_____

_____

_____

_____

_____

_____

_____

 LETTER #64 | ♪COL. 2:14-15 (NKJV)

KINDNESS

[a. Kind: 1a) of a sympathetic or helpful nature
1b) of a forbearing nature: gentle
1c) arising from or characterized by sympathy or forbearance][176]

♪Colossians 3:12–17 (NKJV)[177]

12 Therefore, as the elect of God, holy and beloved, put on tender mercies, kindness,[G5544] humility, meekness, longsuffering; 13 bearing with one another, and forgiving one another, if anyone has a complaint against another; even as Christ forgave you, so you also must do. 14 But above all these things put on love, which is the bond of perfection. 15 And let the peace of God rule in your hearts, to which also you were called in one body; and be thankful. 16 Let the word of Christ dwell in you richly in all wisdom, teaching and admonishing one another in psalms and hymns and spiritual songs, singing with grace in your hearts to the Lord. 17 And whatever you do in word or deed, do all in the name of the Lord Jesus, giving thanks to God the Father through Him.

[G5544] χρηστότης chrēstótēs, khray-stot'-ace; from G5543; usefulness, i.e. morally, excellence (in character or demeanor):— gentleness, good(-ness), kindness.
[G5543] χρηστός chrēstós, khrase-tos'; from G5530; employed, i.e. (by implication) useful (in manner or morals):—better, easy, good(-ness), gracious, kind.[178]

Dear Worship Leader,

It's rare to find good customer service today. Whenever my wife and I come across anyone in public service who's kind, courteous, and cheerful, we usually stop what we're doing to commend them. It's what I enjoyed most about working at Nordstrom, which is known for its stellar customer service and return policy. We were trained to go over and above the customers' expectations. Many times it left them speechless.

The spirit of kindness and going the extra mile originated with Jesus. He taught about it in the Sermon on the Mount (Matthew 5:38–48; 7:7–12). Kindness is a fruit of the Spirit (Galatians 5:22–23). In the KJV, it's also translated as mercy, lovingkindness, goodness, and gentleness. ♪Colossians 3:12 tells us to put on the attire of tender mercies, kindness, humility, meekness, and longsuffering and wear them like a vest. Verse 14 adds, above all these, put on love. God wants our attitudes and attire to match our kingdom affluence and identity. God calls us the elect of God, holy and beloved (v. 12). We are a forgiven people (v. 13). As kingdom citizens ruled by peace, we are called to unity, thankfulness, and grace (vv. 15–16).

If you legitimately found a check with your name on it for $1 million in your mailbox today, how would that change your outlook and attitude? As you rush to the bank to make the deposit, do you think you'd be kinder to the person that cuts you off in traffic or more

---

[176] Merriam-Webster dictionary | www.merriam-webster.com | www.learnersdictionary.com
[177] Exod. 34:5–7; 2 Chron. 5:13; 7:3, 6; 20:21; Luke 6:32–36; Gal. 6:1; Eph. 2:7; 4:2, 32; Titus 3:2, 4; 1 Cor. 15:33; 1 Pet. 2:3; Gen. 24:14; 2 Sam. 9 (1, 3, 7); 1 Kings 3:6; Neh. 9 (17); Prov. 31:26; Acts 28:2; 2 Cor. 6:6; Titus 3:1–7; 2 Pet. 1:7
[178] *Strong's Exhaustive Concordance of the Bible* | Blue Letter Bible | www.blueletterbible.org

forgiving to the person that calls you owing $100? And your newfound wealth would surely change what you wear and how you live. Well, here's the truth: in Christ, we *are* rich through His word (v. 16) and in His name (v. 17). Romans 2:4 speaks to the riches of His goodness, forbearance, and longsuffering—His [G5543] χρηστός chrēstós goodness that leads us to repentance and forever changes us!

Love, grace, and peace …

♪Colossians 3:16,

Rodney

Take a moment to meditate, muse, and memorize God's word. What is the Holy Spirit saying to you right now?

_____

_____

_____

_____

_____

_____

_____

_____

_____

_____

_____

_____

LETTER #65 | ♪COL. 2:16–17 (NKJV)

LOVE

[n. Love: 1a) unselfish loyal and benevolent concern for the good of another: such as (1) the fatherly concern of God for humankind (2) brotherly concern for others 1b) a person's adoration of God][179]

John 13:31–35 (NKJV)[180]

31 So, when he had gone out, Jesus said, "Now the Son of Man is glorified, and God is glorified in Him. 32 "If God is glorified in Him, God will also glorify Him in Himself, and glorify Him immediately. 33 "Little children, I shall be with you a little while longer. You will seek Me; and as I said to the Jews, 'Where I am going, you cannot come,' so now I say to you. 34 "A new commandment I give to you, that you love[G25] one another; as I have loved[G25] you, that you also love[G25] one another. 35 "By this all will know that you are My disciples, if you have love[G26] for one another."

[G26] ἀγάπη **agápē,** ag-ah'-pay; from G25; love, i.e. affection or benevolence; specially (plural) a love-feast:—(feast of) charity(-ably), dear, love.
[G25] ἀγαπάω **agapáō,** ag-ap-ah'-o; perhaps from ἄγαν ágan (much) (or compare H5689); to love (in a social or moral sense):—(be-) love(-ed). Compare G5368.[181]

Dear Worship Leader,

Jesus wants us to be known by our [G26] ἀγάπη agápē love. As sheep branded with His mark of identification, ἀγάπη love is His signet. In fact, God is ἀγάπη love (1 John 4:8, 16). It was ἀγάπη love that led Jesus to the cross in John 19. It's an unconditional godlike love. It's one of sacrifice, suffering, and selflessness. As followers of Jesus, we share in ἀγάπη love.

Loving God, self, and others encompasses every aspect of our lives. The first and greatest commandment is to [G25] ἀγαπάω agapáō love the Lord our God with all our hearts, souls, and minds (Matthew 22:37–38). The second is like it. It's to ἀγαπάω love our neighbors as ourselves (Matthew 22:39). Christ's ἀγάπη love compels us, constrains us, and consumes us (2 Corinthians 5:14–15). God is ἀγάπη.

More than our singing, musicianship, talents, skills, or giftings, let us be characterized and distinguished by ἀγάπη. In the Message Bible, 1 Corinthians 13:1–3 says that without ἀγάπη we are nothing—nothing but the creaking of a rusty gate—without ἀγάπη we've gotten nowhere, and without ἀγάπη we are bankrupt. Verses 4–8 (NKJV) go on to say:

Ἀγάπη suffers long and is kind; ἀγάπη does not envy; ἀγάπη does not parade itself, is not puffed up; does not behave rudely, does not seek its own, is not provoked, thinks no evil; does not rejoice in iniquity, but rejoices in the truth; bears all things, believes all things, hopes all things, endures all things. Ἀγάπη never

[179] Merriam-Webster dictionary | www.merriam-webster.com | www.learnersdictionary.com
[180] Eph. 3:17–19; Rom. 5:5, 8; 8:1–39 (35, 37, 39); John 3:16, 19, 35; 8:31; 15:8–17; Luke 6:27–36; 7:5, 36–50; 9:23–26, 57–62; 10:25–37; 11:43; 14:15–33; 16:13; Matt. 5:13–16, 43–48; 6:24; 8:18–22; 19:16–22; Mark 10:17–22; 12:28–34
[181] *Strong's Exhaustive Concordance of the Bible* | Blue Letter Bible | www.blueletterbible.org

fails. But whether there are prophecies, they will fail; whether there are tongues, they will cease; whether there is knowledge, it will vanish away.

As the light of the world, I pray ἀγάπη fills our hearts, homes, and those we encounter. Verse 13 concludes, "And now abide faith, hope, ἀγάπη, these three; but the greatest of these is ἀγάπη." It never dies, always wins, and always gets the gold!

Ἀγάπη, χάρις, and εἰρήνη …

♪Colossians 3:16,

Rodney

Take a moment to meditate, muse, and memorize God's word. What is the Holy Spirit saying to you right now?

_____

_____

_____

_____

_____

_____

_____

_____

_____

_____

_____

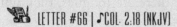 LETTER #66 | ♪COL. 2:18 (NKJV)

LEVITES

[n. Levite: a member of the priestly Hebrew tribe of Levi][182]

1 Chronicles 15:2, 13–16, 26 (NKJV)

2 Then David said, "No one may carry the ark of God but the Levites,[H3881] for the LORD has chosen them to carry the ark of God and to minister before Him forever."

13 "For because you did not do it the first time, the LORD our God broke out against us, because we did not consult Him about the proper order." **14** So the priests and the Levites[H3881] sanctified themselves to bring up the ark of the LORD God of Israel. **15** And the children of the Levites[H3881] bore the ark of God on their shoulders, by its poles, as Moses had commanded according to the word of the LORD. **16** Then David spoke to the leaders of the Levites[H3881] to appoint their brethren to be the singers accompanied by instruments of music, stringed instruments, harps, and cymbals, by raising the voice with resounding joy.

26 And so it was, when God helped the Levites[H3881] who bore the ark of the covenant of the LORD, that they offered seven bulls and seven rams.

[H3881] לִוִּיִּי **Lêvîyiy,** lay-vee-ee'; or לֵוִי **Lêvîy;** patronymically from H3878; a Levite or descendant of Levi:—Leviite.[183]

Dear Worship Leader,

As New Testament believers, because of Christ's finished work on the cross, we are all prophets, priests, and kings in God's kingdom (1 Peter 2:9–10). There's no more distinction or wall of separation (Matthew 27:51). We all have access to the Father through Christ (Ephesians 3:12). Spiritually, there's no more male or female, Jew or Greek; we are all one in Him (Galatians 3:28). Christ is forever our High Priest, and through Him we can come to the throne of grace boldly to obtain mercy and find grace to help us in time of need (Hebrews 4:16). That's what the Protestant Reformation was all about. We no longer need priests to represent us and speak to God on our behalf. Through Christ we can now speak to Him ourselves, anytime we want. What glorious good news!

Similarly, through Christ, we are all spiritual Levites and can "carry the ark of God"—that which represents the very presence of God—wherever we go (1 Corinthians 3:16). We are all ministers of worship before Him. God wants a sacrifice of praise from us all (Hebrews 13:15). In fact, He wants us to present our bodies a living sacrifice, holy and acceptable to Him, which He calls our reasonable service (Romans 12:1–2). It just makes good sense. Romans 11:36 (NKJV) says, "For of Him and through Him and to Him are all things, to whom be glory forever. Amen." We're all created by Him to bring Him glory!

Our New Testament freedom today is best illustrated and appreciated with a backdrop of knowledge regarding the Old Testament law and dispensation. King David carried the ark of God on a "new cart" in 1 Chronicles 13:7, and as a result, Uzza died trying to save the ark

---

[182] Merriam-Webster dictionary | www.merriam-webster.com | www.learnersdictionary.com
[183] *Strong's Exhaustive Concordance of the Bible* | Blue Letter Bible | www.blueletterbible.org

from falling (13:9–12). Thus, David was chastised and corrected the issue in chapter 15. Let's thank God today for the New Testament "covenant of grace" (John 1:17; Romans 4:16; 5:20; 6:14–15; Galatians 2:21; 5:4)!

Love, grace, and peace …

♪Colossians 3:16,

Rodney

Take a moment to meditate, muse, and memorize God's word. What is the Holy Spirit saying to you right now?

_____

_____

_____

_____

_____

_____

_____

_____

_____

_____

_____

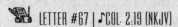 LETTER #67 | ♪ COL. 2:19 (NKJV)

LEADERSHIP

[v. Lead: 1a) to guide on a way especially by going in advance
1b) to direct on a course or in a direction
1c) to serve as a channel for
2) to go through: live //lead a quiet life][184]

———— ✺ ————

1 Timothy 1:18–20; 2:1–4 (NKJV)[185]

18 This charge I commit to you, son Timothy, according to the prophecies previously made concerning you, that by them you may wage the good warfare, 19 having faith and a good conscience, which some having rejected, concerning the faith have suffered shipwreck, 20 of whom are Hymenaeus and Alexander, whom I delivered to Satan that they may learn not to blaspheme. 1 Therefore I exhort first of all that supplications, prayers, intercessions, and giving of thanks be made for all men, 2 for kings and all who are in authority, that we may lead[G1236] a quiet and peaceable life[G979] in all godliness and reverence. 3 For this is good and acceptable in the sight of God our Savior, 4 who desires all men to be saved and to come to the knowledge of the truth.

———— ✺ ————

[G1236] διάγω diágō, dee-ag'-o; from G1223 and G71; to pass time or life:—lead life, living
[G979] βίος bíos, bee'-os; a primary word; life, i.e. (literally) the present state of existence; by implication, the means of livelihood:—good, life, living.[186]

Dear Worship Leader,

When we think of leadership, the first words that come to our minds usually aren't words like prayer, quiet, peaceable, godliness, and reverence. Yet when Paul begins writing to Timothy about leadership, those are some of the first words that he pens (2:1–2). Paul understands that with great authority comes great responsibility. He knows the danger, disaster, and destruction that come with suffering shipwreck (1:19). By name, he calls out Hymenaeus and Alexander as poor examples who rejected faith and good conscience and were being disciplined for blasphemy (1:20). This led Paul to his knees in prayer. Not out of formality but out of necessity.

We all need prayer warriors waging battle for us in the spiritual realm (1:18; 2:1). In the Greek, Paul uses the word [G444] ἄνθρωπος ánthrōpos for "men," which means human being—to be sure to include both male and female—because we all need this superpower! He then highlights prayer for kings and all those in authority. His request is simple but profound—that leaders would lead through the *lifestyle* of a quiet and peaceable life in all godliness and reverence (2:2). One without moral scandal, conflict, or controversy. To the world, there's nothing flashy, sexy, or Hollywood about that. Nothing hot for the headlines or breaking news.

Yes, for some of us, a drama-free, quiet and peaceable life may seem rather boring. But Paul wants the message of the gospel to resound louder than our lives. He doesn't want our

---

[184] Merriam-Webster dictionary | www.merriam-webster.com | www.learnersdictionary.com
[185] 1 Thess. 1:6–10; 4:9–12; 5:25; 1 Tim. 2–3; 4:12; 6:6; Titus 1–2; 3:1–7; 1 Sam. 16:14–18; Exod. 18:21; 28:3; Acts 6:3; Num. 11:16; John 13:1–17; Heb. 12:11; 13:18; James 3:17; Matt. 6:5, 7; 2 Thess. 3:1; Eph. 6:14–20 (19–20); 1 Pet. 5:8
[186] *Strong's Exhaustive Concordance of the Bible* | Blue Letter Bible | www.blueletterbible.org

faith outshined by foolishness. He wants the attention and glory to go to God our Savior, not to gossip or "tea" surrounding personal indiscretion (2:3). God wants all men, ἄνθρωπος, led to salvation and to the knowledge of the truth (2:4). Not the knowledge of our loud contrary living. Good leaders simply model the way through self-leadership first.

Love, grace, and peace …

♪Colossians 3:16,

Rodney

Take a moment to meditate, muse, and memorize God's word. What is the Holy Spirit saying to you right now?

_____

_____

_____

_____

_____

_____

_____

_____

_____

_____

_____

 LETTER #68 | ♪ COL. 2:20–22 (NKJV)

MENTORSHIP

[n. Mentor 1) someone who teaches or gives help and advice to a less experienced and often younger person
2a) trusted counselor or guide
2b) tutor, coach][187]

Titus 2:1–8 (NKJV)

1 But as for you, speak the things which are proper for sound doctrine: 2 that the older men[G4246] be sober, reverent, temperate, sound in faith, in love, in patience; 3 the older women[G4247] likewise, that they be reverent in behavior, not slanderers, not given to much wine, teachers of good things— 4 that they admonish the young women to love their husbands, to love their children, 5 to be discreet, chaste, homemakers, good, obedient to their own husbands, that the word of God may not be blasphemed. 6 Likewise, exhort the young men to be sober-minded, 7 in all things showing yourself to be a pattern of good works; in doctrine showing integrity, reverence, incorruptibility, 8 sound speech that cannot be condemned, that one who is an opponent may be ashamed, having nothing evil to say of you.

[G4246] πρεσβύτης presbýtēs, pres-boo'-tace; from the same as G4245; an old man:—aged (man), old man.
[G4247] πρεσβῦτις presbŷtis, pres-boo'-tis; feminine of G4246; an old woman:—aged woman.[188]

Dear Worship Leader,

Who's in your personal community? I like to have three types of people in my village and on my team. I like to have *mentors* like Paul, *mentees* like Timothy, and *accountability partners* like Barnabas. That tends to cover all bases and positions. The Paul type represents someone ahead of me. The Timothy type represents someone behind or after me. The Barnabas type represents someone alongside me. Although there's lots of flexibility and reciprocity with them, each type has its own slant. I'm primarily receiving from Paul, giving to Timothy, and reflecting with Barnabas. Together their deposits, withdrawals, and transfers help me to stay fueled up for the kingdom of God.

However, of all the relationships, I have to admit there's something uniquely special about spending quality time with older wise men and women in the faith. It's thirst-quenching and life-giving to glean from their reservoirs of wisdom, knowledge, and understanding. Walking with them is like entering a time machine, for they serve as tour guides through the treasures and channels of history. We get to benefit from the lessons they've learned without all the hardships and penalties. If someone ahead falls into a ditch, it's wise to learn from their mistake and avoid the same trap. That's how each generation gets better and further along the path. The wise one hears and increases learning, and one of understanding attains wise counsel (Proverbs 1:5).

With mentoring, faithfully displaying both a servant's heart and a teachable spirit are necessary (2 Timothy 2:2). In the book *Thanks for the Feedback* by Douglas Stone and Sheila Heen, we learn that everyone needs a winning ACE: appreciation, coaching, and evaluation. The person that embraces healthy feedback will grow,

---

[187] Merriam–Webster dictionary | www.merriam-webster.com | www.learnersdictionary.com
[188] *Strong's Exhaustive Concordance of the Bible* | Blue Letter Bible | www.blueletterbible.org

develop, and mature. Ultimately, the acid test to mentoring is running with the baton and passing it on.

Love, grace, and peace …

♪Colossians 3:16,

Rodney

Take a moment to meditate, muse, and memorize God's word. What is the Holy Spirit saying to you right now?

_____

_____

_____

_____

_____

_____

_____

_____

_____

_____

_____

_____

_____

LETTER #69 | ♪COL. 2:23 (NKJV)

MUSIC

[n. Music: the science or art of ordering tones or sounds in succession, in combination, and in temporal relationships to produce a composition having unity and continuity][189]

---

1 Samuel 16:16, 18, 23 (NKJV)[190]

16 "Let our master now command your servants, who are before you, to seek out a man who is a skillful player[H5059] on the harp. And it shall be that he will play[H5059] it with his hand when the distressing spirit from God is upon you, and you shall be well."

---

18 Then one of the servants answered and said, "Look, I have seen a son of Jesse the Bethlehemite, who is skillful in playing,[H5059] a mighty man of valor, a man of war, prudent in speech, and a handsome person; and the LORD is with him."

---

23 And so it was, whenever the spirit from God was upon Saul, that David would take a harp and play[H5059] it with his hand. Then Saul would become refreshed and well, and the distressing spirit would depart from him.

[H5059] נָגַן **nâgan,** naw-gan'; a primitive root; properly, to thrum, i.e. beat a tune with the fingers; expectation. to play on a stringed instrument; hence (generally), to make music:— player on instruments, sing to the stringed instruments, melody, ministrel, play(-er, -ing).[191]

Dear Worship Leader,

Music is a gift from God. It's a universal language to humankind. As musicians and singers, the power we carry is often unrealized. The scientific data behind how music is stored in the brain, releases opioids, and connects with long-term memory is well-documented and astonishing.

The documentary *Alive Inside* (www.aliveinside.org), directed by Michael Rossato-Bennett (starring Dan Cohen, Oliver Sacks, and Bobby McFerrin) opened my eyes, in a new way, to music's capacity to reawaken the deepest part of our minds and souls. It chronicles individuals who've been revived through the simple act of listening to music. It demonstrates music's ability to combat memory loss and restore a sense of self.

Music & Memory (www.musicandmemory.org), founded by Dan Cohen, is a nonprofit organization that helps people in nursing homes who suffer from a wide range of cognitive and physical challenges to find renewed meaning and connection in their lives through the gift of personalized music playlists. According to research, studies show that listening to favorite music can help reduce chronic pain, decrease agitation, anxiety, sleeplessness, and depression. It can also prevent distressed behaviors, aid in the reduction of antipsychotic medications, and even improve swallowing. All glory to God for the blessed benefits of music (Romans 11:36; ♪Colossians 1:16)!

---

[189] Merriam-Webster dictionary | www.merriam-webster.com | www.learnersdictionary.com

[190] 2 Kings 3:15; Luke 1:46–56; 15:25; Zeph. 3:17; Num. 21:17; 1 Cor. 14:15; James 5:13; Rev. 5:9; 14:3; 15:2–4; Ezra 3:10–11; Job 38:7; Acts 16:25; 2 Chron. 5; 20; 29–30; 1 Sam. 2; 18; Dan. 3; Exod. 15; Deut. 31–32; 2 Sam. 22; Judg. 5

[191] *Strong's Exhaustive Concordance of the Bible* | Blue Letter Bible | www.blueletterbible.org

♫ See if you can relate. Music/singing is a channel, gateway, and key to help activate, engage, stimulate, and unlock the following:

- ♫ Memory: memorization, "memory lane," emotional recall
- ♫ Understanding: muse/meditate, think, process, learn, comprehend
- ♫ Sensory and motor skills: mobility, auditory/visual perception, speech
- ♫ Imagination: mood, relax, reflect, renew, rekindle dreams/visions
- ♫ Consciousness: mind/heart/soul reawakening, resurfacing "self"

Love, grace, and peace …

♪Colossians 3:16,

Rodney

Take a moment to meditate, muse, and memorize God's word. What is the Holy Spirit saying to you right now?

_____

_____

_____

_____

_____

_____

_____

_____

_____

_____

_____

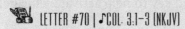 LETTER #70 | ♪COL. 3:1–3 (NKJV)

MEDITATION

[v. Meditate: 1) to focus one's thoughts on: reflect on or ponder over
2) to plan or project in the mind: intend, purpose][192]

Psalm 77:6 (NKJV)

6 I call to remembrance my song in the night; I meditate[H7878] within my heart,[H3824] And my spirit makes diligent search.

Deuteronomy 32:44–47 (NKJV)[193]

44 So Moses came with Joshua the son of Nun and spoke all the words of this song in the hearing of the people.
45 Moses finished speaking all these words to all Israel,
46 and he said to them: "Set your hearts[H3824] on all the words which I testify among you today, which you shall command your children to be careful to observe—all the words of this law.
47 "For it is not a futile thing for you, because it is your life, and by this word you shall prolong your days in the land which you cross over the Jordan to possess."

[H7878] שִׂיחַ **sîyach,** see'-akh; a primitive root; to ponder, i.e. (by implication) converse (with oneself, and hence, aloud) or (transitively) utter:—commune, complain, declare, meditate, muse, pray, speak, talk (with).
[H3824] לֵבָב **lêbâb,** lay-bawb'; from H3823; used also like H3820 the heart (as the most interior organ);:— bethink themselves, breast, comfortably, courage, (faint), (tender-) heart(-ed), midst, mind, × unawares, understanding.[194]

Dear Worship Leader,

Hiding the Word in your heart is not a futile thing to do because it is your life and the scriptures will add divine quality and quantity to your days (Deuteronomy 32:47). Heartily meditating on it is where spiritual grounding begins. Biblical meditation, or musing, is the launching pad for memorization, manifestation, and ministry. I call this the kingdom's M4 assault weaponry against the enemy. It's the sword of the Spirit, the word of God, alive and actively at work within us (Ephesians 6:17). Music, or musing, has the potential to assist us in battle. Our inner man/woman can sing truth to us multiple times throughout the day (Psalm 77:6).

One of the last things Moses did before his death in Deuteronomy 34 was to write a song in chapter 31 (31:19) and teach it to the children of Israel (31:22, 30). The song is found in chapter 32 (vv. 1–43). God told Moses to write it and teach it because He wanted His word put in their mouths (31:19). So even after Moses's death, this song would outlive Moses and be used by God to testify against the Israelites as a witness in their disobedience (31:19–21). Can you believe it? Moses's final investment into their lives was a song! And God said it would not be forgotten in the mouths of their children (31:21)!

Now the whole point of the song was for the Israelites to set their hearts on the Word in obedience and command their children to be careful to do the same (32:46). This wasn't music for music's sake. Music was the medium

---

[192] Merriam-Webster dictionary | www.merriam-webster.com | www.learnersdictionary.com
[193] Gen. 24:63; Josh. 1:8; 1 Kings 18:27; Ps. 1:2; 4:4; 5:1; 7:1; 9:16; 19:14; 39:3; 49:3; 63:6; 64:1; 77:6, 12; 104:34; 119:15, 23, 27, 48, 78, 97, 99, 148; 143:5; 145:5; Isa. 33:18; Mal. 3:16; Mark 13:11; Luke 21:14; Phil. 4:8; 1 Tim. 4:15
[194] *Strong's Exhaustive Concordance of the Bible* | Blue Letter Bible | www.blueletterbible.org

God used to convey a message to His people, for them to manifest godly fruit. That's why God delivered them from Egypt and into a land flowing with milk and honey, because He wanted them to be fruitful and prosperous just like the land (31:20). May music make us all rich in the Word by daily musing on it in our hearts!

Love, grace, and peace …

♪Colossians 3:16,

Rodney

Take a moment to meditate, muse, and memorize God's word. What is the Holy Spirit saying to you right now?

_____

_____

_____

_____

_____

_____

_____

_____

_____

_____

_____

_____

SPIRITUAL CHECKUP: INSPIRE

Review the last ten letters and record any key highlights. Has the Holy Spirit revealed any ...

Instruction?

_____

_____

_____

_____

Needs?

_____

_____

_____

_____

Scripture?

_____

_____

_____

_____

Principles?

_____

_____

_____

_____

Interests?

_____

_____

_____

_____

Reproof?

_____

_____

_____

_____

Encouragement?

_____

_____

_____

_____

 LETTER #71 | ♪COL· 3:4 [NKJV]

MARRIAGE

[n. Marriage: the state of being united as spouses in a consensual and contractual relationship recognized by law][195]

Ephesians 5:22–27 (NKJV)

22 Wives,[G1135] submit to your own husbands,[G435] as to the Lord.
23 For the husband[G435] is head of the wife,[G1135] as also Christ is head of the church; and He is the Savior of the body.
24 Therefore, just as the church is subject to Christ, so let the wives[G1135] be to their own husbands[G435] in everything.
25 Husbands,[G435] love[G25] your wives,[G1135] just as Christ also loved[G25] the church and gave Himself for her,
26 that He might sanctify and cleanse her with the washing of water by the word,
27 that He might present her to Himself a glorious church, not having spot or wrinkle or any such thing, but that she should be holy and without blemish.

[G1135] γυνή **gynē,** goo-nay'; probably from the base of G1096; a woman; specially, a wife:—wife, woman.
[G435] ἀνήρ **anḗr,** an'-ayr; a primary word (compare G444); a man (properly as an individual male):—fellow, husband, man, sir.
[G25] ἀγαπάω **agapáō,** ag-ap-ah'-o; perhaps from ἄγαν ágan (much) (or compare H5689); to love (in a social or moral sense):—(be-) love(-ed). Compare G5368.[196]

Dear Worship Leader,

The institution of marriage, between the husband and wife, is under major attack because it is the earthly representation and illustration of Christ's ἀγαπάω agapáō love for the church (5:25). No other covenantal relationship better demonstrates this sacrificial, unconditional, life-giving passion than a husband loving his wife. Proverbs 18:22 (NKJV) says, "He who finds a wife finds a good thing, And obtains favor from the Lord."

As a husband, I try to always start with and emphasize the husband's role first because he is ultimately responsible for the marriage. He is modeling after Christ, who first loved us (1 John 4:19). *He leads her* as her head, as Christ is the head of the church and the Savior of the body (Ephesians 5:23). *He loves her* just as Christ loved the church and gave Himself for her—that He might sanctify, cleanse, and present her to Himself holy and without blemish (5:25–27). He loves her like he loves his own body and his own self (5:28). He nourishes and cherishes her as the Lord does the church (5:29). *He lives with her* and dwells with her according to knowledge, honoring her as the weaker vessel, and as being heirs together of the grace of life (1 Peter 3:7). Like Christ and the church, the two have become one (Ephesians 5:30–32). As believers, this is a living portrait of Christ's love for us as His adorned bride.

Dr. Doug Weiss says there are six necessary marital structures, including the following:

---

[195] Merriam-Webster dictionary | www.merriam-webster.com | www.learnersdictionary.com | Same-sex marriages are now recognized by law in a growing number of countries and were legally validated throughout the US by the Supreme Court decision in *Obergefell v. Hodges* in 2015. In many other parts of the world, marriage continues to be allowed only between men and women.

[196] *Strong's Exhaustive Concordance of the Bible* | Blue Letter Bible | www.blueletterbible.org

↑ dating—prioritizing fun dates together as lovers and friends
↑ social—getting together with other couples socially, for fun
↑ feelings—intimately communicating feelings with one another
↑ spiritual—spiritual prayer, faith, and engagement together at home
↑ sexual—initiating, responding, and enjoying one another sexually
↑ money—communicating about money, budgets, and financial plans

Love, grace, and peace …

♪Colossians 3:16,

Rodney

Take a moment to meditate, muse, and memorize God's word. What is the Holy Spirit saying to you right now?

_____

_____

_____

_____

_____

_____

_____

_____

_____

_____

_____

_____

 LETTER #72 | ♪COL. 3:5 [NKJV]

MIND

[n. Mind: 1) recollection, memory
2) the element or complex of elements in an individual that feels, perceives, thinks, wills, and especially reasons
3) intention, desire
4) the normal or healthy condition of the mental faculties
5) disposition, mood][197]

Philippians 4:6–9 (NKJV)[198]

**6 Be anxious for nothing, but in everything by prayer and supplication, with thanksgiving, let your requests be made known to God;
7 and the peace of God, which surpasses all understanding, will guard your hearts and minds[G3540] through Christ Jesus.
8 Finally, brethren, whatever things are true, whatever things are noble, whatever things are just, whatever things are pure, whatever things are lovely, whatever things are of good report, if there is any virtue and if there is anything praiseworthy— meditate on these things.
9 The things which you learned and received and heard and saw in me, these do, and the God of peace will be with you.**

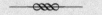

[G3540] νόημα nóēma, no'-ay-mah; from G3539; a perception, i.e. purpose, or (by implication) the intellect, disposition, itself:— device, mind, thought.
[G3539] νοιέω noiéō, noy-eh'-o; from G3563; to exercise the mind (observe), i.e. (figuratively) to comprehend, heed:—consider, perceive, think, understand.[199]

Dear Worship Leader,

Philippians 4:6–9 is an excellent go-to passage when we're tempted to be anxious or worried. In these liberating words of Paul, we find the [G1515] εἰρήνη eirēnē, i-ray'-nay peace of God (4:7) and the God of εἰρήνη peace (4:9)! As sheep, our minds can easily become distressed from the storms of life. We begin to focus on the thunder and lightning, the winds and waves, and the back and forth rocking of the boat. We get seasick and start panicking. But that's not the life of the believer. That's how doubters live. We belong to the God of εἰρήνη peace! And εἰρήνη is a fruit of the Spirit that surpasses all understanding and human intellect (4:7)! God is sovereign and in complete control! Whatever has us afraid is on a leash! Every storm and circumstance we face has an expiration date!

As children of εἰρήνη, God says to let nothing worry or distract us (4:6). Instead, He says to pray about everything. Our minds can't house both worry and prayer at the same time. We must choose. Instead of wasting energy on the bad, let's put it to good use. Lay your requests on the altar before God with praise and thanksgiving. Be reminded of how good He is! Watch His εἰρήνη calm the mental storm and become your gatekeeper and guard (4:7). Then the only way through the gate to your heart/ mind is Christ Jesus, the Prince of [H7965] שָׁלוֹם shâlôm, shaw-lome' Peace (Isaiah 9:6; 26:3).

---

[197] Merriam-Webster dictionary | www.merriam-webster.com | www.learnersdictionary.com
[198] Ps. 1; 18–19; 23; 27; 37; 42; 56; 91; 103; 118; 119 (11); 136; Prov. 3:5–6 | Rom. 15:5–6, 13, 33; 16:20; 1 Thess. 5:23; Heb. 13:20–21; 2 Cor. 1:3; 13:11; 1 Pet. 5:10; Acts 7:2 | Luke 12:22–34; 18:1; 2 Cor. 9:8; Jude 1:24–25; Matt. 6:25–34; 14:22–33; 22:37; Gal. 5:22–26; Phil. 2:5; 1 Tim. 4:15; ♪Col. 1:21; 2:18; 3:1–17; Mark 5:15; 1 Cor. 1:10; 2:16
[199] *Strong's Exhaustive Concordance of the Bible* | Blue Letter Bible | www.blueletterbible.org

Paul offers us a grocery list of good brain food to meditate, muse on, and eat—whatever is true, noble, just, pure, lovely, of good report, anything of virtue and praiseworthy (4:8). Use these daily for muscle building mind exercises. Writing from prison, Paul is speaking from experience. He says that when we follow his example (4:9), the God of εἰρήνη will be with us!

Ἀγάπη, χάρις, and εἰρήνη …

♪Colossians 3:16,

Rodney

Take a moment to meditate, muse, and memorize God's word. What is the Holy Spirit saying to you right now?

_____

_____

_____

_____

_____

_____

_____

_____

_____

_____

_____

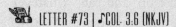 LETTER #73 | ♪COL. 3:6 (NKJV)

NECESSARY

[a. Necessary: 1) so important that you must do it or have it: absolutely needed: required
2) of an inevitable nature: inescapable][200]

Luke 10:38–42 (NKJV)

38 Now it happened as they went that He entered a certain village; and a certain woman named Martha welcomed Him into her house.
39 And she had a sister called Mary, who also sat at Jesus' feet and heard His word.
40 But Martha was distracted with much serving, and she approached Him and said, "Lord, do You not care that my sister has left me to serve alone? Therefore tell her to help me."
41 And Jesus answered and said to her, "Martha, Martha, you are worried and troubled about many things.
42 "But one thing is needed,[G5532] and Mary has chosen that good part, which will not be taken away from her."

[G5532] χρεία chreía, khri'-ah; from the base of G5530 or G5534; employment, i.e. an affair; also (by implication) occasion, demand, requirement or destitution:—business, lack, necessary(-ity), need(-ful), use, want.
[G5534] χρή chrē̆, khray; third person singular of the same as G5530 or G5531 used impersonally; it needs (must or should) be:—ought.[201]

Dear Worship Leader,

Mary or Martha: which one are you? In your current season of life, are you like Martha: worried and troubled about many things (10:41)? She's welcomed Jesus into her house (10:38) and is working hard with much serving, but at what cost? Scripture calls it a distraction (10:40). I've been there.

On the other hand, are you like Mary? Mary is doing one thing: sitting at Jesus's feet hearing His word (10:39). While Martha might be in the background making noises with pots and pans, sweating profusely while doing a service, Mary is silently settled and seated in service. Exasperated, Martha doesn't even directly ask her sister Mary to help (10:40). Instead, she interrupts Jesus's preaching to question His care, complain about Mary, and demand Jesus tells Mary to get on the same page as her. Jesus's response is interesting. He says that only one thing is needed and that Mary "has chosen that good part, which will not be taken away from her (10:42)." In other words, Mary is doing what is needed. Martha is the one off-track and needs her attitude and priorities adjusted. And no, He's not stopping His sermon for Mary to also be derailed!

Clearly, Jesus is not teaching against serving or working hard in the kingdom. Prior to this story is the parable of the Good Samaritan, which is all about loving and serving our neighbor (10:25–37). But the Master Conductor, Jesus, is trying to get Martha and the rest of us on track—and on board with Him. Serving food is great, but not at the expense of being at the Savior's feet eating the Word. That's why we invited Him! There's a time to cook and clean but also a time to take the apron off and sit in Jesus's presence. It's foundational to everything else. Let's prioritize spending time with Jesus. We *need* His word. Isaiah 40:8 (NKJV) says,

[200] Merriam-Webster dictionary | www.merriam-webster.com | www.learnersdictionary.com
[201] *Strong's Exhaustive Concordance of the Bible* | Blue Letter Bible | www.blueletterbible.org

"The grass withers, the flower fades, But the word of our God stands forever." Only one thing is needed.

Love, grace, and peace …

♪Colossians 3:16,

Rodney

Take a moment to meditate, muse, and memorize God's word. What is the Holy Spirit saying to you right now?

_____

_____

_____

_____

_____

_____

_____

_____

_____

_____

_____

_____

_____

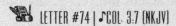 LETTER #74 | ♪COL. 3:7 (NKJV)

ORGANISM

[n. Organism: 1) a complex structure of interdependent and subordinate elements whose relations and properties are largely determined by their function in the whole 2) an individual constituted to carry on the activities of life by means of parts or organs more or less separate in function but mutually dependent: a living being][202]

Romans 12:3–8 (NKJV)[203]

3 For I say, through the grace given to me, to everyone who is among you, not to think of himself more highly than he ought to think, but to think soberly, as God has dealt to each one a measure of faith.
4 For as we have many members in one body,[G4983] but all the members do not have the same function,
5 so we, being many, are one body[G4983] in Christ, and individually members of one another.
6 Having then gifts differing according to the grace that is given to us, let us use them: if prophecy, let us prophesy in proportion to our faith;
7 or ministry, let us use it in our ministering; he who teaches, in teaching;
8 he who exhorts, in exhortation; he who gives, with liberality; he who leads, with diligence; he who shows mercy, with cheerfulness.

[G4983] σῶμα sōma, so'-mah; from G4982; the body (as a sound whole), used in a very wide application, literally or figuratively:—bodily, body, slave.[204]

Dear Worship Leader,

Here's a sobering truth: Life in Christ is not all about you or me. We're a part of something much bigger, the church of Jesus Christ—the body of Christ. The body of Christ is a living organism with many members serving in one body, Christ. All the members do not have the same function or gift, but we are all interdependent and members of one another. No one part can function independently of the body as a whole. Just as the human body needs oneness, order, and organization, so do we. Every member, every person, and every gift matters.

We belong to Christ. He is our Head and we are His body (Ephesians 5:23, 30). In order for the body to function properly, there must be submission to Him and to one another. Before Paul discusses the individual members of the family and community, he teaches us that we are to be "submitting to one another in the fear of God (5:21, 24)." When cells go rogue or wild, they become cancerous and dangerous to the whole body. Nothing works well without submission. Without it there's massive chaos in the family, home, company, community, government, and church!

We can't even have an effective church service without submission and cooperation. As important as the music or worship area is, we need other people and other ministries for us to be successful in what we do. This is why we must think of ourselves soberly—nothing more, nothing less. For example, if a section

---

[202] Merriam-Webster dictionary | www.merriam-webster.com | www.learnersdictionary.com
[203] 1 Cor. 6:12–20; 7:32–35; 10:14–17; 11:3; 12:12–31; Rom. 12:3–21; Eph. 1:22–23; 2:11–18; 4:1–16; 5:22–33; ♪Col. 1:15–18; 2:19; 3:15; Heb. 10:19–25; Acts 2 (40–47); 27:3; Luke 10:25–37; John 10:11–16; Phil. 2:20; 4:10; 1 Tim. 3:5
[204] *Strong's Exhaustive Concordance of the Bible* | Blue Letter Bible | www.blueletterbible.org

of the choir stays home, a major part would be missing. We would still have a choir, and the choir could still sing, but we'd probably be limited to singing in unison or two-part harmony. The same is true for us as members of the body. Our service impacts the whole. Hebrews 10:24–25 says to consider one another, we are not an only child.

Love, grace, and peace …

♪Colossians 3:16,

Rodney

Take a moment to meditate, muse, and memorize God's word. What is the Holy Spirit saying to you right now?

_____

_____

_____

_____

_____

_____

_____

_____

_____

_____

_____

_____

_____

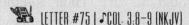 LETTER #75 | ♪COL. 3:8–9 (NKJV)

ORGANIZATION

[n. Organization: 1) the act or process of organizing or of being organized
2a) association, society
2b) an administrative and functional structure (such as a business or a political party) also: the personnel of such a structure][205]

Hebrews 13:7, 17, 24 (NKJV)

7 Remember those who rule[G2233] over you, who have spoken the word of God to you, whose faith follow, considering the outcome of their conduct.

17 Obey those who rule[G2233] over you, and be submissive, for they watch out for your souls, as those who must give account. Let them do so with joy and not with grief, for that would be unprofitable for you.

24 Greet all those who rule[G2233] over you, and all the saints. Those from Italy greet you.

[G2233] ἡγέομαι hēgéomai, hayg-eh'-om-ahee; middle voice of a (presumed) strengthened form of G71; to lead, i.e. command (with official authority); figuratively, to deem, i.e. consider:—account, (be) chief, count, esteem, governor, judge, have the rule over, suppose, think.[206]

Dear Worship Leader,

The church is both an organism and an organization. As worship leaders we add value to both worlds. *The organism is primarily the body or "people" side.* It requires people skills and loving your neighbor as yourself. That means learning names, smiling, speaking, and greeting others. It's prioritizing and engaging others. It's saying, "Thank you" and "You're welcome." It's apologizing and asking for forgiveness at times. It's giving eye contact when others are speaking and showing genuine interest in their lives. It's initiating, answering, and returning calls. Yes, that involves emails, texts, and private messaging sometimes. It's becoming a people investor. Relationships are the economy of the kingdom. It's spending quality time getting to know and enjoy the people you serve. This is caring for others and ministering to them in their time of need. It's demonstrating empathy. People want to know they matter and are not just a number on the roster.

At the same time, the church is also an organization and must be responsible as such. *The organization is primarily the business or "program" side.* Wherever money is spent or exchanged, eyes will be watching. It's paying tithes and taxes. There must be rules, structure, hierarchy, and financial integrity. That means recruiting and releasing people sometimes. It means doing regular evaluations and annual budgets every year. Staff, artists, and guests want to know the church's checks are good and will not "bounce" due to insufficient funds. Our teams want to enjoy organized meetings and rehearsals with a clear agenda. It's getting songs, lyrics, keys, etc. to the right people on time. It's starting and ending on time. If members feel that programs are wasteful and unproductive, eventually they sow elsewhere.

---

[205] Merriam-Webster dictionary | www.merriam-webster.com | www.learnersdictionary.com
[206] *Strong's Exhaustive Concordance of the Bible* | Blue Letter Bible | www.blueletterbible.org

The key to both worlds is stewardship, or what I call "Connect 4!" It's the art of loving people and using things, not loving things and using people. (See Letter #20.)

Love, grace, and peace …

♪Colossians 3:16,

Rodney

Take a moment to meditate, muse, and memorize God's word. What is the Holy Spirit saying to you right now?

_____

_____

_____

_____

_____

_____

_____

_____

_____

_____

_____

_____

_____

LETTER #76 | ♪COL. 3:10 (NKJV)

ORDER

[v. Order: 1) to put in order: arrange
2a) to give an order to: command
2b) destine ordain
2c) to command to go or come to a specified place
2d) to give an order for][207]

Titus 1:5 (NKJV)[208]

5 For this reason I left you in Crete, that you should set in order[G1930] the things that are lacking, and appoint elders in every city as I commanded you—

[G1930] ἐπιδιορθόω epidiorthóō, ep-ee-dee-or-tho'-o; from G1909 and a derivative of G3717; to straighten further, i.e. (figuratively) arrange additionally:—set in order.[209]

1 Corinthians 14:40 (NKJV)

40 Let all things be done decently and in order.[G5010]

[G5010] τάξις táxis, tax'-is; from G5021; regular arrangement, i.e. (in time) fixed succession (of rank or character), official dignity:—order.
[G5021] τάσσω tássō, tas'-so; a prolonged form of a primary verb (which latter appears only in certain tenses); to arrange in an orderly manner, i.e. assign or dispose (to a certain position or lot):—addict, appoint, determine, ordain, set.

Dear Worship Leader,

God is a God of order. There is order within God Himself, the Godhead. The theological term for unity between God the Father, God the Son, and God the Holy Spirit—as one God in three Persons—is Trinity (1 John 5:7; Matthew 28:19). John 3:16 teaches us that God gave His only begotten Son, Jesus. He was sent to us from God the Father (John 3:17; 4:34; 17). When Jesus was baptized, the Father and Holy Spirit were both present (Matthew 3:16–17). Jesus Christ left earth so the Holy Spirit could come and reside in us (John 16:5–15).

There is order in the Godhead and order in God's church. One way to dishonor God is to dishonor or disrespect those in authority. Even if leaders are harsh, God calls us to honor them through submission, just like Jesus did on our behalf (1 Peter 2:18–25). As long as God has us on assignment under a leader, He wants us to represent Him by loving and serving that leader through the Spirit and in a peaceable manner—as much as depends on us (Romans 12:18; Titus 3:1–2). We want to honor our leaders in the same way we would want to be honored. David repented from even cutting the robe of his demented leader (1 Samuel 24:4–7). David understood that dishonoring the anointing on King Saul is dishonoring the same anointing that would one day be on him.

We're called to do things decently and in order, with dignity and respect. In the same way you want your music in order, God wants your spirit and service in order. Proverbs 25:28 (NKJV) says, "Whoever has no rule over his own

[207] Merriam-Webster dictionary | www.merriam-webster.com | www.learnersdictionary.com
[208] 1 Cor. 12:27–31; Titus 2:15 | Luke 1:8; 1 Cor. 14:40; ♪Col. 2:5, 9; Heb. 5:6, 10; 6:20; 7:11, 17, 21 | Matt. 28:16; Luke 7:8; Acts 13:48; 15:2; 22:10; 28:23; Rom. 13:1; 1 Cor. 16:15 | Eph. 5:27; Gal. 4:6; Rom. 1:20; 3:15; 1 Tim. 3:5; 5:17
[209] *Strong's Exhaustive Concordance of the Bible* | Blue Letter Bible | www.blueletterbible.org

spirit Is like a city broken down, without walls." In a court of law, winning isn't based only on being right but also on doing right, or else getting thrown out for being in contempt of court. May Christ return to find His church and bride winning and in order.

Love, grace, and peace …

♪Colossians 3:16,

Rodney

Take a moment to meditate, muse, and memorize God's word. What is the Holy Spirit saying to you right now?

_____

_____

_____

_____

_____

_____

_____

_____

_____

_____

_____

_____

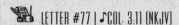 LETTER #77 | ♪COL. 3:11 (NKJV)

PREPARATION

[n. Preparation: the action or process of making something ready for use or service or of getting ready for some occasion, test, or duty.][210]

Ezra 7:6–10 (NKJV)[211]

6 this Ezra came up from Babylon; and he was a skilled scribe in the Law of Moses, which the Lord God of Israel had given. The king granted him all his request, according to the hand of the Lord his God upon him.

7 Some of the children of Israel, the priests, the Levites, the singers, the gatekeepers, and the Nethinim came up to Jerusalem in the seventh year of King Artaxerxes.

8 And Ezra came to Jerusalem in the fifth month, which was in the seventh year of the king.

9 On the first day of the first month he began his journey from Babylon, and on the first day of the fifth month he came to Jerusalem, according to the good hand of his God upon him.

10 For Ezra had prepared[H3559] his heart to seek the Law of the Lord, and to do it, and to teach statutes and ordinances in Israel.

[H3559] כּוּן kûwn, koon; a primitive root; properly, to be erect (i.e. stand perpendicular); hence (causatively) to set up, in a great variety of applications, whether literal (establish, fix, prepare, apply), or figurative (appoint, render sure, proper or prosperous):—certain(-ty), confirm, direct, faithfulness, fashion, fasten, firm, be fitted, be fixed, frame, be meet, ordain, order, perfect, (make) preparation, prepare (self), provide, make provision, (be, make) ready, right, set (aright, fast, forth), be stable, (e-) stablish, stand, tarry, × very deed.[212]

Dear Worship Leader,

When we prepare well, we serve well and set up ourselves for maximal ministry impact. Preparation and consecration are early signs that God is up to something— something higher, greater, and deeper. The heavens are stirring. There are labor pains. God is birthing mission, vision, values, and assignment through us. All of life has been readying us for this moment. Now is not the time for passivity or procrastination. It's time to push. A baby is on the way! A mighty move of God. Divine purpose. Predestination. Generational blessing and legacy!

Below is a practical list of things to do in preparation for service.

- Personal heart preparation and life example of true spiritual worship.
- Prayer and petition for the heartbeat and voice of God, and for His people.
- Prepare to serve through pastoral care and personal investment.
- Receive vision, instruction, and plan from the leadership's heart.
- Confirm singers, musicians, rehearsal, theme/topic, and service order.
- Personal study, prayer, and research regarding songs/topic/theme.
- Work on song list/selections, keys, arrangement, flow, and transitions.
- Communicate plan to singers, musicians, tech team, and leadership.
- Work on learning music and lyrics through great repetition and practice.

---

[210] Merriam-Webster dictionary | www.merriam-webster.com | www.learnersdictionary.com

[211] Josh. 1:11; 4:4; 8:4; Ps. 37:23; 40:2; 51:10; 57:7; 108:1; 112:7; 119:133; 141:2; Prov. 4:26; 16:3, 9; 24:27; 30:25

[212] *Strong's Exhaustive Concordance of the Bible* | Blue Letter Bible | www.blueletterbible.org

- Prerehearsal planning with band director and tech director (for AVL).
- Spiritually arm the team with prayer, devotion, testimony, and scripture.
- Personally worship with the team in rehearsal; practice His presence.
- Rehearse service and flow in detail with singers, musicians, and tech team.
- Prepare the team for flexibility, ad-libs, and spontaneous worship.
- Assign someone with leadership potential to assist with small things.
- Reiterate heart/vision with appreciation, coaching, and evaluation.
- Finalize any ministerial and administrative details (attire, call time, etc.).
- Send words of inspiration, encouragement, and prayer to the team.
- Self-care and preparation to serve with integrity of heart and skill of hand.
- Preservice prayer with singers, musicians, tech team, and leadership.
- Serve with spiritual sensitivity to leadership and the heart/hand of God.

Love, grace, and peace …

♪Colossians 3:16,

Rodney

Take a moment to meditate, muse, and memorize God's word. What is the Holy Spirit saying to you right now?

_____

_____

_____

_____

_____

_____

_____

_____

LETTER #78 | ♪COL. 3:12–13 (NKJV)

PRAYER

[n. Prayer: 1a) words spoken to God especially in order to give thanks or to ask for something
1b) a fixed set of words that are spoken to God
2) the act of speaking to God: the act of praying
3) a strong hope or wish][213]

Matthew 21:12–13, 21–22 (NKJV)[214]

12 Then Jesus went into the temple of God and drove out all those who bought and sold in the temple, and overturned the tables of the money changers and the seats of those who sold doves.
13 And He said to them, "It is written, 'My house shall be called a house of prayer,'[G4335] but you have made it a 'den of thieves.'"

21 So Jesus answered and said to them, "Assuredly, I say to you, if you have faith and do not doubt, you will not only do what was done to the fig tree, but also if you say to this mountain, 'Be removed and be cast into the sea,' it will be done.
22 "And whatever things you ask in prayer,[G4335] believing, you will receive."

————— ❡ —————

[G4335] προσευχή proseuché, pros-yoo-khay'; from G4336; prayer (worship); by implication, an oratory (chapel):—X pray earnestly, prayer.
[G4336] προσεύχομαι proseúchomai, pros-yoo'-khom-ahee; from G4314 and G2172; to pray to God, i.e. supplicate, worship:—pray (X earnestly, for), make prayer.[215]

Dear Worship Leader,

If the church is anything, it is a house of prayer. That's what scripture calls it (Isaiah 56:7). In fact, that's what Jesus calls it Himself (Matthew 21:13). Yes, that involves preaching, teaching, and singing, but when reduced to its lowest common denominator, the church is a community of prayer warriors. We know how to wage war and get God's attention!

The church was born out of prayer (Acts 1:12–2:4). It grew and labored through prayer (Acts 2:42–47). Prayer is its secret weapon against the enemy. Many miracles were performed through the power of being on one accord in prayer (Acts 5:12–16). The apostles chose deacons like Stephen to lead and help with the business of the church so they could continually devote themselves to prayer and the Word (Acts 6:1–7). We have the same need now.

As worship leaders, the secret sauce to our leadership is prayer and ministry of the Word (Acts 6:4). I hope and pray that our excellent musicianship is founded upon prayer and the very word of God. *This is an identity issue.* You and I have to see ourselves as men and women of prayer. Without prayer we aren't much different from every other talented musician and artist outside the body of Christ. Prayer is our connection to a power beyond this world. Much prayer, much power! For us, everything is bathed in prayer. When persecution arose and Peter was imprisoned, it was the church's constant prayer that eventually led him to freedom and had Peter knocking on their door during the prayer meeting (Acts 12:5–17)!

---

[213] Merriam-Webster dictionary | www.merriam-webster.com | www.learnersdictionary.com
[214] Luke 6:12; 18:1; Matt. 14:23; 19:13; 26:36–46; Mark 6:46; 1 Cor. 14:15; 1 Tim. 2:8; James 5:13–18; ♪Col. 4:2, 12
[215] *Strong's Exhaustive Concordance of the Bible* | Blue Letter Bible | www.blueletterbible.org

We pray without ceasing (1 Thessalonians 5:17, 25). Not as a rule but as a lifestyle. How else will we know what leader to select, song to sing, church to attend, step to take personally or professionally? It's how we hear God and how God hears us.

Love, grace, and peace …

♪Colossians 3:16,

Rodney

Take a moment to meditate, muse, and memorize God's word. What is the Holy Spirit saying to you right now?

_____

_____

_____

_____

_____

_____

_____

_____

_____

_____

_____

_____

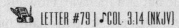 LETTER #79 | ♪COL. 3:14 (NKJV)

PSALMS

[n. Psalm: a sacred song or poem used in worship, especially: one of the biblical hymns collected in the Book of Psalms][216]

Psalm 3:1–8 (KJV)[217]

[[A Psalm[H4210] of David, when he fled from Absalom his son.]]

1 LORD, how are they increased that trouble me! many are they that rise up against me.
2 Many there be which say of my soul, There is no help for him in God. Selah.
3 But thou, O LORD, art a shield for me; my glory, and the lifter up of mine head.
4 I cried unto the LORD with my voice, and he heard me out of his holy hill. Selah.
5 I laid me down and slept; I awaked; for the LORD sustained me.
6 I will not be afraid of ten thousands of people, that have set themselves against me round about.
7 Arise, O LORD; save me, O my God: for thou hast smitten all mine enemies upon the cheek bone; thou hast broken the teeth of the ungodly.
8 Salvation belongeth unto the LORD: thy blessing is upon thy people. Selah.

[H4210] מִזְמוֹר **mizmôwr,** miz-more'; from H2167; properly, instrumental music; by implication, a poem set to notes:—psalm.

[H2167] זָמַר **zâmar,** zaw-mar'; a primitive root (perhaps identical with H2168 through the idea of striking with the fingers); properly, to touch the strings or parts of a musical instrument, i.e. play upon it; to make music, accompanied by the voice; hence to celebrate in song and music:—give praise, sing forth praises, psalms.[218]

Dear Worship Leader,

The book of Psalms is a songbook of prayers and poetry. It's the hymnal of the Bible, a journal set to music. That's why ♪Colossians 3:16 and Ephesians 5:19 both instruct us to teach, admonish, and speak to one another from it—because it's filled with wisdom and life lessons regarding everyday experiences from people just like you and me. It's God's word in song—us singing to God, God to us, and us to one another. Selah (3:2, 4, 8), used seventy-one times in psalms, is a musical term for interlude, suspension, and pause.

The entire book of Psalms has 150 chapters. Traditionally, it was divided into five smaller sections or books: 1–41, 42–72, 73–89, 90–106, and 107–150. Psalm 1:1–6 is a great starting place and summary of the book. It contrasts the delightful prosperity of walking in God's blessing (vv. 1–3) versus the perishing of the ungodly (vv. 4–6). This psalm spotlights lovingly obeying God's word and meditating on it day and night. (Psalm 19:14 is an awesome prayer song in this regard.)

Psalm 119 is the longest chapter in the Bible, with 176 short verses that point us to God, His principles, and His truth (also called commandments, judgments, law, precepts, righteousness, sayings, statutes, testimonies, way, and word). Psalm 119:11 (KJV) says, "Thy word have I hid in mine heart, that I might not sin against thee." The entire chapter is an acrostic poem with twenty-two stanzas matching the twenty-two letters of the Hebrew alphabet. Each stanza, eight verses, sequentially

---

216 Merriam-Webster dictionary | www.merriam-webster.com | www.learnersdictionary.com
217 Ps. 95:2; 105:2; 1 Chron. 16:7, 9; Luke 20:42; 24:13–49 (27, 44); Acts 1:20; 13:33, 35; 1 Cor. 14:26; James 5:13
218 *Strong's Exhaustive Concordance of the Bible* | Blue Letter Bible | www.blueletterbible.org

introduces a Hebrew letter—with each line beginning with that Hebrew letter. It's quite a creative work of art.

Although King David is not the only author of psalms, scripture does title him the sweet psalmist of Israel (2 Samuel 23:1). God called him a man after His own heart (1 Samuel 13:14; Acts 13:22). What songs do you have in your heart?

Love, grace, and peace ...

♪Colossians 3:16,

Rodney

Take a moment to meditate, muse, and memorize God's word. What is the Holy Spirit saying to you right now?

_____

_____

_____

_____

_____

_____

_____

_____

_____

_____

_____

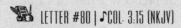 LETTER #80 | ♪COL. 3:15 (NKJV)

PROVERBS

[n. Proverbs: a collection of moral sayings and counsels forming a book of canonical Jewish and Christian Scripture][219]

Proverbs 1:1–7 (NKJV)

1 The proverbs[H4912] of Solomon the son of David, king of Israel:
2 To know wisdom and instruction,
To perceive the words of understanding,
3 To receive the instruction of wisdom,
Justice, judgment, and equity;
4 To give prudence to the simple,
To the young man knowledge and discretion—
5 A wise man will hear and increase learning,
And a man of understanding will attain wise counsel,
6 To understand a proverb[H4912] and an enigma,
The words of the wise and their riddles.
7 The fear of the LORD is the beginning of knowledge,
But fools despise wisdom and instruction.

[H4912] מָשָׁל **mâshâl,** maw-shawl'; apparently from H4910 in some original sense of superiority in mental action; properly, a pithy maxim, usually of metaphorical nature; hence, a simile (as an adage, poem, discourse):—byword, like, parable, proverb.
[H4910] מָשַׁל **mâshal,** maw-shal'; a primitive root; to rule:—(have, make to have) dominion, governor, × indeed, reign, (bear, cause to, have) rule(-ing, -r), have power.[220]

Dear Worship Leader,

King Solomon, son of King David, spoke three thousand proverbs and wrote 1005 songs (1 Kings 4:32). God gave him wisdom, great understanding, and largeness of heart like the sand on the seashore (4:29). His wisdom excelled the wisdom of all the men of the East and all the wisdom of Egypt (4:30). Men of all nations, from all the kings of the earth who had heard of his wisdom, came to hear the wisdom of Solomon (4:34). He is the author of the book of Proverbs, a book known for its rich wisdom and profound insight. Since Proverbs has thirty-one chapters, for daily doses of wisdom and instruction, many are known to read a chapter each day—one that corresponds to the current numerical day of the month. For some, reading from Proverbs every day might seem extreme, but just how important is wisdom to you? Observe how valuable this was for Solomon as leader and king.

On that night God appeared to Solomon, and said to him, "Ask! What shall I give you?"

And Solomon said to God: "You have shown great mercy to David my father, and have made me king in his place.

"Now, O LORD God, let Your promise to David my father be established, for You have made me king over a people like the dust of the earth in multitude.

"Now give me wisdom and knowledge, that I may go out and come in before this people; for who can judge this great people of Yours?"

---

219 Merriam-Webster dictionary | www.merriam-webster.com | www.learnersdictionary.com
220 *Strong's Exhaustive Concordance of the Bible* | Blue Letter Bible | www.blueletterbible.org

Then God said to Solomon: "Because this was in your heart, and you have not asked riches or wealth or honor or the life of your enemies, nor have you asked long life—but have asked wisdom and knowledge for yourself, that you may judge My people over whom I have made you king—

"wisdom and knowledge are granted to you; and I will give you riches and wealth and honor, such as none of the kings have had who were before you, nor shall any after you have the like." (2 Chronicles 1:7–12 NKJV)

Love, grace, and peace …

♪Colossians 3:16,

Rodney

Take a moment to meditate, muse, and memorize God's word. What is the Holy Spirit saying to you right now?

_____

_____

_____

_____

_____

_____

_____

_____

_____

_____

SPIRITUAL CHECKUP: INSPIRE

Review the last ten letters and record any key highlights. Has the Holy Spirit revealed any …

Instruction?

_____

_____

_____

_____

Needs?

_____

_____

_____

_____

Scripture?

_____

_____

_____

_____

Principles?

_____

_____

_____

_____

Interests?

_____

_____

_____

_____

Reproof?

_____

_____

_____

_____

Encouragement?

_____

_____

_____

_____

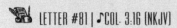 LETTER #81 | ♪COL. 3:16 (NKJV)

POLITICS

[n. Politics: 1) activities that relate to influencing the actions and policies of a government or getting and keeping power in a government
2a) the art or science of government
2b) the art or science concerned with guiding or influencing governmental policy
2c) the art or science concerned with winning and holding control over a government][221]

Genesis 41:37–42 (NKJV)[222]

37 So the advice was good in the eyes of Pharaoh and in the eyes of all his servants.
38 And Pharaoh said to his servants, "Can we find such a one as this, a man in whom is the Spirit of God?"
39 Then Pharaoh said to Joseph, "Inasmuch as God has shown you all this, there is no one as discerning and wise as you.
40 "You shall be over my house, and all my people shall be ruled according to your word; only in regard to the throne[H3678] will I be greater than you."
41 And Pharaoh said to Joseph, "See, I have set you over all the land of Egypt."
42 Then Pharaoh took his signet ring off his hand and put it on Joseph's hand; and he clothed him in garments of fine linen and put a gold chain around his neck.

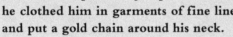

[H3678] כִּסֵּא kiççê', kis-say'; or כִּסֵּה kiççêh; from H3680; properly, covered, i.e. a throne (as canopied):—seat, stool, throne.[223]

Dear Worship Leader,

Like governmental politics, church politics can be challenging and disillusioning. The level that some will stoop to climb the organizational ladder of success or be seated on the "throne" of position, power, and prominence can be altogether disgraceful, dishonoring, and disheartening. This dog-eat-dog mindset is earthly, sensual, and demonic (James 3:15).

James 3:16 (NKJV; emphasis mine) says, "For where envy and self-seeking exist, confusion and *every evil thing* are there." Philippians 2:3 (NKJV; emphasis mine) further advises, "Let *nothing* be done through selfish ambition or conceit, but in lowliness of mind let each esteem others better than himself." First John 2:15–16 (NKJV; emphasis mine) commands, "Do not love the world or the things in the world. If *anyone* loves the world, the love of the Father is not in him. For *all that is in the world*—the lust of the flesh, the lust of the eyes, and the pride of life—is not of the Father but is of the world." Proverbs 16:18 (NKJV) warns, "Pride goes before destruction, And a haughty spirit before a fall."

Pride caused Satan to fall like lightning from heaven (Luke 10:18). The letter *i* is always at the center of the word pride. Isaiah 14:13–14 (NKJV; emphasis mine) exposes Lucifer's dangerous political agenda by saying, "For you have said in your heart: '*I will* ascend into heaven, *I will* exalt my throne above the stars of God; *I will* also sit on the mount of the congregation On the farthest sides of the north; *I will* ascend above the heights of the clouds, *I will* be like the Most High.'"

---

221 Merriam-Webster dictionary | www.merriam-webster.com | www.learnersdictionary.com

222 Gen. 39:2, 3, 21, 23; Acts 7:9 | Gen. 39:4, 9; 40:8; 41:16, 25, 32, 37–57; 45:5–11; 50:19–21, 22–26; Heb. 11:21–22

223 *Strong's Exhaustive Concordance of the Bible* | Blue Letter Bible | www.blueletterbible.org

Satan is an example of corrupt politics. Joseph is an example of clean kingdom politics. Filled with the Spirit of God, he modeled service, humility, and patience—along with the meekness and purity of wisdom from above (James 3:13, 17). This is the one God rewards and the attitude God promotes.

Love, grace, and peace …

♪Colossians 3:16,

Rodney

Take a moment to meditate, muse, and memorize God's word. What is the Holy Spirit saying to you right now?

_____

_____

_____

_____

_____

_____

_____

_____

_____

_____

_____

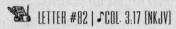 LETTER #82 | ♪COL. 3:17 (NKJV)

QUIET

[a. Quiet: 1) free from noise or uproar: still
2) marked by little or no motion or activity: calm
3) secluded][224]

Matthew 14:19–23 (NKJV)[225]

**19 Then He commanded the multitudes to sit down on the grass. And He took the five loaves and the two fish, and looking up to heaven, He blessed and broke and gave the loaves to the disciples; and the disciples gave to the multitudes.
20 So they all ate and were filled, and they took up twelve baskets full of the fragments that remained.
21 Now those who had eaten were about five thousand men, besides women and children.
22 Immediately Jesus made His disciples get into the boat and go before Him to the other side, while He sent the multitudes away.
23 And when He had sent the multitudes away, He went up on the mountain by Himself to pray. Now when evening came, He was alone[G3441] there.**

[G3441] μόνος **mónos,** mon'-os; probably from G3306; remaining, i.e. sole or single; by implication, mere:—alone, only, by themselves.
[G3306] μένω **ménō,** men'-o; a primary verb; to stay (in a given place, state, relation or expectancy):—abide, continue, dwell, endure, be present, remain, stand, tarry (for), × thine own.[226]

Dear Worship Leader,

Similar to how some people are afraid of the dark, some of us are afraid of the quiet or simply uncomfortable being left alone. The busyness of life has a way of hypnotizing us into conforming to the loud chaotic pattern of this world (Romans 12:1–2). Our schedules have the capacity to control us instead of us controlling them. Before long, minutes turn into hours, days, weeks, months, and years of being totally consumed with seeking and securing more and more "things."

Matthew 6:33 (NKJV) says, "But seek first the kingdom of God and His righteousness, and all these things shall be added to you." At the end of this earthly life, on their deathbed, no one in their right mind wishes they had more earthly things for the afterlife. We brought nothing into this world, and it's certain we can carry nothing out of it (1 Timothy 6:7). The rich fool in Luke 12:13–21 unwisely trusted in the things he possessed. He didn't simply have possessions; his possessions had him. Notice what God said to him in Luke 12:20–21 (NKJV).

But God said to him, "Fool! This night your soul will be required of you; then whose will those things be which you have provided?" "So is he who lays up treasure for himself, and is not rich toward God."

In Matthew 6:19–21 (NKJV) Jesus offers us personal advice.

---

[224] Merriam-Webster dictionary | www.merriam-webster.com | www.learnersdictionary.com
[225] Exod. 20:21; 24:12–18; 33:11; 1 Kings 19:11–12; Matt. 6:5–15; 26:36; Mark 6:46; 14:32; Luke 6:12; 18:1; John 17; Ps. 19:13–14; 27:14; 46:10; 139:23–24; Acts 1:13–14; 3:1; 6:4; 12:5; ♪Col. 4:2; James 5:13–18; Lam. 3:26; Isa. 40:31
[226] *Strong's Exhaustive Concordance of the Bible* | Blue Letter Bible | www.blueletterbible.org

Do not lay up for yourselves treasures on earth, where moth and rust destroy and where thieves break in and steal; but lay up for yourselves treasures in heaven, where neither moth nor rust destroys and where thieves do not break in and steal. For where your treasure is, there your heart will be also.

If we have a refrigerator, freezer, or any type of surplus storage, compared with the rest of the world, we are rich. Let's all prioritize the eternal first with quiet time alone with Jesus.

Love, grace, and peace …

♪Colossians 3:16,

Rodney

Take a moment to meditate, muse, and memorize God's word. What is the Holy Spirit saying to you right now?

_____

_____

_____

_____

_____

_____

_____

_____

_____

_____

_____

 LETTER #83 | ♪COL. 3:18 (NKJV)

RELEASER

[v. Release: to set free from restraint, confinement, or servitude][227]

Acts 20:31–38 (NKJV)[228]

31 "Therefore watch, and remember that for three years I did not cease to warn everyone night and day with tears.

32 "So now, brethren, I commend[G3908] you to God and to the word of His grace, which is able to build you up and give you an inheritance among all those who are sanctified.

33 "I have coveted no one's silver or gold or apparel.

34 "Yes, you yourselves know that these hands have provided for my necessities, and for those who were with me.

35 "I have shown you in every way, by laboring like this, that you must support the weak. And remember the words of the Lord Jesus, that He said, 'It is more blessed to give than to receive.'"

36 And when he had said these things, he knelt down and prayed with them all.

37 Then they all wept freely, and fell on Paul's neck and kissed him,

38 sorrowing most of all for the words which he spoke, that they would see his face no more. And they accompanied him to the ship.

[G3908] παρατίθημι paratíthēmi, par-at-ith'-ay-mee; from G3844 and G5087; to place alongside, i.e. present (food, truth); by implication, to deposit (as a trust or for protection):—allege, commend, commit (the keeping of), put forth, set before.[229]

Dear Worship Leader,

I get emotional whenever I read or hear Acts 20:32. It reminds me of Bishop Arthur M. Brazier. He was my pastor in Chicago, Illinois, during my teenage years. He quoted this verse at the start of most sermons. He was a man of great grace and fervent faith. I remember a time I went to his office with a complaint. He would not allow me to "lick my wounds" or "play the victim role." Instead, he heard my concern and commended me to another trusted leader in the church—to shepherd and develop me on a more personal, ongoing basis. He set me free from the enemy's snare. Bishop is now gone home to be with the Lord, but I am forever indebted to him. He fathered me through that moment (1 Corinthians 4:15). I'm still in relationship with the precious family he sent me to.

I've been extremely blessed with many overseers who cared for me and released me to grow in my faith, gifts, talents, and calling—far too many to name in this letter. I would not be who I am today without their love. Every time I minister, I do so standing on their shoulders. They all share in my reward.

Are you a releaser or a dictator? Are you more like Moses or Pharaoh (Exodus 3:10–22)? Are you secure enough to release others in their gifts, talents, and calling, or do you have to be the superstar on the court? As a teenager, I couldn't wait to get my hands on the microphone. I wanted the world to see what I could offer. But as I've grown and matured in the faith, I now get greater joy in seeing what

---

[227] Merriam-Webster dictionary | www.merriam-webster.com | www.learnersdictionary.com

[228] Acts 20:17–38; 1 Thess. 2 (8) | Luke 23:46; Acts 14:23; 20:32; 2 Tim. 2:2 | 1 Cor. 2:1–5; 2 Cor. 3:1–3; Philem. 1:8–22

[229] *Strong's Exhaustive Concordance of the Bible* | Blue Letter Bible | www.blueletterbible.org

others have to offer. God still uses me, but I gladly share the microphone and platform. Just as my leaders invested in me, I invest in others. Acts 20:36–38 only happens as a result of releasing others. The gratitude and love one has for a releaser cannot be fully communicated in words only; it sometimes comes with tears.

Love, grace, and peace …

♪Colossians 3:16,

Rodney

Take a moment to meditate, muse, and memorize God's word. What is the Holy Spirit saying to you right now?

_____

_____

_____

_____

_____

_____

_____

_____

_____

_____

_____

_____

_____

 LETTER #84 | ♪COL. 3:19 (NKJV)

ROLES

[n. Role: 1) a function or part performed especially in a particular operation or process
2) the part that someone has in a family, society, or other group][230]

Ephesians 4:11–16 (NKJV)[231]

**11 And He Himself gave some to be apostles, some prophets, some evangelists, and some pastors and teachers,
12 for the equipping of the saints for the work of ministry, for the edifying of the body of Christ,
13 till we all come to the unity of the faith and of the knowledge of the Son of God, to a perfect man, to the measure of the stature of the fullness of Christ;
14 that we should no longer be children, tossed to and fro and carried about with every wind of doctrine, by the trickery of men, in the cunning craftiness of deceitful plotting,
15 but, speaking the truth in love, may grow up in all things into Him who is the head—Christ—
16 from whom the whole body, joined and knit together by what every joint[G860] supplies, according to the effective working by which every part does its share, causes growth of the body for the edifying of itself in love.**

[G860] αφή **haphé,** haf-ay'; from G680; probably a ligament (as fastening):—joint.
[G680] ἅπτομαι **háptomai,** hap'-tom-ahee; reflexive of G681; properly, to attach oneself to, i.e. to touch (in many implied relations):—touch.[232]

Dear Worship Leader,

There are a lot of ways to build your team, develop your teammates, and share the workload. Like the human body, every joint has a function and part to play (1 Corinthians 12:21–22). It's the leader's job to organize the team in the best way that fits each member's gifting and the overall vision/mission for the team (Mark 3:13–19). Below is a short list of some of the various roles and responsibilities shared in scripture for kingdom building and advancement.

▶ building the tabernacle—Exodus 31:1–11; 35:30–36:1
▶ building the temple—1 Kings 5:1–18; 2 Chronicles 2:1–18
▶ carters of the ark—1 Chronicles 15:1–28; 2 Samuel 6:12–15
▶ celebratory praise service—1 Chronicles 16:4–6
▶ ceremonial worship—1 Chronicles 16:37–43
▶ rebuilding the wall—Nehemiah 3:1–32

When it comes to the overall success of the team, no task, duty, or assignment is too small. Every position matters. Every gift matters. Every person matters. Every joint matters. Everyone can help. Try walking or working without the use of your pinky toes or fingers. Although they are small in size, they have a huge impact.

Practically, here are some duties (or committees) I've seen shared among worship/praise teams:

---

[230] Merriam-Webster dictionary | www.merriam-webster.com | www.learnersdictionary.com
[231] ♪Col. 2:19; Eph. 2:21 | 2 Cor. 9:10; Gal. 3:5; ♪Col. 2:19; 2 Pet. 1:5, 11 | 1 Chron. 13; 15:13; 2 Sam. 6:1–11, 16–23
[232] *Strong's Exhaustive Concordance of the Bible* | Blue Letter Bible | www.blueletterbible.org

- birthdays, anniversaries, baby showers, celebrations
- prayer, prayer requests, praise reports, testimonies
- icebreakers, fellowships, fun, group outings, special events
- outreach projects, volunteer opportunities, donations
- administration (guidelines, scheduling, notes, contact information)
- orientation, spiritual gifts, assimilation of new members, attire
- creative team, songwriting, arranging, recording, and teaching parts
- recruitment, assessment, training and development, evaluations
- devotional prayer, praise, discipleship, spiritual growth
- technical support (assists audiovisual team with lyrics, format, etc.)
- section leaders (serving, coaching, encouragement, caring)
- hospitality, comfort and care, prayer partners, small groups

Love, grace, and peace …

♪Colossians 3:16,

Rodney

Take a moment to meditate, muse, and memorize God's word. What is the Holy Spirit saying to you right now?

_____

_____

_____

_____

_____

_____

_____

_____

_____

_____

LETTER #85 | ♪COL. 3:20 (NKJV)

RECOVERY

[n. Recovery: the process of combating a disorder (such as alcoholism) or a real or perceived problem][233]

2 Corinthians 7:9–12 (NKJV)[234]

9 Now I rejoice, not that you were made sorry, but that your sorrow led to repentance.[G3341] For you were made sorry in a godly manner, that you might suffer loss from us in nothing.
10 For godly sorrow produces repentance[G3341] leading to salvation,[G4991] not to be regretted; but the sorrow of the world produces death.
11 For observe this very thing, that you sorrowed in a godly manner: What diligence it produced in you, what clearing of yourselves, what indignation, what fear, what vehement desire, what zeal, what vindication! In all things you proved yourselves to be clear in this matter.
12 Therefore, although I wrote to you, I did not do it for the sake of him who done the wrong, nor for the sake of him who suffered wrong, but that our care for you in the sight of God might appear to you.

[G3341] μετάνοια metánoia, met-an'-oy-ah; from G3340; (subjectively) compunction (for guilt, including reformation); by implication, reversal (of (another's) decision):—repentance.
[G4991] σωτηρία sōtēría, so-tay-ree'-ah; feminine of a derivative of G4990 as (properly, abstract) noun; rescue or safety (physically or morally):—deliver, health, salvation, save, saving.[235]

Dear Worship Leader,

One day I stumbled into the liberating truth of 2 Corinthians 7:11. In it lies what I call the Seven Signs of Godly Sorrow. Worldly sorrow leads us to the world—into more sin, guilt, and shame. But godly sorrow leads us to God, into repentance and salvation. These are the signs that we have the right type of sorrow: diligence, clearing of yourselves, indignation, fear, vehement desire, zeal, and vindication!

Godliness aggressively pursues *Christ* through *community* and *counseling*. In my recovery work, one of the greatest breakthrough statements I've ever heard is this: *the antidote to addiction is not sobriety but intimacy.* Selah. In other words, God doesn't simply want the idol, stronghold, or addiction out of your hands. He wants your heart. He wants it all. He wants us near and drawing close to Him. Friendship with the world is enmity with God (James 4:4). The Spirit who dwells in us yearns jealously (4:5). God resists the proud but gives grace to the humble (4:6). James 4:7–10 (NKJV) says,

Therefore submit to God. Resist the devil and he will flee from you. Draw near to God and He will draw near to you. Cleanse your hands, you sinners; and purify your hearts, you double-minded. Lament and mourn and weep! Let your laughter be turned to mourning and your joy to gloom. Humble yourselves in the sight of the Lord, and He will lift you up.

A life of recovery is a lifetime commitment to the following:

---

233 Merriam-Webster dictionary | www.merriam-webster.com | www.learnersdictionary.com
234 Ps. 1; 19:7–14; 32; 42; 51; Prov. 4; 28:13; 1 John 1:9; Mark 2:17; Luke 15:17–24; John 8:1–12; Rom. 8; 2 Pet. 1:8
235 *Strong's Exhaustive Concordance of the Bible* | Blue Letter Bible | www.blueletterbible.org

- ▶ pursuing true freedom and intimacy with God, self, and others
- ▶ humbly falling toward the cross of Christ and the Christ of the cross
- ▶ breaking up with the world and falling in love with Jesus.
- ▶ confession and repentance—having a change of mind and heart
- ▶ positive coping—creating healthy habits, patterns, behaviors, and boundaries—forming new neurological pathways in the brain
- ▶ personal weakness/brokenness and dependence on the Spirit of God

We are safe in the Shepherd's care. Not just in crisis, but *for life.*

Love, grace, and peace …

♪Colossians 3:16,

Rodney

Take a moment to meditate, muse, and memorize God's word. What is the Holy Spirit saying to you right now?

_____

_____

_____

_____

_____

_____

_____

_____

_____

_____

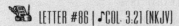 LETTER #86 | ♪COL. 3:21 (NKJV)

SERVANTS

[n. Servant: one that serves others //a public servant, especially: one that performs duties about the person or home of a master or personal employer][236]

John 13:12–17 (NKJV)[237]

12 So when He had washed their feet, taken His garments, and sat down again, He said to them, "Do you know what I have done to you?

13 "You call Me Teacher and Lord, and you say well, for so I am.

14 "If I then, your Lord and Teacher, have washed your feet, you also ought to wash one another's feet.

15 "For I have given you an example, that you should do as I have done to you.

16 "Most assuredly, I say to you, a servant[G1401] is not greater than his master; nor is he who is sent greater than he who sent him.

17 "If you know these things, blessed are you if you do them.

[G1401] δοῦλος **doûlos,** doo'-los; from G1210; a slave (literal or figurative, involuntary or voluntary; frequently, therefore in a qualified sense of subjection or subserviency):—bond(-man), servant.

[G1210] δέω **déō,** deh'-o; a primary verb; to bind (in various applications, literally or figuratively):—bind, be in bonds, knit, tie, wind. See also G1163, G1189.[238]

Dear Worship Leader,

As followers of Jesus, we are cross-bearing, foot-washing servants. This can be easy to forget sometimes as artists, musicians, and worship leaders because of the fame, fortune, or favor often associated with such highly esteemed positions. However, as servant leaders, we must be careful to remember that we aren't kingdom stars, superstars, legends, or celebrities. We are simply servants.

In John 13, we have King Jesus—Teacher, Lord, and Master—washing the feet of His disciples. Serving as a foot washer was one of the dirtiest, lowest, and most humbling jobs to have. Imagine how filthy their feet must have been walking on dusty roads in sandals all day, for many miles. Yet this is the position and example of our Savior. For servanthood, ego [G1473] ἐγώ egṓ, eg-o' must die (13:14–15). Galatians 2:20 (NKJV) says, "I have been crucified with Christ; it is no longer I [G1473 ἐγώ egṓ, eg-o'] who live, but Christ lives in me; and the life which I now live in the flesh I live by faith in the Son of God, who loved me and gave Himself for me."

In scripture we find many contrasts in the kingdom of God. We're crucified but alive. We're living but living sacrifices. We're rich in Christ but blessed if we're poor in spirit. We're weak but strong. We're loved and accepted in Christ but hated and rejected by the world. We're free from sin but slaves of righteousness. God uses the foolish things of the world to shame and confound the wise. If we seek to save our lives, we will lose them, but if we lose

---

[236] Merriam-Webster dictionary | www.merriam-webster.com | www.learnersdictionary.com

[237] John 13:1–17; Acts 20:17–24; 2 Cor. 8:9; 11:22–33; 12:7–10; Rom. 6; 8:18; 12; 2 Tim. 2:1–13; 1 Pet. 2; 5:1–11; Matt. 5:3; 10; Gal. 5:13; Phil. 2:5–11; ♪Col. 3:12–14; Eph. 1:6; Luke 9:23, 48; 17:33; 22:24–27; 1 Cor. 1:27; Mark 9:33–37

[238] *Strong's Exhaustive Concordance of the Bible* | Blue Letter Bible | www.blueletterbible.org

our lives for His sake, we will find them. If we suffer with Him, ultimately we'll reign with Him. The last will be first, the first will be last, and the least will be great. *The greatest among you will be your servant* (Matthew 23:11). King Jesus models this truth best at the feet of His disciples.

Love, grace, and peace …

♪Colossians 3:16,

Rodney

Take a moment to meditate, muse, and memorize God's word. What is the Holy Spirit saying to you right now?

_____

_____

_____

_____

_____

_____

_____

_____

_____

_____

_____

_____

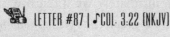 LETTER #87 | ♪COL. 3:22 (NKJV)

STEAM

~Part 1~

[n. Steam: the strength, force, or energy that allows someone to continue, to go faster, etc. // I was making good progress this morning, but now I'm starting to run out of steam.][239]

———∽∽∽———

Matthew 25:14–19 (NKJV)[240]

14 "For the kingdom of heaven is like a man traveling to a far country, who called his own servants and delivered his goods to them.
15 "And to one he gave five talents, to another two, and to another one, to each according to his own ability; and immediately he went on a journey.
16 "Then he who had received the five talents went and traded with them, and made[G2770] another five talents.
17 "And likewise he who had received two gained[G2770] two more also.
18 "But he who had received one went and dug in the ground, and hid his lord's money.
19 "After a long time the lord of those servants came and settled accounts with them.

———∽∽∽———

[G2770] κερδαίνω kerdaínō, ker-dah'-ee-no; from G2771; to gain (literally or figuratively):—(get) gain, win.[241]

Dear Worship Leader,

STEAM is an acronym for promoting personal growth. We maximize steam and stewardship of our time, talents, and treasures as we pursue personal investment in these five ways:

STEAM Principle	Explanation	Examples
System (1 Cor. 9:24–27) We are serious …	• lead/challenge self • self-discipline/work • personal growth plan • SMART goals • strategy, hands/feet • sacrifice, investment	• projects, counseling • integrity of heart, personality, character • skill of hand, gifts, strengths, craft, talent • routine, organic
Training (1 Kings 4:29–34) We are tenacious …	• gain info and insight • increase skill/ wisdom • research, data/stats, history, culture • student, homework • hunger, heart	• workshops, seminars, conferences, classes • online, books, audio, podcasts, webcasts • lessons, coaching • tools, resources
Experience (Rom. 5:3–5) We are embracing …	• time in/on the field • high quantity/ quality • practice within area • learn while doing • on-the-job-training • exercise, pressure	• volunteer in/ outside your home church • local neighborhood, community events • county, city, state • nationally, globally
Aspiration (Eph. 2:8–10) We are affirming …	• motivation/passion • inner drive/fire/ flame • calling, purpose, vision, dream, desire, divine fingerprint • target, aim, shoot • predestined, design	• prayer/fasting • Experiencing God study and The Purpose Driven Life study (spiritual gifts, heart, abilities, personality, experiences= SHAPE)
Mentoring (2 Tim. 2:1–7) We are meeting …	• apprenticeship model • accountable, faithful, teachable, servant, reputation • favor, relational networking, influence	• someone ahead that you admire • someone alongside that you respect • someone behind that you believe in

———

[239] Merriam-Webster dictionary | www.merriam-webster.com | www.learnersdictionary.com
[240] Matt. 20:8; 25:14–30; Luke 19:11–27 | Luke 12:42; 16:1–8; Rom. 16:23; 1 Cor. 4:1–2; Gal. 4:2; Titus 1:7; 1 Pet. 4:10
[241] *Strong's Exhaustive Concordance of the Bible* | Blue Letter Bible | www.blueletterbible.org

Love, grace, and peace …

♪Colossians 3:16,

Rodney

Take a moment to meditate, muse, and memorize God's word. What is the Holy Spirit saying to you right now?

_____

_____

_____

_____

_____

_____

_____

_____

_____

_____

_____

_____

_____

_____

_____

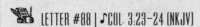 LETTER #88 | ♪COL. 3:23–24 (NKJV)

STEAM

~Part 2~

[n. Steam: the strength, force, or energy that allows someone to continue, to go faster, etc. // I was making good progress this morning, but now I'm starting to run out of steam.][242]

Matthew 25:20–23 (NKJV)[243]

20 "So he who had received five talents came and brought five other talents, saying, 'Lord, you delivered to me five talents; look, I have gained five more talents besides them.'

21 "His lord said to him, 'Well done, good[G18] and faithful[G4103] servant; you were faithful[G4103] over a few things, I will make you ruler over many things. Enter into the joy of your lord.'

22 "He also who had received two talents came and said, 'Lord, you delivered to me two talents; look, I have gained two more talents besides them.'

23 "His lord said to him, 'Well done, good[G18] and faithful[G4103] servant; you have been faithful[G4103] over a few things, I will make you ruler over many things. Enter into the joy of your lord.'

[G18] ἀγαθός agathós, ag-ath-os'; a primary word; "good" (in any sense, often as noun):—benefit, good(-s, things), well. Compare G2570.
[G4103] πιστός pistós, pis-tos'; from G3982; objectively, trustworthy; subjectively, trustful:—believe(-ing, -r), faithful(-ly), sure, true.[244]

Dear Worship Leader,

The Lord gifted me this resource after my administrative assistant, Loukisha Bridges, asked for a practical tool and bridge to help individuals on our worship team thrive and not merely survive. We want to be like the good and faithful servants in Matthew 25 who gained talents. They multiplied the Lord's investment, gave Him interest on His return, and didn't dig a hole in the ground to hide their gift. So they heard, "Well done, good and faithful servant."

Operating at full STEAM requires a *system* that keeps us sharp. It incorporates key elements of our craft into our daily or weekly regimes. It's being intentional and consistent over time. Good singers sing at home, in the car, at work, in church, at the store, in the mall, etc. They're constantly singing, humming, and listening to music. That's part of their system. It's one reason they're great at what they do. They do it all the time!

You might ask, "How will I know what habits or practices I need to incorporate into my life?" That's where *training* comes in. Good singers become good by studying good to great singers. They learn to do and think like skilled singers. Every trade has a culture and philosophy. Immerse yourself into it.

That leads us to *experience.* It can really prove to be an excellent teacher! Singing in the shower is one thing. Singing in front of a crowd is another animal. We only get better by doing what we study and love. Start small, stay at it, and grow from there.

---

[242] Merriam-Webster dictionary | www.merriam-webster.com | www.learnersdictionary.com
[243] Phil. 2:13; Matt. 13; Mark 4:19; 1 Cor. 3:7; ♪Col. 2:19; 2 Cor. 8:7; 9:6–8; 1 Thess. 3:12; 2 Pet. 1:8; 3:18; Heb. 6:10
[244] *Strong's Exhaustive Concordance of the Bible* | Blue Letter Bible | www.blueletterbible.org

This requires *aspiration* and drive. I've learned that only God can give this. Good singers have to want to learn to sing. We sow, plant, and water seeds, but only God gives increase.

That's why *mentoring* is critical. For full STEAM, we need those ahead seeding and sowing into the soul/soil of our lives.

Love, grace, and peace …

♪Colossians 3:16,

Rodney

Take a moment to meditate, muse, and memorize God's word. What is the Holy Spirit saying to you right now?

_____

_____

_____

_____

_____

_____

_____

_____

_____

_____

_____

_____

 LETTER #89 | ♪COL. 3:25 (NKJV)

SEX

[n. Sex: physical activity that is related to and often includes sexual intercourse]245

Proverbs 5:15–23 (NKJV)

15 Drink water from your own cistern,
And running water from your own well.
16 Should your fountains be dispersed abroad,
Streams of water in the streets?
17 Let them be only your own,
And not for strangers with you.
18 Let your fountain be blessed,
And rejoice with the wife of your youth.
19 As a loving deer and a graceful doe,
Let her breasts satisfy you at all times;
And always be enraptured with her love.
[H160]

20 For why should you, my son, be enraptured by an immoral woman,
And be embraced in the arms of a seductress?
21 For the ways of man are before the eyes of the LORD,
And He ponders all his paths.
22 His own iniquities entrap the wicked man,
And he is caught in the cords of his sin.
23 He shall die for lack of instruction,
And in the greatness of his folly he shall go astray.

[H160] אַהֲבָה ’ahăbâh, a-hab-aw; feminine of H158 and meaning the same:—love.
[H158] אַהַב ’ahab, ah'-hab; from H157; affection (in a good or a bad sense):—love(-r).
[H157] אָהַב ’âhab, aw-hab'; or אָהֵב ’âhêb ; a primitive root; to have affection for (sexually or otherwise):—(be-) love(-d, -ly, -r), like, friend.246

Dear Worship Leader,

Let's have the love and "sex talk." I'm not sure why the church doesn't teach on it more. Sex is not a taboo subject or a sin. It's not a dirty or profane word. It's not a worldly concept or a consequence from the fall of man. It was happening in the Garden of Eden prior to the serpent showing up in Genesis 3. In Genesis 2:21–25, Adam and his woman, husband and wife, were lovingly and exclusively enjoying each other as one flesh—naked and not ashamed. There was no shame in them being naked and intimate with one another. They were cleaving to each other in the paradise and perfection of God's presence. A portrait of true intimacy, purity, and love.

Sex is God's idea. It was meant for pleasure and procreation. Within the covenant of marriage, there is no greater or deeper connection than being one flesh with one spouse, one person, one man or woman of the opposite sex, for the duration of your life—as long as you both shall live. Selah. Sex is not meant for children or for the unmarried to be playing around with it. It's so special, precious, powerful, and binding that God reserved it for the marriage bed only. Hebrews 13:4 (NKJV) says, "Marriage is honorable among all, and the bed undefiled; but fornicators and adulterers God will judge."

Fire is not a problem for the fireplace. It becomes a problem when it leaves the fireplace and begins burning up the rest of the house. We have a problem today because the fire of sex has left God's fireplace (Proverbs 6:27–30). So our houses are on fire! Our churches are on fire! Our government is on fire! Our entire culture is on fire! The fire of unrestrained

---

245 Merriam-Webster dictionary | www.merriam-webster.com | www.learnersdictionary.com
246 *Strong's Exhaustive Concordance of the Bible* | Blue Letter Bible | www.blueletterbible.org

passion has broken up our families, destroyed our homes, and left our children in chaos and confusion. Someone needs to call 911! We need divine intervention. When sex is experienced God's way, there's heaven on earth. When it's not, there's hell.

Love, grace, and peace …

♪Colossians 3:16,

Rodney

Take a moment to meditate, muse, and memorize God's word. What is the Holy Spirit saying to you right now?

_____

_____

_____

_____

_____

_____

_____

_____

_____

_____

_____

_____

_____

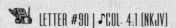 LETTER #90 | ♪COL. 4:1 [NKJV]

SAFETY

[n. Safety: 1) freedom from harm or danger; the state of being safe
2) the state of not being dangerous or harmful
3) a place that is free from harm or danger: a safe place][247]

Proverbs 18:10–12; 29:25 (KJV)[248]

10 The name of the LORD is a strong tower: the righteous runneth into it, and is safe.[H7682]
11 The rich man's wealth is his strong city, and as an high wall in his own conceit.
12 Before destruction the heart of man is haughty, and before honour is humility.

25 The fear of man bringeth a snare: but whoso putteth his trust in the LORD shall be safe.[H7682]

[H7682] שָׂגַב **sâgab,** saw-gab'; a primitive root; to be (causatively, make) lofty, especially inaccessible; by implication, safe, strong; used literally and figuratively:—defend, exalt, be excellent, (be, set on) high, lofty, be safe, set up (on high), be too strong.[249]

Dear Worship Leader,

Let's take a "praise break" to thank the Lord our God for safety!

Some trust in chariots, and some in horses: but we will remember the name of the LORD our God. (Psalm 20:7 KJV)

The LORD is my rock, and my fortress, and my deliverer; my God, my strength, in whom I will trust; my buckler, and the horn of my salvation, and my high tower. I will call upon the LORD, who is worthy to be praised: so shall I be saved from mine enemies. (Psalm 18:2–3 KJV)

Lord, with all of the damage suffered or caused in this life, You have proven Yourself to be the ultimate First Responder! Whether burned, bruised, battered, broken, or brokenhearted, You've been faithful, merciful, and gracious!

He that covereth his sins shall not prosper: but whoso confesseth and forsaketh them shall have mercy. (Proverbs 28:13 KJV)

And the LORD passed by before him, and proclaimed, The LORD, The LORD God, merciful and gracious, longsuffering, and abundant in goodness and truth, (Exodus 34:6 KJV)

The LORD is merciful and gracious, slow to anger, and plenteous in mercy. He will not always chide: neither will he keep his anger for ever. He hath not dealt with us after our sins; nor rewarded us according to our iniquities. For as the heaven is high above the earth, so great is his mercy toward them that fear him. As far as the east is from the west, so far hath he removed our transgressions from us. Like as a father pitieth his children, so the LORD pitieth them that fear him. For he knoweth our frame; he remembereth that we are dust. (Psalm 103:8–14 KJV)

[247] Merriam-Webster dictionary | www.merriam-webster.com | www.learnersdictionary.com
[248] Ps. 9:9; 18:2; 46:7, 11; 48:3; 59:9, 16–17; 62:2, 6; 94:22; 144:1–2 | Ps. 106:1; 107:1; 118:1–4, 29; 136:1–26 | Ps. 7:17; 20:7; 102:15, 21; 113:1–2; 116:4, 13, 17; 118:10–12, 26; 122:4; 124:8; 129:8; 135:1; 148:5, 13 | 1 Tim. 1:12–17
[249] *Strong's Exhaustive Concordance of the Bible* | Blue Letter Bible | www.blueletterbible.org

Thank You that we are numbered with the forgiven. The redeemed. Those washed in the blood of the Lamb! Where would we be without Your love, grace, mercy, and blessing?

The LORD bless thee, and keep thee: The LORD make his face shine upon thee, and be gracious unto thee: The LORD lift up his countenance upon thee, and give thee peace. (Numbers 6:24–26 KJV)

Love, grace, and peace …

♪Colossians 3:16,

Rodney

Take a moment to meditate, muse, and memorize God's word. What is the Holy Spirit saying to you right now?

_____

_____

_____

_____

_____

_____

_____

_____

_____

_____

_____

_____

SPIRITUAL CHECKUP: INSPIRE

Review the last ten letters and record any key highlights. Has the Holy Spirit revealed any …

Instruction?

_____

_____

_____

_____

Needs?

_____

_____

_____

_____

Scripture?

_____

_____

_____

_____

Principles?

_____

_____

_____

_____

Interests?

_____

_____

_____

_____

Reproof?

_____

_____

_____

_____

Encouragement?

_____

_____

_____

_____

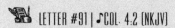 LETTER #91 | ♪COL. 4:2 (NKJV)

SONGWRITING

[n. Song: 1) the act or art of singing
2) poetical composition
3a) a short musical composition of words and music
3b) a collection of such compositions
4a) a melody for a lyric poem or ballad
4b) a poem easily set to music][250]

———— ∞∞∞ ————

Psalm 40:1–3 (NKJV)[251]

To the Chief Musician. A Psalm of David.
1 I waited patiently for the LORD;
And He inclined to me,
And heard my cry.
2 He also brought me up out of a horrible pit,
Out of the miry clay,
And set my feet upon a rock,
And established my steps.
3 He has put a new song[H7892] in my mouth—
Praise to our God;
Many will see it and fear,
And will trust in the LORD.

———— ∞∞∞ ————

1 Kings 4:32 (NKJV)

32 He spoke three thousand proverbs, and his songs[H7892] were one thousand and five.

———— ∞∞∞ ————

[H7892] שִׁיר shîyr, sheer; or feminine שִׁירָה shîyrâh; from H7891; a song; abstractly, singing:—musical(-ick), × sing(-er, -ing), song.[252]

Dear Worship Leader,

When it comes to songwriting, I often hear people say, "I can't write songs. I'm not a songwriter." Let's settle this. According to Psalm 40:3, God can put a new song in your mouth for His praise, glory, and honor. Will you believe this verse with me, for yourself? I already believe it for you! I've personally witnessed God do this for many believers that originally claimed to be "nonsingers" or "nonmusicians." My question is always "Do you have a testimony?" If you have a testimony (Psalm 40:1–2), you have a song, actually more than one! Your seeds/soil just need to be fertilized in the Spirit, the Word, prayer, and faith.

- Ask God to give you a verse from the Bible.
  - It can be a meaningful or misquoted verse that you want to meditate and memorize. You can also take it from a recent reading, sermon, devotion, or study. For demonstration, I usually have individuals start with Psalm 119. I ask them to pick a number from 1 to 176, and we start songwriting from the corresponding verse. Like verse 11 or 54, they're all short poetic verses that are easy to put to rhythm and melody.
- Ask God to give you a rhythm for that verse.
  - Read the verse out loud *in repetition*. Do this several times. Think about its meaning and significance. What is the Holy Spirit saying to you through this verse? Meditate/muse on it.
  - Read the verse out loud *in rhythm*. Add emphasis and inflection. Do this until you hear a beat, pulse, cadence, rhythm, or tempo develop. Don't stop until it does!
- Ask God to give you a melody for that rhythm and verse.

[250] Merriam-Webster dictionary | www.merriam-webster.com | www.learnersdictionary.com
[251] Ps. 28:7; 32:7; 33:3; 40:3; 42:8; 69:30; 77:6; 81:2; 95:2; 96:1; 98:1, 4–5; 105:2; 118:14; 137:3–4; 144:9; 149:1
[252] *Strong's Exhaustive Concordance of the Bible* | Blue Letter Bible | www.blueletterbible.org

    ○ Sing the verse out loud *in repetition*. Yes, in faith, it's time to actually sing something! You're simply adding musical notes to the rhythm you've already established. Do this repeatedly until you hear a melody develop. Don't stop until it does!

Congratulations! You've just written a scripture song! And there's nothing more potent than a song drawn from the eternal wellspring of life, Christ, the Word of God Himself! Be sure to save it, sing it, submit to it, and share it. I'm so excited for you!

Love, grace, and peace …

♪Colossians 3:16,

Rodney

Take a moment to meditate, muse, and memorize God's word. What is the Holy Spirit saying to you right now?

_____

_____

_____

_____

_____

_____

_____

_____

_____

_____

_____

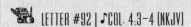 LETTER #92 | ♪COL. 4:3–4 (NKJV)

SCRIPTURE

[n. Scripture: 1a) the books of the Bible—often used in plural; a passage from the Bible
1b) a body of writings considered sacred or authoritative][253]

———— ⬤⬤⬤ ————

2 Timothy 4:6–13 (NKJV)

6 For I am already being poured out as a drink offering, and the time of my departure is at hand.
7 I have fought the good fight, I have finished the race, I have kept the faith.
8 Finally, there is laid up for me the crown of righteousness, which the Lord, the righteous Judge, will give to me on that Day, and not to me only but also to all who have loved His appearing.
9 Be diligent to come to me quickly;
10 for Demas has forsaken me, having loved this present world, and has departed for Thessalonica—Crescens for Galatia, Titus for Dalmatia.
11 Only Luke is with me. Get Mark and bring him with you, for he is useful to me for ministry.
12 And Tychicus I have sent to Ephesus.
13 Bring the cloak that I left with Carpus at Troas when you come—and the books,[G975] especially the parchments.

———— ⬤⬤⬤ ————

[G975] βιβλίον biblíon, bib-lee'-on; a diminutive of G976; a roll:—bill, book, scroll, writing.[254]

Dear Worship Leader,

In 2 Timothy 4, the apostle Paul is preparing to die as a martyr for the faith. Even so, he requests that Timothy bring him the books, and especially the parchments, so he could still grow, read, learn, write, and study the scriptures (4:13)!

Are you a lifelong learner and student of the Bible? I once heard that if we study any subject matter for just fifteen minutes a day, in the span of three years we would be at the mastery level. That's over 16,000 minutes of study or more than 270 hours! As a graduate of Criswell College in Dallas, Texas, where I received my MA in Christian studies, Mrs. W. A. Criswell, Betty, was said to be known for the following words: "No Bible, no breakfast!" Now imagine if we lived by that rule.

The Holy Bible is the number one bestseller and is by far the greatest historical book of all time! How well do you know the Bible?

- Learn to recite the books of the Bible in order, by memory. Consider learning them through song; even a fun, playful, silly song will work!
  - 39 books in the Old Testament (OT)
    - 5—the Law/Pentateuch (Genesis–Deuteronomy)
    - 12—history (Joshua–Esther)
    - 5—poetry and wisdom (Job–Song of Solomon)
    - 5—major prophets (Isaiah–Daniel)
    - 12—minor prophets (Hosea–Malachi)
  - 27 books in the New Testament (NT)
    - 4—Gospels (Matthew–John)

---

[253] Merriam-Webster dictionary | www.merriam-webster.com | www.learnersdictionary.com
[254] *Strong's Exhaustive Concordance of the Bible* | Blue Letter Bible | www.blueletterbible.org

- 1—church history (Acts)
- 13—Pauline epistles (Romans–Philemon)
- 8—general epistles (Hebrews–Jude)
- 1—prophecy (Revelation)
- Commit to a daily, weekly, monthly, or annual reading plan that interests you.
- Memorize and share verses regularly with others in your circle.
- Enroll in a Bible study class/course online at a church/seminary.
  - Learn the Hebrew language for a deep dive into the Old Testament and/or Greek for the New Testament.
  - Volunteer to assist the instructor and maybe lead someday.
- Invest in good Bible study materials, resources, and tools.

Love, grace, and peace …

♪Colossians 3:16,

Rodney

Take a moment to meditate, muse, and memorize God's word. What is the Holy Spirit saying to you right now?

_____
_____
_____
_____
_____
_____
_____
_____
_____
_____

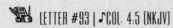 LETTER #93 | ♪ COL. 4:5 (NKJV)

SUCCESS

[n. Success: 1a) degree or measure of succeeding
1b) favorable or desired outcome also: the attainment of wealth, favor, or eminence
2) one that succeeds][255]

Psalm 1:1–6 (NKJV)

1 Blessed is the man
Who walks not in the counsel of the ungodly,
Nor stands in the path of sinners,
Nor sits in the seat of the scornful;
2 But his delight is in the law of the Lord,
And in His law he meditates day and night.
3 He shall be like a tree
Planted by the rivers of water,
That brings forth its fruit in its season,
Whose leaf also shall not wither;
And whatever he does shall prosper.[H6743]
4 The ungodly are not so,
But are like the chaff which the wind drives away.
5 Therefore the ungodly shall not stand in the judgment,
Nor sinners in the congregation of the righteous.
6 For the Lord knows the way of the righteous,
But the way of the ungodly shall perish.

[H6743] צָלַח **tsâlach,** tsaw-lakh'; or צָלֵחַ tsâlêach; a primitive root; to push forward, in various senses (literal or figurative, transitive or intransitive):—break out, come (mightily), go over, be good, be meet, be profitable, (cause to, effect, make to, send) prosper(-ity, -ous, -ously).[256]

Dear Worship Leader,

What is success or prosperity to you? How you and I answer this question is crucial because we don't want to spend our lives building the tower of Babel only to have the Lord come down and destroy it due to His displeasure (Genesis 11:1–9). Unless the Lord builds our house, we labor in vain when we build it (Psalm 127:1). True success is measured by God's plan and measuring stick. It's living a life on track with His purpose and will for our lives (Matthew 12:50). Matthew 6:33 (NKJV) wisely instructs, "But seek first the kingdom of God and His righteousness, and all these things shall be added to you." This is filling life's basket with the big rocks first (Psalm 128).

Jesus is our Conductor. He's guiding the train, the orchestra, and the choir of our lives. Constant communication with Him is key to life's success. That's why Psalm 1 is foundational for the believer. As a lighthouse, it illuminates for us what the blessed life looks like. The way we walk, stand, and sit is different from the world. Our delight, what lights us up, is the same thing that lights up heaven: God's will and word (Psalm 37:3–7, 11, 23). We meditate/muse on what pleases God. We're tuned to His frequency. In Psalm 1, verse 3 only happens as a result of verses 1 and 2. Our fruitfulness in verse 3 is God being faithful to the foundation previously laid with His counsel, His path, His seat—His law, light, and word.

As long as King Uzziah sought the Lord, God made him to prosper (2 Chronicles 26:5, 16). Joseph had favor and success because the Lord was with him (Genesis 39:2–3, 21, 23). Peter and John were perceived as uneducated and

---

255 Merriam-Webster dictionary | www.merriam-webster.com | www.learnersdictionary.com
256 *Strong's Exhaustive Concordance of the Bible* | Blue Letter Bible | www.blueletterbible.org

untrained men but were bold because they had been with Jesus (Acts 4:13). Like Joshua, in Joshua 1:8, we too can be strong and very courageous with God's word as our firm foundation. Only then does God guarantee good success.

Love, grace, and peace …

♪Colossians 3:16,

Rodney

Take a moment to meditate, muse, and memorize God's word. What is the Holy Spirit saying to you right now?

_____

_____

_____

_____

_____

_____

_____

_____

_____

_____

_____

_____

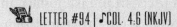 LETTER #94 | ♪COL. 4:6 (NKJV)

THEOLOGY

[n. Theology: the study of religious faith, practice, and experience, especially: the study of God and of God's relation to the world][257]

Ephesians 1:17–23 (NKJV)[258]

17 that the God[G2316] **of our Lord Jesus Christ, the Father of glory, may give to you the spirit of wisdom and revelation in the knowledge of Him,**
18 the eyes of your understanding being enlightened; that you may know what is the hope of His calling, what are the riches of the glory of His inheritance in the saints,
19 and what is the exceeding greatness of His power toward us who believe, according to the working of His mighty power
20 which He worked in Christ when He raised Him from the dead and seated Him at His right hand in the heavenly places,
21 far above all principality and power and might and dominion, and every name that is named, not only in this age but also in that which is to come.
22 And He put all things under His feet, and gave Him to be head over all things to the church,
23 which is His body, the fullness of Him who fills all in all.

[G2316] θεός theós, theh'-os; of uncertain affinity; a deity, especially (with G3588) the supreme Divinity; figuratively, a magistrate; by Hebraism, very:—X exceeding, God, god(-ly, -ward).[259]

Dear Worship Leader,

Our theology, what we believe about God, affects every decision we make, both personally and professionally. It is the highest and greatest revelation one can have, that of God Himself. That's what's so awesome about the following exchange between God and Moses in Exodus 33:17–23 (NKJV):

So the LORD said to Moses, "I will also do this thing that you have spoken; for you have found grace in My sight, and I know you by name." And he said, "Please, show me Your glory." Then He said, "I will make all My goodness pass before you, and I will proclaim the name of the LORD before you. I will be gracious to whom I will be gracious, and I will have compassion on whom I will have compassion." But He said, "You cannot see My face; for no man shall see Me, and live." And the LORD said, "Here is a place by Me, and you shall stand on the rock. "So it shall be, while My glory passes by, that I will put you in the cleft of the rock, and will cover you with My hand while I pass by. "Then I will take away My hand, and you shall see My back; but My face shall not be seen."

Here's Isaiah's experience with God in Isaiah 6:1–4 (NKJV):

In the year that King Uzziah died, I saw the Lord sitting on a throne, high and lifted up, and the train of His robe filled the temple. Above it stood seraphim; each one had six wings: with two he covered his face, with two he covered his feet, and with two he flew. And one cried to another and said: "Holy, holy, holy is the

---

257 Merriam-Webster dictionary | www.merriam-webster.com | www.learnersdictionary.com
258 Exod. 3:1–4:17; 6:2–7:7; 14:30–15:21; 19:1–25 (9, 20); 20:1–26 (21); 33:1–23 (11, 15–16); Num. 12:3–8; Ps. 103:7
259 *Strong's Exhaustive Concordance of the Bible* | Blue Letter Bible | www.blueletterbible.org

Lord of hosts; The whole earth is full of His glory!" And the posts of the door were shaken by the voice of him who cried out, and the house was filled with smoke.

Have you ever had God reveal Himself to you in a special way? If not, ask Him to. As worship leaders, experiencing God and growing in the knowledge of Him are paramount to our effectiveness. A serious study of the attributes of God will set you on a life-changing course that will revolutionize your worship leading. I am forever indebted to God for books like *Our God Is Awesome* by Tony Evans and *The Knowledge of the Holy* by A. W. Tozer. They helped jumpstart my pursuit of God.

Love, grace, and peace …

♪Colossians 3:16,

Rodney

Take a moment to meditate, muse, and memorize God's word. What is the Holy Spirit saying to you right now?

_____

_____

_____

_____

_____

_____

_____

_____

_____

_____

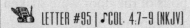 LETTER #95 | ♪COL. 4:7–9 (NKJV)

TABERNACLE

[n. Tabernacle: 1a) a tent sanctuary used by the Israelites during the Exodus 1b) a dwelling place][260]

Exodus 25:8–9; 29:43–46 (NKJV)[261]

8 "And let them make Me a sanctuary, that I may dwell[H7931] among them.
9 "According to all that I show you, that is, the pattern of the tabernacle[H4908] and the pattern of all its furnishings, just so you shall make it.

43 "And there I will meet with the children of Israel, and the tabernacle shall be sanctified by My glory.
44 "So I will consecrate the tabernacle of meeting and the altar. I will also consecrate both Aaron and his sons to minister to Me as priests.
45 "I will dwell[H7931] among the children of Israel and will be their God.
46 "And they shall know that I am the LORD their God, who brought them up out of the land of Egypt, that I may dwell[H7931] among them. I am the LORD their God.

[H4908] מִשְׁכָּן mishkân, mish-kawn'; from H7931; a residence (including a shepherd's hut, the lair of animals, figuratively, the grave; also the Temple); specifically, the Tabernacle (properly, its wooden walls):—dwelleth, dwelling (place), habitation, tabernacle, tent.
[H7931] שָׁכַן shâkan, shaw-kan'; a primitive root (apparently akin (by transmission) to H7901 through the idea of lodging; compare H5531, H7925); to reside or permanently stay (literally or figuratively):—abide, continue, (cause to, make to) dwell(-er), have habitation, inhabit, lay, place, (cause to) remain, rest, set (up).[262]

Dear Worship Leader,

Our God personally loves us and wants to dwell with us. Prior to the Lord delivering the Israelites from bondage, He made it abundantly clear that He wanted His people free to worship and serve Him. That was His message to Pharaoh in Exodus 5:1 (NKJV). "Let My people go that they may hold a feast to Me in the wilderness." Along with the ten plagues He sent to Pharaoh, He repeatedly sent the same message over and over again. "Let My people go (Exodus 7:16; 8:1, 20–21; 9:1, 13; 10:3–4)!" Know this: God is unwaveringly resolute about our full deliverance and us dwelling with Him freely.

That's why He instructed the children of Israel to make a sanctuary and tabernacle (Exodus 25:8–9). We have a God who wants to be close to us. He loves us. But His love for us does not cancel out His holiness and the truth that He hates sin. That's where the problem lies. We have a holy and sinless God loving a sinful and unholy people. The tabernacle was a way of temporarily offering a bridge between fallen humankind and a perfect God. It's really a foreshadow of the Man Christ Jesus—Mediator between God and men (1 Timothy 2:5–6). A careful study of the tabernacle's elements and pattern will reveal God's relentless desire to passionately pursue us and close the sin gap—all in an effort to dwell with and tabernacle among us!

• the courtyard (for main access to the tabernacle)

---

[260] Merriam-Webster dictionary | www.merriam-webster.com | www.learnersdictionary.com
[261] Exod. 25–40; Lev. 16; Heb. 6:19–20; 7:24–27; 8–13 (8:6; 9:15; 10:19; 12:24); ♪Col. 1:13, 20; 2:14–15; 3:1; Rev. 21:3
[262] Strong's Exhaustive Concordance of the Bible | Blue Letter Bible | www.blueletterbible.org

- o   the bronze altar (for priests to offer sacrifices)
- o   the bronze laver (for priests to cleanse themselves)
- the holy place (outer room—for priests to perform daily tasks)
  - o   the golden lampstand (for daily continual oil burning)
  - o   the altar of incense (for offering incense twice a day)
  - o   the table of the bread of the presence (fresh weekly bread)
  - o   the veil/curtain (barrier of separation crossed once a year)
- the most holy place (inner room—for God's very presence)
  - o   the Ark of the Covenant (mercy seat and Day of Atonement)

Love, grace, and peace …

♪Colossians 3:16,

Rodney

Take a moment to meditate, muse, and memorize God's word. What is the Holy Spirit saying to you right now?

_____

_____

_____

_____

_____

_____

_____

_____

_____

_____

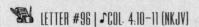 LETTER #96 | ♪COL. 4:10–11 (NKJV)

TRANSITION

[n. Transition: a change or shift from one state, subject, place, etc. to another][263]

—ⴲⴲⴲ—

Acts 15:36–41 (NKJV)

36 Then after some days Paul said to Barnabas, "Let us now go back and visit our brethren in every city where we have preached the word of the Lord, and see how they are doing."
37 Now Barnabas was determined to take with them John called Mark.
38 But Paul insisted that they should not take with them the one who had departed[G868] from them in Pamphylia, and had not gone with them to the work.
39 Then the contention became so sharp that they parted from one another. And so Barnabas took Mark and sailed to Cyprus;
40 but Paul chose Silas and departed, being commended by the brethren to the grace of God.
41 And he went through Syria and Cilicia, strengthening the churches.

—ⴲⴲⴲ—

[G868] ἀφίστημι aphístēmi, af-is'-tay-mee; from G575 and G2476; to remove, i.e. (actively) instigate to revolt; usually (reflexively) to desist, desert, etc.:—depart, draw (fall) away, refrain, withdraw self.[264]

2 Timothy 4:9–11 (NKJV)

9 Be diligent to come to me quickly;
10 for Demas has forsaken me, having loved this present world, and has departed for Thessalonica—Crescens for Galatia, Titus for Dalmatia.
11 Only Luke is with me. Get Mark and bring him with you, for he is useful to me for ministry.

Dear Worship Leader,

As the old hymn states, "Time is filled with swift transition." Transitions are probably one of the most difficult things to do well—for individuals, families, places of employment, and even churches. There are usually so many factors involved. It requires a lot of grace and forgiveness on everyone's part. Early on, I was told to try to always leave in a way that I would be welcomed back. I believe gratitude and blessing are keys to this. We want to enter a place or position saturated with gratitude and blessing, and that's exactly how we want to exit. Unfortunately, many times there are numerous hurdles to overcome combating our desire to do so.

We live in a fallen world with fallen people—filled with fallen experiences and tendencies. James 4:1 (NKJV) puts it plainly by asking, "Where do wars and fights come from among you? Do they not come from your desires for pleasure that war in your members?" We are people of war. We have wars and fights on the inside controlling the wars and fights on the outside. Once you add to that personality differences, personal preferences, political agendas, wounded emotions, unmet expectations, offenses, triggers, reminders, and a host of other misunderstandings and miscommunication, you'll see why the only means of winning is through the divine grace of God.

From Genesis to Revelation, transitions are everywhere. The only one that always did it perfectly and without error every

263 Merriam-Webster dictionary | www.merriam-webster.com | www.learnersdictionary.com
264 *Strong's Exhaustive Concordance of the Bible* | Blue Letter Bible | www.blueletterbible.org

time was Jesus—full of grace and truth (John 1:14, 17). And even so, He suffered and endured transition on an old rugged cross, from hostile sinners against Himself (Hebrews 12:2–3). Paul and Barnabas's contention over taking Mark became so sharp that they parted ways! But before his martyrdom, Paul specifically asked for Mark (2 Timothy 4:11). Selah. What a portrait of God's amazing grace! May we all grow in forgiveness and grace amid life's swift transitions.

Love, grace, and peace …

♪Colossians 3:16,

Rodney

Take a moment to meditate, muse, and memorize God's word. What is the Holy Spirit saying to you right now?

_____

_____

_____

_____

_____

_____

_____

_____

_____

_____

_____

 LETTER #97 | ♪COL. 4:12 (NKJV)

UNDERSTANDING

[n. Understanding: the knowledge and ability to judge a particular situation or subject][265]

1 Kings 3:11–14 (NKJV)[266]

11 Then God said to him: "Because you have asked this thing, and have not asked long life for yourself, nor have asked riches for yourself, nor have asked the life of your enemies, but have asked for yourself understanding[H995] to discern justice,
12 "behold, I have done according to your words; see, I have given you a wise and understanding[H995] heart, so that there has not been anyone like you before you, nor shall any like you arise after you.
13 "And I have also given you what you have not asked: both riches and honor, so that there shall not be anyone like you among the kings all your days.
14 "So if you walk in My ways, to keep My statutes and My commandments, as your father David walked, then I will lengthen your days."

[H995] בִּין **bîyn,** bene; a primitive root; to separate mentally (or distinguish), i.e.(generally) understand:—attend, consider, be cunning, diligently, direct, discern, eloquent, feel, inform, instruct, have intelligence, know, look well to, mark, perceive, be prudent, regard, (can) skill(-full), teach, think, (cause, make to, get, give, have) understand(-ing), view, (deal) wise(-ly, man).[267]

Dear Worship Leader,

Imagine with me: what if the Lord appeared to you in a dream one night and said, "Ask! What shall I give you?"

Take a moment now to close your eyes and ponder that question.

What types of answers flood your mind? Remember this is the Lord of the heavens and the earth. There is nothing outside His realm that He can't offer you or do for you. Nothing too hard for Him. Nothing too big or small. Nothing.

Well, as you may already know, this actually happened to King Solomon at the very beginning of his reign over the children of Israel. I absolutely love this story.

If I were a grieving son, a young adult, a new leader, and now the most powerful man in the kingdom, I truly wonder what my answer would be. Solomon, in his dream—while still asleep—answered, "Give to Your servant an understanding heart to judge Your people, that I may discern between good and evil (3:9)." Wow. Not quite what I would have expected. But for Solomon, understanding was that big of a deal! More important to him than longevity, riches, or revenge over his enemies. And because of such, God rewarded him with more.

Unfortunately, not all leaders are in this for the same reason. Some are in it for selfish gain: fame, fortune, fanfare, power, prestige, and position. Serving the King of kings without

---

[265] Merriam-Webster dictionary | www.merriam-webster.com | www.learnersdictionary.com
[266] 1 Kings 3:1–28; 4:29; 2 Chron. 1:1–12; 26:5; Prov. 2:10–12; 6:27–7:5 | Prov. 2:11; 4:6; 6:22, 24; 7:5 | 1 Cor. 14:15, 20; Eph. 1:18; 4:18; ♪Col. 1:9; 2:2; James 3:13; 1 Chron. 12:32; Ps. 32:9; 119:34, 73, 99, 104, 125, 130, 144, 169
[267] *Strong's Exhaustive Concordance of the Bible* | Blue Letter Bible | www.blueletterbible.org

notoriety and honor is nowhere in their dreams. What about us? What do we really want? What's your innermost desire and motive? Solomon loved the Lord (3:3). He worshiped Him before and after this dream (3:4, 15). In writing Proverbs, Solomon uses the word "understanding" fifty-two times (NKJV)! That's a lot of wealth. Just how rich do you want to be?

Love, grace, and peace …

♪Colossians 3:16,

Rodney

Take a moment to meditate, muse, and memorize God's word. What is the Holy Spirit saying to you right now?

_____

_____

_____

_____

_____

_____

_____

_____

_____

_____

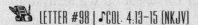 LETTER #98 | ♪COL. 4:13-15 (NKJV)

UNITY

[n. Unity: the state of being in full agreement: harmony][268]

Psalm 133:1–3 (NKJV)[269]

A Song of Ascents. Of David.
1 Behold, how good and how pleasant it is
For brethren to dwell together in unity![H3162]
2 It is like the precious oil upon the head,
Running down on the beard,
The beard of Aaron,
Running down on the edge of his garments.
3 It is like the dew of Hermon,
Descending upon the mountains of Zion;
For there the LORD commanded the blessing—
Life forevermore.

[H3162] יַחַד **yachad**, yakh'-ad; from H3161; properly, a unit, i.e. (adverb) unitedly:—alike, at all (once), both, likewise, only, (al-) together, withal.

[H3161] יָחַד **yâchad**, yaw-khad'; a primitive root; to be (or become) one:—join, unite.[270]

Proverbs 6:16–19 (NKJV)

16 These six things the LORD hates,
Yes, seven are an abomination to Him:
17 A proud look,
A lying tongue,
Hands that shed innocent blood,
18 A heart that devises wicked plans,
Feet that are swift in running to evil,
19 A false witness who speaks lies,
And one who sows discord among brethren.

Dear Worship Leader,

Unity has to be contended and fought for within the body. It doesn't come or remain easily. Ephesians 4:3 calls for us to be diligent, to endeavor—to eagerly make every effort to keep and maintain the unity of the Spirit in the bond of peace! As leaders we must spiritually be on guard, on watch, and on duty to protect the unity of the Spirit in the bond, or band of peace.

Please don't mistake peace for passivity. Full armor requires having our feet shod with the preparation of the gospel of peace (Ephesians 6:15). With these feet, we can trample on serpents and scorpions and over all the power of the enemy (Luke 10:19). When Christ was raised from the dead and seated at the right hand of the Father in heavenly places, far above all principality and power and might and dominion, and every name that is named, not only in this age but also in that which is to come, the Father put all things under His feet and gave Him to be the head over all things to the church, which is His body, the fullness of Him who fills all in all (Ephesians 1:20–23). Through Christ we're authorized to step on the enemy's head in fight for His people, His church!

So fight! Selah. Roll up your sleeves and give it your best shot. Too much is at stake. The benefits from being on one accord are too great to bypass, and the collateral damage from not being on one accord is too devastating and heartbreaking. So you've got this! It's going to take blood, sweat, and tears, but you've got

---

[268] Merriam-Webster dictionary | www.merriam-webster.com | www.learnersdictionary.com
[269] 2 Chron. 5:11–14; Matt. 18:15–20; Acts 1:12–14 (14); 2:1–4 (1), 41–47 (46); 4:24, 31; 5:12–16 (12); 7:57; 8:4–8 (6); 12:20; 15:23–29 (25); 18:12; 19:29; Luke 14:18; Phil. 2:1–4 (2); 1 Cor. 1:10–17 (10); 11:17–22; 12:1–31; 14:1–40
[270] *Strong's Exhaustive Concordance of the Bible* | Blue Letter Bible | www.blueletterbible.org

this! You were made for this battle! You were called for this! It won't be easy, but that's what the anointing is for. You were oiled for this fight, for this calling, and for this service. So with all humility and gentleness, with patience, bearing with one another in love, fight (Ephesians 4:2)! Until hell and the enemy are on the run, unity is restored, and heaven shows up!

Love, grace, and peace …

♪Colossians 3:16,

Rodney

Take a moment to meditate, muse, and memorize God's word. What is the Holy Spirit saying to you right now?

_____

_____

_____

_____

_____

_____

_____

_____

_____

_____

_____

_____

 LETTER #99 | ♪COL. 4:16 (NKJV)

VISION

[n. Vision: 1) the ability to see: sight or eyesight
2) something that you see or dream especially as part of a religious or supernatural experience][271]

Habakkuk 2:1–4 (NKJV)[272]

**1 I will stand my watch
And set myself on the rampart,
And watch to see what He will say to me,
And what I will answer when I am corrected.
2 Then the LORD answered me and said:**

"Write the vision[H2377]
**And make it plain on tablets,
That he may run who reads it.
3 For the vision**[H2377] **is yet for an appointed time;
But at the end it will speak, and it will not lie.
Though it tarries, wait for it;
Because it will surely come,
It will not tarry.
4 "Behold the proud,
His soul is not upright in him;
But the just shall live by his faith.**

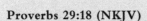

Proverbs 29:18 (NKJV)

18 Where there is no revelation,[H2377] **the people cast off restraint;
But happy is he who keeps the law.**

[H2377] חָזוֹן **châzôwn,** khaw-zone'; from H2372; a sight (mentally), i.e. a dream, revelation, or oracle:—vision.[273]

Dear Worship Leader,

So much of life is driven by vision. Every movie and show we stream on television and watch at the cinema was first conceived in someone's mind long before we saw it. No building, business, or home just magically appears. Before it became a tangible architecture in the physical realm, it had to first be envisioned as an intangible architecture in the heart and soul of some visionary somewhere.

We see this principle at work all throughout scripture, even from the very beginning. Hebrews 11:3 (NKJV) says, "By faith we understand that the worlds were framed by the word of God, so that the things which are seen were not made of things which are visible." That's how the heavens and earth were created. A creative God spoke it all into existence (Genesis 1; John 1:3). All we are, and all we have, is a product of someone's faith, seed, and vision. That is why it's fitting that we honor those who sowed, planted, and watered the fields we now harvest. We benefit today from a vision they birthed long before we got here. Aren't you grateful they had the courage and wisdom to cast well?

But that's what leaders do; we cast vision. For every song we write or teach, for every service we lead, for every project or ministry team we oversee, it all requires divine vision, revelation, and inspiration.

The people *need* a vision. Not two visions. That leads to division. As worship leaders and pastors, our vision for the house we serve has to be submitted and subservient to those that

---

271 Merriam-Webster dictionary | www.merriam-webster.com | www.learnersdictionary.com
272 Joel 2:28; Acts 2:17; 16:9–10; Dan. 1:17; Matt. 12:22–30; Mark 3:22–27; Eph. 4:16; ♪Col. 1:16; 2:2, 19; Rom. 11:36
273 *Strong's Exhaustive Concordance of the Bible* | Blue Letter Bible | www.blueletterbible.org

rule over us (Hebrews 13:7). If we can't do that in good conscience, for the sake of unity in the body, gracefully and graciously transition out! But if our hearts are knit together in love/ labor, cast vision there in faith so that others may also eat.

Love, grace, and peace …

♪Colossians 3:16,

Rodney

Take a moment to meditate, muse, and memorize God's word. What is the Holy Spirit saying to you right now?

_____

_____

_____

_____

_____

_____

_____

_____

_____

_____

_____

_____

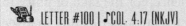 LETTER #100 | ♪COL. 4:17 (NKJV)

WORLD CHANGER

[n. World: the earth with its inhabitants and all things upon it][274]

Matthew 28:16–20 (NKJV)[275]

16 Then the eleven disciples went away into Galilee, to the mountain which Jesus had appointed for them.
17 When they saw Him, they worshiped Him; but some doubted.
18 And Jesus came and spoke to them, saying, "All authority has been given to Me in heaven and on earth.[G1093]
19 "Go therefore and make disciples of all[G3956] the nations,[G1484] baptizing them in the name of the Father and of the Son and of the Holy Spirit,
20 "teaching them to observe all things that I have commanded you; and lo, I am with you always, even to the end of the age." Amen.

[G1093] γῆ **gē,** ghay; contracted from a primary word; soil; by extension a region, or the solid part or the whole of the terrene globe (including the occupants in each application):— country, earth(-ly), ground, land, world.

[G3956] πᾶς **pâs,** pas; including all the forms of declension; apparently a primary word; all, any, every, the whole:—all (manner of, means), alway(-s), any (one), × daily, + ever, every (one, way), as many as, + no(-thing), X thoroughly, whatsoever, whole, whosoever.

[G1484] ἔθνος **éthnos,** eth'-nos; probably from G1486; a race (as of the same habit), i.e. a tribe; specially, a foreign (non-Jewish) one (usually, by implication, pagan):—Gentile, heathen, nation, people.[276]

Dear Worship Leader,

Does your vision only include impacting the people in your community who look like you, talk like you, and sound like you? Is it limited only to the ceiling and four walls of your local church or community center? I hope it includes all of that but that it doesn't stop there. Culturally, we're all probably most comfortable around people that understand our lingo, enjoy similar food, and frequent the same malls. And while being salt and light to this closed select group of individuals is really a good start, let's ask the Holy Spirit to expand our thinking and take us further. Can you imagine having a vision broad enough to include the whole world—people all over the globe? What about the worldwide web (www)?

Well, in what's known as "the Great Commission" in Matthew 28:19–20, Jesus commands His disciples to go and make more disciples of all nations. That means He wants the eleven to increase their scope of ministry, enlarge their circle, and embrace people of all [G1484] ἔθνος éthnos—all races, tongues, and nationalities—for the sake of the gospel. Why is "therefore" found at the top of verse 19? Because, in verse 18, the resurrected Jesus says that He's been given all authority in all places, heaven and earth. Therefore, He's handing them keys authorizing them to go viral with the good news gospel—to all places, for all people, with all power!

In closing, the vision God has given me and my wife is discipleship through music, based

---

274 Merriam-Webster dictionary | www.merriam-webster.com | www.learnersdictionary.com
275 Mark 16:14–18; Luke 24:36–49; John 20:19–23; Acts 1:6–8; 17:6; 1 John 2:15–17; John 15:18–25; Matt. 16:26; Ps. 9:8; 17:14; 18:15; 19:4; 22:27; 24:1; 33:8; 49:1; 50:12; 77:18; 89:11; 90:2; 93:1; 96:10, 13; 97:4; 98:7, 9; 100:1–5 (3)
276 *Strong's Exhaustive Concordance of the Bible* | Blue Letter Bible | www.blueletterbible.org

on ♪Colossians 3:16. It's to develop and disciple all nations, imprinting hearts and minds with kingdom truth. As worshippers, warriors, and world changers, with grace in our hearts to the Lord, singing psalms and hymns and spiritual songs, teaching and admonishing one another, *so the word of Christ dwells in us richly in all wisdom.*

Love, grace, and peace …

♪Colossians 3:16,

Rodney

Take a moment to meditate, muse, and memorize God's word. What is the Holy Spirit saying to you right now?

_____

_____

_____

_____

_____

_____

_____

_____

_____

_____

_____

_____

SPIRITUAL CHECKUP: INSPIRE

Review the last ten letters and record any key highlights. Has the Holy Spirit revealed any ...

Instruction?

_____

_____

_____

_____

Needs?

_____

_____

_____

_____

Scripture?

_____

_____

_____

_____

Principles?

_____

_____

_____

_____

Interests?

_____

_____

_____

_____

Reproof?

_____

_____

_____

_____

Encouragement?

_____

_____

_____

_____

LIFE APPLICATION LETTER #1 | ♪COL. 4:18 (NKJV)

Χριστός

[G5547] Χριστός Christós, khris-tos'; from G5548; anointed, i.e. the Messiah, an epithet of Jesus:—Christ.[277]

Luke 4:14–22 (NKJV)[278]

14 Then Jesus returned in the power of the Spirit to Galilee, and news of Him went out through all the surrounding region.
15 And He taught in their synagogues, being glorified by all.
16 So He came to Nazareth, where He had been brought up. And as His custom was, He went into the synagogue on the Sabbath day, and stood up to read.
17 And He was handed the book of the prophet Isaiah. And when He had opened the book, He found the place where it was written:
18 "The Spirit of the LORD is upon Me, Because He has anointed[G5548] Me
To preach the gospel to the poor;
He has sent Me to heal the brokenhearted,
To proclaim liberty to the captives
And recovery of sight to the blind,
To set at liberty those who are oppressed;
19 To proclaim the acceptable year of the LORD."
20 Then He closed the book, and gave it back to the attendant and sat down. And the eyes of all who were in the synagogue were fixed on Him.
21 And He began to say to them, "Today this Scripture is fulfilled in your hearing."
22 So all bore witness to Him, and marveled at the gracious words which proceeded out of His mouth. And they said, "Is this not Joseph's son?"

Dear Worship Leader,

Now it's your turn. Read, write, and discuss anything that stands out to you from the passage above and/or the references below. What is the Spirit saying to you? How does it apply to your life today?

_____

_____

_____

_____

_____

_____

_____

_____

_____

_____

_____

_____

_____

_____

[277] *Strong's Exhaustive Concordance of the Bible* | Blue Letter Bible | www.blueletterbible.org
[278] Isa. 9:6; 53; 61:1–2 | Acts 4:23–31 (27); 10:34–43 (38); 2 Cor. 1:15–22 (21); Heb. 1:5–14 (9) | ♪Col. 1:1–4, 7, 24, 27–28; 2:2, 5–6, 8, 11, 17, 20; 3:1, 3–4, 11, 13, 16, 24; 4:3, 12

[G5548] χρίω chríō, khree'-o; probably akin to G5530 through the idea of contact; to smear or rub with oil, i.e. (by implication) to consecrate to an office or religious service:—anoint.[279]

[279] *Strong's Exhaustive Concordance of the Bible* | Blue Letter Bible | www.blueletterbible.org

LIFE APPLICATION LETTER #2 | ♪COL. 3:16 (NKJV)

YIELDING

[v. Yield: to bear or bring forth as a natural product especially as a result of cultivation][280]

————⚬⚬⚬————

John 15:1–17 (NKJV)[281]

1 "I am the true vine, and My Father is the vinedresser.
2 "Every branch in Me that does not bear[G5342] fruit He takes away; and every branch that bears[G5342] fruit He prunes, that it may bear[G5342] more fruit.
3 "You are already clean because of the word which I have spoken to you.
4 "Abide in Me, and I in you. As the branch cannot bear[G5342] fruit of itself, unless it abides in the vine, neither can you, unless you abide in Me.
5 "I am the vine, you are the branches. He who abides in Me, and I in him, bears[G5342] much fruit; for without Me you can do nothing.
6 "If anyone does not abide in Me, he is cast out as a branch and is withered; and they gather them and throw them into the fire, and they are burned.
7 "If you abide in Me, and My words abide in you, you will ask what you desire, and it shall be done for you.
8 "By this My Father is glorified, that you bear[G5342] much fruit; so you will be My disciples.
9 "As the Father loved Me, I also have loved you; abide in My love.
10 "If you keep My commandments, you will abide in My love, just as I have kept My Father's commandments and abide in His love.

Dear Worship Leader,

Again, read, write, and discuss anything that stands out. What is the Spirit saying to you? How does it apply to your life? Finally, use letter #91 to help you write a scripture song from one of the verses.

_____

_____

_____

_____

_____

_____

_____

_____

_____

_____

_____

_____

_____

_____

_____

---

[280] Merriam-Webster dictionary | www.merriam-webster.com | www.learnersdictionary.com
[281] Matt. 13:1–9, 18–23; Mark 4:1–9, 13–20; Luke 8:4–8, 11–15 | Heb. 12:11; Rom. 12:1–2; John 12:20–26; Ps. 1; 128; 2 Pet. 1:5–11; 3:18; Gal. 5:22; 6:9; Eph. 2:10; 4:15; Luke 2:52; James 1:21–27; Acts 9:36–43; 13:36; 2 Tim. 3:16–17

11 "These things I have spoken to you, that My joy may remain in you, and that your joy may be full.

12 "This is My commandment, that you love one another as I have loved you.

13 "Greater love has no one than this, than to lay down one's life for his friends.

14 "You are My friends if you do whatever I command you.

15 "No longer do I call you servants, for a servant does not know what his master is doing; but I have called you friends, for all things that I heard from My Father I have made known to you.

16 "You did not choose Me, but I chose you and appointed you that you should go and bear[G5342] fruit, and that your fruit should remain, that whatever you ask the Father in My name He may give you.

17 "These things I command you, that you love one another.

———⊶⊷———

[G5342] φέρω phérō, fer'-o; a primary verb (for which other, and apparently not cognate ones are used in certain tenses only; namely, οἴω oíō oy'-o; and ἐνέγκω enénkō en-eng'-ko; to "bear" or carry (in a very wide application, literally and figuratively, as follows):—be, bear, bring (forth), carry, come, + let her drive, be driven, endure, go on, lay, lead, move, reach, rushing, uphold.[282]

[282] *Strong's Exhaustive Concordance of the Bible* | Blue Letter Bible | www.blueletterbible.org

 LIFE APPLICATION LETTER #3

YOUR LETTER

[v. Write: to communicate with someone by sending a letter, email, etc.][283]

2 Corinthians 3:1–3 (NKJV)[284]

1 Do we begin again to commend ourselves? Or do we need, as some others, epistles of commendation to you or letters of commendation from you?
2 You are our epistle written[G1449] in our hearts, known and read by all men;
3 clearly you are an epistle of Christ, ministered by us, written[G1449] not with ink but by the Spirit of the living God, not on tablets of stone but on tablets of flesh, that is, of the heart.

[G1449] ἐγγράφω engráphō, eng-graf'-o; from G1722 and G1125; to "engrave", i.e. inscribe:—write (in).[285]

Dear Worship Leader,

This time I want you to write your own letter. For the many people who poured into me, I am their letter—living proof of their ministry. The same is true for you. The focus is not the length of your letter; it's the depth, authenticity, vulnerability, and transparency of it. Write from your heart. Write from a place of divine revelation, inspiration, personal testimony, and experience. Flow in grace and truth—and truth in love. Edify the body of Christ and build it up. Use any of the letters in scripture as your model and guide. And if it helps, you can also use any of mine as a starting place as well. My letters are by no means perfect, but they were written from the bottom of my heart. But now it's your turn. Someone needs to hear your voice. So write as led by the Lord and filled with His Spirit. You may use whatever passage or verse you'd like as your launching pad. And as the Lord prompts you, be willing to share it with someone else. In fact, ask Him to lead you to the right person(s) at the right time. His word will not return void. It will accomplish all that He purposes and plans. And only in heaven will you be able to fully see with your own eyes all the fruit you will have produced. So sow in faith; God will give the increase.

_____

_____

_____

_____

_____

_____

---

[283] Merriam-Webster dictionary | www.merriam-webster.com | www.learnersdictionary.com
[284] 1 Thess. 2:1–20 (8, 19–20); Acts 4:13–22 (13); 20:17–38; Isa. 55:8–11; 2 Cor. 7:8–12 (8); 9:6–15 (8); Gal. 6:11–15 (11); Luke 12:11–12; 2 Pet. 1:16–21 (21); 3:14–18 (15–16); ♪Col. 4:16–18 (18)
[285] *Strong's Exhaustive Concordance of the Bible* | Blue Letter Bible | www.blueletterbible.org

 LIFE APPLICATION LETTER #4

ZENITH

[n. Zenith: culminating point: acme][286]

---

2 Timothy 4:1–8 (NKJV)[287]

1 I charge you therefore before God and the Lord Jesus Christ, who will judge the living and the dead at His appearing and His kingdom:

2 Preach the word! Be ready in season and out of season. Convince, rebuke, exhort, with all longsuffering and teaching.

3 For the time will come when they will not endure sound doctrine, but according to their own desires, because they have itching ears, they will heap up for themselves teachers;

4 and they will turn their ears away from the truth, and be turned aside to fables.

5 But you be watchful in all things, endure afflictions, do the work of an evangelist, fulfill your ministry.

6 For I am already being poured out as a drink offering, and the time of my departure is at hand.

7 I have fought the good fight, I have finished[G5055] the race, I have kept the faith.

8 Finally, there is laid up for me the crown of righteousness, which the Lord, the righteous Judge, will give to me on that Day, and not to me only but also to all who have loved His appearing.

[G5055] τελέω teléō, tel-eh'-o; from G5056; to end, i.e. complete, execute, conclude, discharge (a debt):—accomplish, make an end, expire, fill up, finish, go over, pay, perform.

Dear Worship Leader,

As a final writing exercise, I want you to kick up your feet and dream a little. What would be your zenith? A culminating point for you? What would it look like for you to finish your course? Are you just starting out? Do you need a course correction? Practically, what next steps are you going to take so that you can finish strong? Whatever the answer, write it down and lay it on the altar before the Lord. Like you, I want to fight a good fight, finish my course, and keep the faith. After which, there is laid up for me the crown of righteousness, which the Lord, the righteous Judge, will give to me on that day, and not to me only but also to all who have loved His appearing (2 Timothy 4:7–8).

I finish these letters with the words of Jude 1:24–25 (KJV). "Now unto him that is able to keep you from falling, and to present you faultless before the presence of his glory with exceeding joy, To the only wise God our Saviour, be glory and majesty, dominion and power, both now and ever. Amen."

_____

_____

_____

_____

_____

_____

---

[286] Merriam-Webster dictionary | www.merriam-webster.com | www.learnersdictionary.com

[287] Acts 20:24; Phil. 3:12; John 4:34; 5:36; 17:4, 23; 19:28, 30; Matt. 25:1–46 (21, 23); 2 Tim. 4:17; 1 Cor. 9:24–27; Heb. 11:1–40; 12:1–2; 2 Cor. 11:22–33; ♪Col. 1:28; 4:17; 2 Tim. 3:10–11 | 1 Tim. 1:12–17; 1 Pet. 5:10; Eph. 3:20–21

[G5056] τέλος télos, tel'-os; from a primary τέλλω téllō (to set out for a definite point or goal); properly, the point aimed at as a limit, i.e. (by implication) the conclusion of an act or state (termination (literally, figuratively or indefinitely), result (immediate, ultimate or prophetic), purpose); specially, an impost or levy (as paid):—+ continual, custom, end(-ing), finally, uttermost. Compare G5411.[288]

[288] *Strong's Exhaustive Concordance of the Bible* | Blue Letter Bible | www.blueletterbible.org

This is me speaking at Crosspoint Bible Fellowship, 2022.

This is us at the Criswell College Gala, Dallas Arboretum and Botanical Gardens, 2022.

This is us after worship on a Sunday, 2022.

Josiah, age eleven, sixth grade, 2022–23 school year.

The LORD bless you and keep you; The LORD make His face shine upon you, And be gracious to you; The LORD lift up His countenance upon you, And give you peace.

(Numbers 6:24–26 NKJV)

ABOUT THE AUTHOR

Rodney L. Carter is a global worship leader, musician, songwriter, clinician, pastor, preacher/teacher, leader, and mentor. A Chicago native, he's recorded with world-renowned artists and has served in worship leadership ministry for over thirty years. A licensed and ordained minister of the gospel and a graduate of the University of Iowa, he holds a master's degree from Criswell College and is certified as a pastoral counselor. He is married, has a teenage son, and lives in the Dallas/Fort Worth area.

Printed in the United States
by Baker & Taylor Publisher Services

Printed in the United States
by Baker & Taylor Publisher Services